DIAMOND POWER

Gems of Wisdom From America's Greatest Marketer

Sept. 2007

Barry Farber

Best Wishes,

CAREER PRESS

DIAMOND POWER
EDITED BY NICOLE DEFELICE
TYPESET BY EILEEN DOW MUNSON
Cover design by Dorothy Wachtenheim
Printed in the U.S.A. by Book-mart Press

To order this title, please call toll-free 1-800-CAREER-1 (NJ and Canada: 201-848-0310) to order using VISA or MasterCard, or for further information on books from Career Press.

The Career Press, Inc., 3 Tice Road, PO Box 687,
Franklin Lakes, NJ 07417
www.careerpress.com

Library of Congress Cataloging-in-Publication Data

Farber, Barry J.
    Diamond power : gems of wisdom from America's greatest
marketer / by Barry Farber.
        p. cm.
    Includes bibliographical references and index.
    ISBN 1-56414-698-7 (pbk.)
    1. Success—Psychological aspects. I. Title.

BF637.S8F342 2004
158—ds22

2003054651

To Mom and Dad.

I wish I knew then what I know now.

Thanks for everything.

Acknowledgments—

Special thanks to Sharyn Kolberg and
all the wonderful people at Career Press.

Contents

Introduction

Twenty years ago, a coworker made a remark I'll never forget. He called me a diamond in the rough. I'm not sure if it was meant as a compliment or not, but I took it to mean that although I was rough around the edges, I had the potential to shine amongst my peers. Today I'm an even bigger diamond in the rough. I have even more rough edges. The more you learn, the more you find out about your potential, and the more you have to work on. When you sail into uncharted waters, when you have experiences you never had before, it opens a vast amount of knowledge and resources inside you that you were unaware you had in the first place. But by doing that, you're polishing some facets of yourself while other parts are newly exposed and still rough.

Every day becomes a new day to work on your skills and become sharper and more focused. Some parts of myself have smoothed out, but I still have flaws. I don't mind that at all—our flaws are what make us unique.

It's for all of us to decide what we're going to do with what we're given in life. We're all "diamonds in the rough," with untapped potential. *Diamond Power* will show you how to overcome adversity, energize yourself, maintain life-long learning, achieve your personal goals, make relationships work, tap into your hidden creativity, persist until you succeed, and much, much more.

Diamond Power is divided into 20 different areas that help us live better business and personal lives. It is a compilation of information and insight gathered from my 20 years of seminars, books, tapes, and radio and television shows. The experience I've gained has been my training ground, my ongoing university. This has really been an encyclopedia of information that I can draw from. It's helped me develop a literary agency that represents high-profile people, from television personalities to world-champion athletes. It's helped me develop a company that manufactures and licenses innovative products like the world's only FoldzFlat® Pen. It's helped me earn a black belt and compete in martial arts competitions.

But it's not only my knowledge you'll find in this book. I've interviewed people in every field and industry including sports, education, science, business, and the arts—people who have achieved the highest levels of success in their fields—people such as Bruce Jenner on energy, John Gray on relationships, and Dr. Ken Blanchard on service.

Within these chapters you'll find a wealth of practical ideas and suggestions you can use every day. You may find some more useful than others. That's fine. I once read a passage by martial arts expert Bruce Lee, who recommended that the best way to learn was to collect as much information as you can from people you admire, discard what you feel is not useful for your needs and personality, and then create your own style.

Diamond Power is designed so that you can come to one comprehensive source and get the answers you need to be successful in today's fast-paced world. Every single chapter is:

✧ Brimming with useful tips to equip you for success in today's aggressive culture.

✧ Bursting with techniques for driving your personal success every day.

✧ Jam-packed with top priorities to get you started right now on your way to your life's goals.

✧ Filled with inspirational quotes and powerful true stories from people who never gave up when challenged by failure or adversity.

You'll discover topics that will help you:

✧ Find the courage within you to move forward.

✧ Turn obstacles into opportunities.

✧ Discover how to recharge your batteries every day.

✧ Find out your strengths and what makes you unique.

✧ Take action in new directions that will help you change the way you feel about yourself and enable you to make the impossible possible.

✧ Get control of your self-esteem.

✧ Create a mental vision for your life and then make it happen.

What makes this book special is that it is crisp, easy-to-read, and more than just a book of collected wisdom. Each chapter contains "do-able" steps that can be practiced and applied immediately. *Diamond Power* gives you the ability to understand who you are, what makes you unique, and how to tap into the power of the diamond in the rough that we all are.

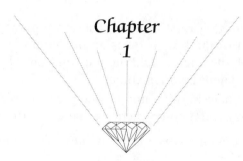

Chapter 1

Courage:
Lessons From Inside the Ring of Fire

Courage is the first of human qualities because it is the quality which guarantees the others.

—Aristotle,
philosopher

What Is Courage?

There are many definitions of courage. They have to do with mental and moral strength to resist danger or hardship—firmness of mind and will in the face of extreme difficulty—and the capacity to meet adversity with fortitude and resilience. My favorite definition of courage is "readiness to deal with things fearlessly by reason of stouthearted temperament or a resolute spirit."

Courage does not mean facing danger without thinking. It does not mean that you go out looking for danger. It does mean that when faced with a dangerous situation, you act with reason. You consider the risks. You do what must be done for your protection and survival and for the protection and survival of others.

It doesn't take saving a life to be a hero, or to prove you have courage. Courage comes in many shapes and sizes. For some, courage takes the form of facing physical danger. For many people, courage is what makes it possible to go after those things that seem impossible to achieve.

Humorist Erma Bombeck once wrote, "There are people who put their dreams in a little box and say, 'Yes, I've got dreams, of course I've got dreams.' Then they put the box away and bring it out once in a while to look in it. And yep, they're still there. These are great dreams but they never even get out of the box. It takes an uncommon amount of guts to put your dreams on the line, to hold them up and say 'How good' or 'How bad am I?' That's where courage comes in."

Courage is not necessarily found in one great heroic act, but is more often embedded in the day-to-day actions that come from the heart.

> *All our dreams can come true, if we have the courage to pursue them.*
>
> —Walt Disney

The Power of Courage

I have studied many different styles of martial arts, and have learned many lessons from all of my martial arts training. But this one is perhaps the most important lesson of them all: The goal of martial arts is to become a master of combat skills—and never to use them. This means that you are always physically and mentally able to defend yourself and those around you, but that you only use your skills when you have no other choice. It is being prepared that gives you the confidence to go out into the world knowing that you have what it takes to face the unknowns of life.

Once adversity strikes, it is too late to prepare yourself. That's why many people fall apart. They don't expect to fail or to face difficulties, and when they do, they have no psychological reserves. So they quit. And when they do, they set up a habit of quitting. Being prepared means that you don't have to quit when you run into problems. You will have the physical and mental reserves you need to get you through.

It is comforting to know that you are prepared. It keeps you grounded in your life and assures you of strong footing on every path you choose. You don't need to flaunt your abilities; it is enough just to know that you have them. It will give you the ability to respond appropriately to any situation, and to cope with any hardship. That in itself is a triumph over evil.

> *I would define true courage to be a perfect sensibility of the measure of danger, and a mental willingness to endure it.*
>
> — William Tecumseh Sherman,
> Civil War general

Does this mean that everyone should become a martial arts master? Of course not (although I highly recommend it.) It means that you should do at least one thing every day to increase your preparedness. Exercise to keep your body prepared. Take some time for yourself to renew your spiritual side, whether it is in silent contemplation, meditation, or prayer. Learn something new every day to keep your mental abilities sharp. All of these tasks enable you to stand strong on the foundation of courage should the need arise.

> *There can be no great courage where there is no confidence or assurance, and half the battle is in the conviction that we can do what we undertake.*
>
> —Orison Swett Marden,
> founder of *Success Magazine*

Courage Comes in Many Guises

Lieutenant John Cagno is a decorated firefighter in North Providence, Rhode Island. A troubled kid who grew up without a father, there was a void in his life he couldn't fill until he was 16 and began volunteering as a firefighter. This was when he found what had been missing—a feeling he could do something worthwhile with his life.

Two years later, he became a paid firefighter. One day, he was climbing an aerial ladder to get to the third floor of a burning building. There were high-tension transmission wires overhead. Although Cagno never actually touched the power line, he came close enough to send 14,000 volts of electricity through his left hand.

He didn't know that he was burned badly over his entire body until the next morning in the hospital.

"I was bandaged everywhere, and the pain was unbearable," he says. "I prayed to God every night to take me to Him. I wasn't even sure if I still had all my limbs intact."

Then one night there was a show on TV about a woman gymnast who had one arm amputated below the elbow. She was performing amazing feats on the uneven parallel bars. "I was facing great uncertainty at that time," says Cagno. "I didn't know which way things were going to go. But I looked at her and thought she's had the courage to go on. She's been injured, she's had tough times, but she's enjoying her life and accomplishing great things." What Cagno saw in that young woman helped him through the most difficult times of his recovery.

"I looked at her and I realized that she made a tremendous handicap into nothing more than an inconvenience," he says. "So I mirrored her actions. I decided to look at my injuries as a little inconvenience. She inspired me and I suddenly knew that no matter what my outcome, I'd be okay. It gave me the strength I needed to keep fighting.

"I was in the hospital for five months," he says. "I came home and couldn't do anything for myself. My mother or my sister had to help me take care of every bodily function. It was painful and humiliating. But my biggest concern was when I could get back to being a firefighter. I didn't know if I would be able to. Would I be able to use my hands? Would I freak out? I didn't know, but I slowly fought my way back."

> *There is no failure for the man who realizes his power, who never knows when he is beaten; there is no failure for the determined endeavor; the unconquerable will. There is no failure for the man who gets up every time he falls, who rebounds like a rubber ball, who persists when everyone else gives up, who pushes on when everyone else turns back.*
>
> —Orison Swett Marden,
> founder of *Success Magazine*

Unfortunately, John Cagno's trials were not yet over, and he would find himself tested again. Several years after Cagno was reinstated as a firefighter, he was riding in one of the town's older fire trucks. The door, which wasn't closing properly, opened as the truck turned the corner, and Cagno fell out. He was able to hook his arm through the window so that he didn't fall under the wheels, but his knee got caught between the door and the jam. The result was that he developed Reflex Sympathetic Dystrophy, which is a damaged nerve that causes intense pain and swelling.

"Of course, I was given pain medication," says Cagno. "But because I've had so many operations during my life, I'm immune to almost everything. So when the doctors told me to take one or two pills, I took three or four. And then three or four again. Pretty soon, no matter how I tried to deny it, I had a problem.

"Just because I'm a firefighter, people think I have a lot of courage. But when I'm fighting a fire, when I face danger in a professional situation, I have tools in place to help me deal with it. When I was faced with drug dependency, I didn't have those tools in place to help give me courage. I had to reach deep inside and confront my demons. I had to face my obstacles and understand my options. I had to confront this situation head on.

John Cagno reached deep inside and admitted his problem. "I could run into a burning building every day of the week," he says. "And I did. But when it came to identifying, to stopping my denial, and then to confronting a problem like that, I put it off and put it off. But I could only put it off so long before I knew that if I didn't do something about it, it would destroy me."

He found a counselor in whom he could confide. The counselor advised him to enter a treatment center.

"When I was injured the first time, the fire chief came in and told me, 'This won't make sense to you now, but things happen for a reason. Something's going to come out of this because you didn't die. You have a purpose, and eventually you'll know what that purpose is.'"

And though he didn't know it at the time, he now says that the purpose was so that he could use his experiences in a positive way, and so he could give hope, strength, and understanding to others. And he has much greater empathy for people who are struggling to find the courage they need to overcome the stumbling blocks of life.

"I'll put it this way," he says. "If there were two doors and somebody said to me, 'Behind door number one is a raging fire. We don't know how bad it is, we don't know if the floor is safe, and we don't know if the ceiling is going to come down and behind door number two is confronting drug dependency.' I'd pick the fire every time."

"I've done a lot of things in my career that other people have judged courageous. I've saved people who were in cardiac arrest. I've rescued people from burning buildings, from horrifying car wrecks. But I think the greatest rescue I ever made was of myself."

> *Let it never be forgotten that glamour is not greatness;*
> *applause is not fame; prominence is not eminence. The*
> *man of the hour is not apt to be the man of the ages. A*
> *stone may sparkle, but that does not make it a diamond;*
> *people may have money, but that does not make them a*
> *success. It is what the unimportant people do that really*
> *counts and determines the course of history. The greatest*
> *forces in the universe are never spectacular. Summer*
> *showers are more effective than hurricanes, but they get no*
> *publicity. The world would soon die but for the fidelity,*
> *loyalty and consecration of those whose names are*
> *unhonored and unsung.*
>
> —James R. Sizoo,
> writer

8 Ways to Build Courage

1. **Understand that in difficult situations, there are always choices.** According to Chinese writer and philosopher Ming-Dao Deng, "Whether we remain ash or become the phoenix is up to us." Are you going to let circumstances break you? Or are you going to break old habits and go to new heights? Your life does not depend as much on what happens to you as on how you respond to what happens to you. Keep in mind that even though an action may be scary at first, simply taking an action is the first step toward building courage.

   Man is not the creature of circumstances, circumstances are the creatures of men. We are free agents, and man is more powerful than matter.

   —Benjamin Disraeli,
   politician and writer

2. **Have the courage to move away from people who think negatively, who want to pull down your ideas.** Misery loves company. If there are people around you who don't give you the support you need, or who consistently tell you that you don't measure up—walk away from them. Don't take their words to heart. It takes courage to step outside a circle of people, but if that circle is defining who you are in a negative way, it's time to move on.

3. **Do not let your fears become bigger than reality.** Remember that old definition of FEAR: **F**alse **E**vidence **A**ppearing **R**eal. Humans are extremely creative; we can think of a million things that can go wrong in any given situation. Use that to your advantage. If you know that a particular obstacle might arise, you can prepare yourself and guard against it. Then let go of the things that are beyond your control. If you let it, fear itself gets larger and larger and keeps you from having the courage to move forward. Use yourself as an example. We've all done things that were frightening at first (made a speech, started a new relationship, began a new career). Most of the time, the result is that you realize they weren't as bad as you thought they would be, and now you can go forward and do them again. You have to believe that taking an action is of greater benefit to you than letting the fear hold you back.

   Make not your thoughts your prisons.

   —William Shakespeare,
   poet and playwright

4. **Go back to your core values.** What are your beliefs? What types of people do you want to deal with in your life? What is integrity to you? What are the values you're searching for? What keeps you going? The strongest people are those who keep their core values in mind every time they make a decision. They make decisions based not only on how they think, not only on how their gut feels, but also on what is inside their hearts. When you make a decision, ask yourself: Can I do this and keep my dignity? My integrity? Can I do it without hurting others? If you can answer yes to these questions, you're probably on the right track.

> *Success means figuring out who you are, not who other people think you are or who you think you should be. It's being able to say, 'This is what I am. It may not be enough for some, but it's enough for me to be able to make a difference.' Think about the power one person has to make a difference—Martin Luther King, Jr., Albert Schweitzer, Eleanor Roosevelt. One person can make a difference in a short period of time if they do what's really true to them—and that takes courage.*
>
> —John James,
> author

5. **Build up your courage step by step.** Courage does not always come in one giant package. Success breeds success; every time you accomplish something, your confidence increases and builds upon itself. When you reach your goal, other people may look at you and say, "I can't believe what you accomplished." They see the one big event. What they don't see is the history of small steps you've taken, each one demanding the courage that got you to this place. Push yourself a little more every day, and your courage will be nurtured and blossom before your eyes. Try greater and greater ventures until you are brave enough to accomplish undertakings far beyond what you thought you could. The rewards will be beyond your imagination.

> *Do not pray for tasks equal to your powers. Pray for powers equal to your tasks.*
>
> —Phillips Brooks,
> pastor

6. **Indulge in quiet confidence.** Courage advances our skill and advances our position in life. But there's also a warning that one must heed, and that is not to get too cocky. Don't mistake hubris—pride taken to the

extreme—for courage. Most people whom others consider to be heroes do not see themselves in that role. They simply took actions that needed to be taken. There is nothing wrong with taking pride in your accomplishments, but let the accomplishments speak for themselves. They say more about you than words could ever express.

7. **Savor the struggle.** Courage doesn't always come easily. Sometimes you must struggle against inertia. There are many times when we are in turmoil, when we are actively searching deep within ourselves to find the courage we need. Courage challenges us. There's an old saying that goes, "You never see the true strength of a tea bag until it's in hot water." Any time you're going to do something that is a courageous act in any way—small or large—there is a struggle to do it. Remember that you gain strength from that struggle. Understand that the struggle in itself will build you, not break you down.

> *I count him braver who overcomes his desires than him who conquers his enemies; for the hardest victory is the victory over self.*
>
> —Aristotle,
> philosopher

8. **Be original.** Think outside of the box. Don't be afraid to be first. True, other people might not understand, or might criticize your way of thinking. But it is only when you stretch outside of your current situation that you come up with new ideas. You don't have to come up with astounding ideas or inventions that no one has ever discovered before. Being original means seeing things from your unique perspective and believing in their value. Being original means pushing old ideas in new directions. It's not easy to do; it takes courage. But the "road not taken" usually offers the best scenery and the most exciting adventures. This is the courage that drives us forward and leads us to better lives.

More on Courage and Fear

> *Courage is a special kind of knowledge: the knowledge of how to fear what ought to be feared and how not to fear what ought not to be feared.*
>
> —Plato,
> philosopher

There is a deep core-based sense of courage and confidence that is not something we are born with. It comes from having tried and failed, and risen to try again. It comes from experience, from having confronted one's fears and lived to tell the tale. It comes from the courage that is born in our hearts.

The word courage comes from the Latin *cuer,* or heart. It means the quality of spirit that enables one to face danger or difficulty instead of withdrawing from it. Courage does not mean the absence of fear. Those who are without fear are reckless and thoughtless, and often cause harm to themselves and others. Those who have courage know fear, yet carry on despite it. They are able to look fear in the face, acknowledge it, and say, "I will not let you stop me."

Courage and fear are inevitably intertwined. We become courageous when we have faith and we take action. When we believe strongly in what we're doing, and we're moving toward a goal that challenges all of our senses, we meet fear head-on.

The problem with courage is one of perception. Most of us think that courage only applies to the big things: to saving someone's life or to bravery in extreme circumstances. But if you struggle day to day to overcome adversities large and small (and we all do), you show a great amount of courage when you press on instead of just giving up. It's the opposite of being discouraged. It's looking inside yourself, being honest with yourself, and knowing that going after your dreams may be difficult and you may not succeed. But in the end, you know that choosing to follow your heart because you know it is right and good is courage.

> *Courage is being scared to death—and saddling up anyway.*
> —John Wayne,
> actor

I Dare You...

Dream big. There are many people in the world who have little dreams. They don't start out as little dreams, but people make them little. Fear and doubt chip away at them until they're nothing more than fleeting memories and wishes of things that might have been.

Make difficult choices in life. There will always be outside circumstances we can't control, but there are also decisions we can make about how we want to live our lives. We can choose to go through door number one, behind which we know lies a path of uncertainty and rough spots. Or we can choose door number two, which leads to a much gentler, easier road.

Neither choice is wrong or right. What's wrong is choosing the easier road without ever having tried something new or different. Every time you step up to try something you've never done before, you learn more than you expect. The uniqueness of the experience gives you insight you could never get unless you take action. When you venture out into new worlds, you open your mind to things you might otherwise never experience. Your knowledge of the world, and of yourself within it, expands tremendously with every new step you take.

> *You gain strength, courage, and confidence by every experience in which you really stop to look fear in the face. You are able to say to yourself, "I lived through this horror, I can take the next thing that comes along." You must do the things you think you cannot do.*
>
> —Eleanor Roosevelt,
> humanitarian and writer

We all have to learn to live through "the next thing that comes along." For there will always be a next thing. You have to go out on a limb to get to where the fruit is—you may have to go out on many limbs in order to survive. The fruit may still be out of reach. Limbs can break. Many things can happen even after you've summoned up the courage to make the climb. If you're alive, you're going to face adversity. You're going to fall down. Adversity will test you over and over again. In the next chapter you'll learn what happens when adversity strikes and how you can turn obstacles into opportunities.

Chapter 2

Adversity:
Turning Obstacles Into Opportunities

Adversity is the diamond dust heaven polishes its jewels with.

—Robert Leighton,
Scottish minister and professor of divinity

What Is Adversity?

The dictionary says that adversity is a condition marked by misfortune, a calamity, or an unfortunate event or circumstance. I say that adversity comes in all shapes and sizes, from life-threatening illnesses, to losing a sale, to failing in business, to rocky relationships. Adversity can be many things according to just when it hits you and under what conditions. Whatever it may be for you, if you have suffered setbacks, hardships, or failures, know that you are not alone. Very few things are true all of the time in all situations, but this is a universal truth: Plans do not become achievements, dreams do not become realities, and ideas do not come to fruition without setbacks, hardships, and failures.

The thing about adversity, though, is that it is the greatest teacher we can ever have. The ocean never stays calm, and still waters do not make for a skilled mariner. No matter what you're facing today, there's something in it that will build fortitude for tomorrow. As Michael Korda once said, "It is on the way down that we learn how things work. On the way up, we are enjoying the ride too much to pay attention." Adversity is not just a lesson for the next time, but a lesson for a lifetime.

People are always blaming their circumstances for what they are. I don't believe in circumstances. The people who get on in this world are the people who get up and look for the circumstances they want, and if they can't find them, make them.

—George Bernard Shaw,
playwright

The Power of Adversity

When adversity strikes, it often feels like we are plunged into a dark void from which we will never emerge. But when things are the darkest, the stars come out and shine their light upon us so that we can see the path before us. Everyone experiences darkness; everyone goes through rough times. What's important to remember is that rough times are the foundations for future progress. Every type of adversity contains within it lessons that can be harnessed to fuel your success in the future. When adversity strikes, it can tear us apart, or it can build us up so that we can face whatever else life may bring. What doesn't kill us makes us stronger.

Adversity is like a hurricane, and we are like trees in the storm. If we stiffen up and stand unbending when it hits, we will break in two. But if we are able to bend in the wind, to listen and learn even while a tempest rages around us, then we may suffer damage, but we will survive the storm.

There is adversity everywhere in the natural world. There are hurricanes, tornadoes, volcanoes, and earthquakes. There are natural predators for every animal. But there is also a balance in nature. Floods may destroy one year's crops, but they may also make the fields more fertile for the next year's growth.

We, too, need to find that balance. If you look at today's high achievers, they have all experienced much adversity and kept on going. They learned its lessons and used them to move forward with their lives. At the end of our lives, what we look back on with the most pride is the way we stood up to adversity and the way we came through the tough times with grace and character. These are the times that challenge us, that can either break us or make us break records.

The human brain has the capability to create our surroundings, to limit the natural adversity we face. But there is no way to completely eliminate adversity, nor should we seek to eliminate it all together. When things come too easily, we lose our hunger. We lose our focus. We get lazy and complacent. We need to learn to be thankful for the good things in our lives, and to appreciate what we can learn from the bad.

Strength comes from struggle, not from taking the path of least resistance. The real test is not whether bad things happen to you or whether you experience failure, but how you deal with adversity and setbacks. No one wants adversity, nor should anyone go looking for trouble. But when it comes, we must learn to make the best of it before it gets the best of us. If we don't use the adversity we've gone through before as momentum to get through even tougher times, then its lessons are wasted. We will have suffered and struggled in vain. Just as advertising legend Joseph Sugarman said:

"Not many people are willing to give failure a second opportunity. The bitter pill of failure...is often more than people can handle...If you're willing to accept failure and learn from it, if you're willing to consider failure as a blessing in disguise and bounce back, you've got the potential of harnessing one of the world's most powerful success forces."

The Courage to Go on Despite the Odds

Imagine that you grew up in the ghettos around Los Angeles as a tough guy known to relish a fight. You've had many brushes with the law, and most people you know expect you to die early or in jail. Then imagine you decide you don't want to live up to those expectations; you want to live a better life. So you join the Los Angeles police force and run an anti-gang unit. You think you've got it beat. Then, while you're out taking a run, you are hit by a car and severely injured. You lose a portion of your left leg, and your hopes for the future.

You can let pain and disability defeat you before the injury does, or you can fight. You can keep yourself psychologically strong enough to come out physically scarred but mentally intact and able to put life in perspective. Now you can say to yourself, no matter what obstacles are thrown in your path, "I can't have a bad day. I know what a bad day is, and this isn't one of them."

Now, imagine that you're 22 and in an abusive marriage. You find the courage to leave, only to discover that your ex has left you destitute. Then, you're offered a job as a pharmaceutical sales representative. You don't think you can handle the job. But you take a leap of faith—and the job. Today, you look on that time as a blessing in disguise, realizing that one of the most important aspects of adversity is that it makes you feel so uncomfortable that you have no choice but to reexamine what you're doing and why you're doing it.

Sergeant John Brown (back at his job and believed to be the first officer in the United States to return to full duty as a police officer with a prosthesis) and Jo Jerman (now one of the highest-ranking vice presidents at a large pharmaceutical company) are the real people who lived the nightmare stories previously discussed. The success they found after experiencing setbacks is not necessarily measured by fame or money, but rather by a shift in attitude and a new way of dealing with the kinds of adversity we all face every day. Dealing with adversity helped give clarity to their lives, helped them appreciate what they have now, and changed the quality of their lives.

> *I have lived through countless storms at sea. Winds over 100 miles an hour, swells reaching 50 feet. And when I thought I could not last another minute, the winds dropped off, the seas flattened, the blue sky appeared, and my quest was reached.*
>
> —Robert D. Ballard,
> undersea explorer

Laughter Really *Is* the Best Medicine

Sometimes the best and healthiest way to deal with adversity is to laugh through it. Not to laugh at it, or ignore it, but to keep your sense of humor and seek out others who can help to lighten your load. When you're having a rough day, the best thing you can do for yourself is call someone who makes you laugh. Laughter changes your perspective and turns your emotions around.

There is scientific proof of this. Studies have shown that laughter decreases your blood pressure and heart rate, increases oxygen in the blood, strengthens the immune system, and creates an enzyme that protects your stomach from stress. There is no greater stress inducer than adversity. Laughter is like a pressure valve; it helps release the pent-up anxiety that keeps us from moving forward. The most successful people are able to let most of that anxiety go and handle adverse situations calmly and confidently.

> *Flops are a part of life's menu and I've never been a girl to miss out on any of the courses.*
>
> —Rosalind Russell,
> actress

A Funny Thing Happened...

Laughter may be the best medicine, but that doesn't mean that professional funnymen are immune from life's ups and downs. Several years ago, Robert Schimmel was managing a stereo store in Scottsdale, Arizona. He went out to Los Angeles to visit his sister, and while he was there they went to a comedy club. On stage were people like Jay Leno, Jerry Seinfeld, Larry Miller, and George Wallace. Schimmel's sister said, "You're as funny as these guys! Why don't you try comedy?" Schimmel answered, "I couldn't do that."

They came back a week later on amateur night. Although Schimmel didn't know it, his sister had put his name on the list of performers. They were sitting in the audience when the announcer said, "And now for our next comic, Robert Schimmel!"

Schimmel went up on stage and talked about his parents for two minutes. The audience laughed. The owner of the club came over and said, "You can work here whenever you want. Just call me up and I'll give you a spot."

Schimmel went back to Arizona and convinced his wife to move to Los Angeles. They packed all their things in a truck and drove off to sunny California. They made straight for the club that had promised him employment, so he could show it to his wife. But when they got there, all they found were smoldering embers. The club had burnt down the night before.

Schimmel did not give up. He got a job selling stereo equipment and went to every amateur night he could find. "I had to do it," says Schimmel. "My vision of becoming a comedian was so clear I felt like I had no choice. If you bet on yourself like that, there's more to win than if you play it safe and let yourself be afraid of failure." Soon, Schimmel was appearing with those comedians he so admired; he was even named Comic of the Year by the *Las Vegas Review Journal*.

Then he had a heart attack. But even that didn't stop him. He worked that frightening experience into an HBO comedy special that contained some of the funniest material he's ever written.

> *A pessimist sees the difficulty in every opportunity; an optimist sees the opportunity in every difficulty.*
>
> —Winston Churchill,
> British prime minister

It's All in How You Look at It

Robert Schimmel didn't think having a heart attack was funny. But he took his adversity and tried to find ways to use it as a productive force in his life. When you are faced with a difficult situation, you can let it defeat you or you can make something good from it. You can see all the difficulties when opportunity comes around or you can see all the opportunities in every difficulty.

That reminds me of a story I read about two young boys who grew up in a broken home, abused by an alcoholic father. Eventually, they moved away from home and led separate lives. Years later, they both participated in a study of people who had grown up in alcoholic homes. One of the boys had become a successful businessman who never drank. His brother had grown up to be an alcoholic, now in dire straits. The psychologist who was conducting the study asked each brother why he had ended up the way he did. Each one of them answered, "What else would you expect when you have a father like mine?"

Suffering has two paths. You can let adversity pull you down, or you can use it as a life force to spur you on to greater accomplishments. That doesn't mean that you deny it, or that you need to repress your emotions. You can't look at a tragic event while it is happening and say, "Oh well, I'm sure there's a lesson in here somewhere." Some people bounce back quicker than others. But we all have a choice to make, and it has been proven over and over again that it is not what happens to us in life that counts, but what we choose to do about it.

We learn wisdom from failure much more than from success. We often discover what will do by finding out what will not do; and probably he who never made a mistake, never made a discovery.

—Samuel Smiles,
writer

Tough Choices

There was a story reported on television about a young boy facing the worst type of adversity you can imagine. Charlie was 10 years old and told he had only six months to a year to live. He was dying from a rare type of thyroid cancer.

Here was a child who was being forced to choose how he wanted to spend the rest of his limited time on Earth. He could have spent his time feeling sorry for himself, traveling to see new sights, or simply playing with his friends. Instead, he asked his mother if he could spend his allowance money, which he had saved, to buy gifts and give them out to the other children on the cancer ward.

A reporter asked little Charlie why he had made this choice, and he replied that it made him feel really good and forget about being sick himself.

Charlie actually lived another four years—time enough to buy many gifts for many children. Many of his doctors felt that his choice to give back to others and his determination to help as many children as he could had a lot to do with his longevity.

In the end, Charlie gave even more than he had imagined. Through his illness, doctors were able to discover the gene mutation that caused his rare form of cancer. This discovery raised hope that it might be possible someday to test children from at-risk families and to remove their thyroid glands before they get cancer.

Charlie lived as long as he did because of the skill of his doctors and because of his amazing attitude. A child, facing the worst adversity possible, made choices that not only kept his body and spirit going, but helped countless others as a result. Think about how your life would change if you didn't fear adversity and if—like Charlie—you actually embraced it as an opportunity for growth and wisdom.

Charlie's strength and determination showed that no matter how bad things get, something good can come from adversity. In fact, sometimes the worse things become, the greater the discoveries you can make about yourself.

> *To be really alive, to truly feel life's offerings, is to know the highs and lows, the exhilaration of the mountaintop and the descent to the valley, and to accept and enjoy not one but both. Life's highs are most invigorating; there is also fertileness to be found in the lowest valley.*
> —David Chow and Richard Spangler,
> *Kung Fu: History, Philosophy and Technique*

One Man's Travels Through Adversity

Tony Wainright is a successful advertising director, director of six public companies, writer of books, movies, and plays, and a consultant to Fortune 500 companies across the United States.

One of his secrets to success is that he doesn't see rejection as failure or adversity. Once there was a company he wanted for an advertising account. The first time he went to see them, he was told the timing was wrong. Wainright pursued this company for six years. He thought about giving up, but he kept going. Then one day, in the sixth year, the company told him, "We're starting a new division. How would you like the account?" He walked out of their offices that day with $30 million worth of their business.

Wainright's confidence and his belief in persistence told him to keep trying. "The analogy I would use is, if you stand by a door, the odds are at some juncture the door will open. If you walk away saying, 'Gee the door is closed and I can't get in,' you'll never get inside. I'm willing to stand by the door."

Wainright wasn't always so confident or successful. When he was 29 years old, three hardships struck him at once. First, he became ill and required major surgery. Then he lost his job. And, most seriously, his second daughter was born with spina bifida and died within a year.

"I got down on my knees and I remember thinking, 'There are two ways to go. I'm either going to pull myself together or I'm not.' I did. The good news is that from adversity two things happened. First, I worked harder than ever before and became successful. Second I never forgot what happened to me. From that moment on, I dedicated part of my life to helping other people—doing things I never would have thought of had I not gone through adversity myself.

"For me, there are three things that helped me get through adversity. One is prayer. Another is the absolute belief that tomorrow will be better than today. And third, though it may sound like a cliché, is that I don't take things personally. Instead, I figure out a way to overcome it. That's the best advice I can give. Don't dwell on things. And don't feel sorry for yourself when something happens. It happens to everyone, and it happens more than once. The ultimate winners are the ones that never give up."

> *Far better to dare mighty things, to win glorious triumphs,*
> *even though checkered by failure, than to take rank with*
> *those poor spirits who neither enjoy much nor suffer*
> *much…in the grey twilight that knows not victory nor*
> *defeat.*
>
> —Theodore Roosevelt,
> U.S. president

Top 10 Things to Do When Adversity Hits

1. **Write down the most important thing you are trying to accomplish, followed by the small steps you can take to get it done.** This will help you concentrate and focus.

2. **Always finish your commitments.** Never stop on the one-yard line. Tough times never last—tough people do. Give up now and you will never find the inner strength you have.

3. **Create a vision of your goal.** Post it somewhere you can see it every day. Focus all your energy on what you're trying to accomplish and what you need to get through each task.

4. **Do more than you're expected to do on a project or in your job.** Increase your service to others, and that action will often turn around some of the adversity and difficulties you're going through.

5. **Think about the benefits of this adversity, knowing what will be accomplished at the end.** How does it benefit you? How does it benefit the people you're serving?

6. **Look for the lessons adversity teaches.** The highest achievers in the world understand that failure is the most valuable teacher they can have.

   The good things which belong to prosperity are to be wished, but the good things that belong to adversity are to be admired.

   —Seneca,
   Roman playwright

7. **Apply the lessons you learn to every part of your life.** Failure in one part of your life might teach you lessons about how to deal with other parts, for example, setbacks in your business may tell you to take your life in a whole new direction or may teach you that you need to improve the way you relate to people.

8. **Live in the present.** Put stickers around the house that say, "What am I thinking about now?" Are you living in today or worrying about tomorrow? Worry is a negative activity that diminishes strength, confidence, and energy. Conquer something today and you don't have to worry about it tomorrow.

9. **Live by Albert Einstein's three rules of work:** 1. Out of clutter, find simplicity. 2. From discord, find harmony. 3. In the middle of difficulty, find opportunity. Most people are so busy knocking opportunity that they don't hear opportunity knocking.

10. **Put the last nine tips to use before adversity strikes.** Use them when times are good and your confidence is high. Remember, success breeds success.

> *If we had no winter, the spring would not be so pleasant. If we did not sometimes taste of adversity, prosperity would not be so welcome.*
>
> —Anne Bradstreet,
> writer

I Dare You...

In a difficult or challenging situation, take action using these five strategies:

1. **Find one or two people who have done what you're trying to do and interview them about how they achieved their goals.**

2. **Read biographies of people who overcame obstacles to succeed in your field.**

3. **Seek out every piece of information you can find about what you're trying to accomplish. (Try the library, tapes, the Internet.)** Surround yourself with information.

4. **When you want to stop working, go another 10 minutes.** Make one more call. Write one more letter. Work through the pain, be it physical or mental. It will make you stronger for the next time.

5. **Discard the word *can't* from your vocabulary.** Where there's an open mind, there's unlimited potential. Negative thoughts block our own achievements: *I can't do that. I'm too tired. I'm not good enough.* Substitute action thoughts: *I'll try one more time. I'm not ready to give up. I deserve to give myself another chance.*

Those who dare to fail miserably can achieve greatly.
>   —John F. Kennedy,
>   U.S. president

If these chapters make you feel better about your own situation, if they give you the courage to go after your dreams, notwithstanding the possibility of failure and adversity, if they provide you with just a few practical tools to help you accomplish your goals, then I am doing my job.

What we get in life most of the time is not new information. We get reminders. Reminders of how lucky we are in the good times, how appreciative we must be of the gifts and talents we have been given, and how much love we are capable of giving and getting. Shakespeare said that every day is a king in disguise. Every day we get a chance and a choice to start with a positive attitude, to make something unique, to put a new twist on life. Every day is a new beginning, every single day.

It is never too late to be what you might have been.
>   —George Eliot,
>   novelist

Every day *is* a new beginning. And every day we have choices to make. We may not always be able to choose what happens to us on any given day, but we can choose the attitude we take towards those events. No matter who we are, what we do, or where we come from, we have the choice. That choice is not how the events before us shape our attitude, it's how our attitude shape the events before us. In the next chapter, we'll examine one of the greatest gifts we possess, if only we choose it—the power of the positive, realistic attitude.

Chapter
3

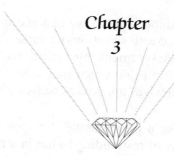

Attitude:
Staying Positive From Start to Finish

This may shock you, but I believe the single most significant decision I can make on a day-to-day basis is my choice of attitude. It is more important than my past, my education, my bankroll, my successes or failures, fame or pain, what other people think of me or say about me, my circumstances, or my position. Attitude is that single string that keeps me going or cripples my progress. It alone fuels my fire or assaults my hope. When my attitudes are right, there's no barrier too high, no valley too deep, no dream too extreme, no challenge too great for me.

—Charles Swindoll,
writer

What Is Attitude?

Attitude is defined as the mental position you take regarding a fact or a state. This means it's not what you look at that counts, but *how* you look at it. It's not what you hear, but *how* you hear it. It's not what you think, but *how* you think it. Your attitude forms every moment of your day, whether you realize it or not. Out of your attitude comes your enjoyment of life and your gratitude for all your blessings; out of attitude also comes your disappointment and anger at how things have turned out. Out of your attitude comes your productivity and satisfaction from accomplishments small and large. Out of attitude also comes the feeling that no accomplishment will ever be good enough.

There are some circumstances in life we can change; there are many we cannot. When we are faced with situations we must accept, we have two choices: We can live in disappointment, bitterness, and anger, or we can look deep within ourselves, find that place that won't be crushed by circumstance, and then pick ourselves up, dust ourselves off, and start all over again.

A positive attitude is not a phony smile, a happy face, and a perky disposition. It is simply a way of responding to life in a manner that allows us to accept the things we cannot change, and change the things we can. A positive attitude enables you to make a difference in the world because when you are able to see things in a positive light, you help others see the light as well.

> *A great attitude does much more than turn on the lights in our worlds; it seems to magically connect us to all sorts of serendipitous opportunities that were somehow absent before the change.*
>
> —Earl Nightingale,
> radio talk show host and writer

The Power of Attitude

Over the past 20 years, I have considered myself extremely lucky. I have been able to work with all types of successful people, ranging from sports, business, the arts, science and medicine, education, and entertainment. I believe that we become what we think about, and who we surround ourselves with every day strongly influences what we think about. That's why it's so important to be very choosy about who we do spend our time with, this short time we have here on Earth. All the people I've met, whether they are clients, mentors, guests, or colleagues, have one thing in common. In one way or another, each of them has a strong, positive, and resilient attitude.

These are people—ordinary people—who have harnessed the incredible power of a positive mental attitude to help them achieve extraordinary success. All of these people believe in one important concept: You become what you think about. All top achievers believe in their ability to succeed, and they are committed to doing and being their best at all times. They possess a quiet confidence and a comfort within themselves that makes you want to be around them. They are not only successful themselves, they elevate your success as well.

It's not just my opinion that attitude is essential for success. A study conducted by Harvard Business School determined that four factors are critical for success in business: information, intelligence, skill, and attitude. When these factors were ranked in importance, this particular study found that information, intelligence, and skill combined amounted to seven percent of business success, and attitude amounted to 93 percent! What is true for business is also true for our lives—our attitude is overwhelmingly the most important factor to our success.

> *There is little difference in people, but that little difference makes a big difference. The little difference is attitude. The big difference is whether it is positive or negative.*
>
> —W. Clement Stone,
> writer

Whose Attitude Is It Anyway?

A businessman walked by the same newsstand every morning and bought a paper from the same vendor. Every morning he gave the vendor a huge smile and a friendly hello, and every morning the vendor ignored him. One day, a colleague (who watched this ritual unfold every day) asked, "Why do you continue to give this guy such a friendly greeting? He never even talks to you."

The man replied, "I'm not going to let that individual determine how I act for the day."

Every day, your attitude is challenged by other people and by outside events. How will you react? Will you let adversity or obstacles stop you from moving forward? Or will you look at the situation objectively and find the lesson that can be learned or the action that can be taken to turn things around? Will you let a negative person influence your day, your life? Or will you remember the words of the great Eleanor Roosevelt, who said, "No one can make you feel inferior without your consent."

Stand Proud and Get Over It

Keith Harrell, author of *Attitude is Everything: 10 Life-Changing Steps to Turning Attitude into Action*, says that he had three great lessons about having a positive attitude in his life.

"Lesson one came on my first day of kindergarten," he says. "The teacher asked all the kids to stand up and say their names. When my turn came, I couldn't say my name. I stuttered. All the kids laughed, and I ran home; to this day, it's the fastest I've ever run in my life.

"My mother was standing on our porch, and I ran straight into her arms. 'I know just how you feel,' she said. 'I just got off the phone with Miss Peterson, and I was coming to get you, because I'm so proud of you.'

"'You're proud of me?'

"'Yes,' said my mother. 'I'm proud because you tried. In life there are going to be challenges, and this was our first challenge. We have to stay positive. We're going to work hard. Because one day my little baby is going to stand tall and he's going to say his name as loud and as strong as all the other boys and girls.'"

"The second lesson came at the end of my school career. I was an All-American State Champion high school basketball player. I played in college, started all four years, and was captain for three. I fully expected to be drafted by an NBA team. I never got the call. I was devastated; I had expected that I would at least get a shot at the big time. At one point I even thought about giving up on life.

"Then my grandmother sat me down and said, 'Get over it. Get your eyes down the road and get another game. You've got to be positive. This setback is nothing but a setup.'"

"So I looked at the skills I had learned from basketball—teamwork, competition, discipline, and goal-setting. I took these skills into job interviews and got a great job with IBM. Fourteen years later, the marketing director called a meeting and announced that IBM, which had never laid off anyone in its 65-year history, had to lay off 40,000 people. 'And,' he said, 'out of the 650 people in this room today, I'm sad to say that 80 percent of you will be gone in 3 months.'"

"I saw fear and defeat take over that room. I raised my hand. The marketing director, puzzled, called on me and said, 'Do you have a question?'"

"'Yes,' I said. 'Once these 80 percent are gone, can I get a bigger office, one with a window view?' The whole room burst out laughing, and everyone began to realize that, even though we still had to go through this downsizing, we had a choice about how we would respond to it."

"Who would have thought that a kindergartner who couldn't even say his own name would one day have his own business, speaking to corporations all over the world about how to handle change, overcome adversity, and harness the power of attitude? Attitude is a choice that we make; it is the control center for your life. Knowing that, I can say that even though I'm not playing with the NBA, I'm playing with the best of my natural born abilities, and I'm slam dunking every day."

Keith Harrell learned his lessons the hard way—but isn't that how most lessons are learned? Something amazing happens when, no matter how bad the situation, we can control how we view it and get through it with a positive attitude. And, as shown by his example at IBM, a good attitude and a sense of humor not only make a difference in your own life, they help others get through adverse situations as well.

> *Life can be wildly tragic at times, and I've had my share. But whatever happens to you, you have to keep a slightly comic attitude. In the final analysis, you have got to not forget to laugh.*
>
> —Katharine Hepburn,
> actress

The 1 Percent Attitude Solution

Until very recently, Don Fink was a high level manager at Citicorp. He has taken time off from his job so he can train full time for the Iron Man competition. The Iron Man is a national competition that includes a 2.4-mile swim, a 112-mile bike ride, and a 26-mile marathon—all in the same day.

It's his attitude that gives Fink the energy to keep going, even when he's physically exhausted. There have been times when Fink was tempted to give up his dream of competing in the race, as many people do. There are those who find the going too difficult and simply give up. Many people don't stick with their goals long enough to find out whether they can really achieve them or not. The motivation that keeps you on track and ultimately produces results comes from focusing on a destination, seeing yourself moving through the process, and expecting to achieve positive results. When that attitude of expectation is so strong, it acts as a magnet, keeping us moving forward and on course.

For Fink, the secret is in his "1 percent improvement" plan. The idea for 1 percent improvement came to him when he began running. He spent three years placing in the middle of the pack. Then he decided he really wanted to break into the top three, to hear his name announced and be awarded his medal in front of the cheering crowd. He trained harder than ever for this race, and came in eighth.

At first, he was satisfied because he had, after all, moved up from middle of the pack to the top 10 finishers. But then a few weeks later he sat down and read the actual race results and times. The person who had come in third, which had been Fink's goal, finished the race 1 minute and 40 seconds before Fink. Doing the math, Fink realized that the third place winner was only 1 percent faster than he was.

"I remember asking myself, 'Can I become 1 percent faster?'" he says. "I thought for a few seconds and then answered, 'Of course I can!'"

It is this 1 percent factor that changes a dream into an achievable goal. It may be too great a leap to set a goal of moving from the middle of the pack to third place in one fell swoop, but it's not too great to focus on the steps necessary to improve that tiny increment of 1 percent.

Don Fink has used the 1 percent improvement concept many times since that race to help him stay focused and motivated. "Every time I found a 1 percent improvement, then and only then would I focus on where to find my next 1 percent improvement," he says. "Ask yourself right now, 'Can I perform 1 percent better at my job? Can I be a 1 percent better husband or wife? Can I be a 1 percent better person?' If the answer is *yes* to any of these questions, write down a list of all the ways you can think of to achieve a 1 percent improvement. Then pick a couple of items from your list and go to work on them."

Perhaps the greatest question of all is, can you make a 1 percent improvement in your attitude? Of course you can.

Harvey Mackay on Attitude

Harvey Mackay, author of *Swim With the Sharks Without Being Eaten Alive*, is also chairman and CEO of Mackay Envelope Corp., a company that has been in business since the 1950s. In an interview, he told me that "attitude is the cornerstone of living." He has hired thousands of people during his career, and it is the top quality he looks for.

Mackay said, "I've studied attitude for over 40 years now. I have a 10-step process for hiring, but number one on my list is attitude.

"You get your choice when you get up every morning. Every single morning you can either be an optimist or a pessimist. You can be happy, you can be sad, you can have the right attitude, or you can have the wrong attitude. When I look to hire someone, I'm looking for someone who makes a good choice every morning, someone who's got a phenomenal attitude and the 'stick-to-it' mentality to hang in through rough times.

"One way I personally keep up a positive attitude is this—I have no negative friends. I always want to be around upbeat people. Norman Vincent Peale, who always had a positive attitude, was a great friend of mine. And Lou Holtz, one of the [most victorious] coaches in college football history, has been my closest friend for 15 years. These two men are the most positive people I've ever known. How can you be negative around people like that?"

> *Ability is what you're capable of doing. Motivation determines what you do. Attitude determines how well you do it.*

> —Lou Holtz,
> football coach

The 3 Most Powerful Words in the English Language

If you are looking for the road to success, you won't find any clear signposts. You won't find any magical answers. There is no wizard to grant your wishes, no yellow brick road that will lead you and others who walk along it directly to the land of Oz, to fame and fortune. Of all the high achievers I work with, not one took the same path as any other.

However, what they did have was an attitude of expectation. They expect things to turn out well and have confidence in their own abilities to make that happen.

What happens when you ask someone how a project is going to turn out, or if they're going to accomplish their goals, the answer you usually hear is, "I'm going to try my very best." But when you ask people who believe in themselves, people who have achieved success against the odds, they will answer with the three most powerful words in the English language: "Yes I will."

They are so positive, and their expectations are so strong, they will prevail over any obstacles in their way. Other people recognize their strength and either move out of the way to let them through, or find a way to hop on board.

> *Like the waves of the sea are the ways of fate as we voyage through life. 'Tis the set of the soul which decides its goal and not the calm or the strife.*

> —Ella Wheeler Wilcox,
> writer

Top 7 Things to Do to Improve Your Attitude

1. **Read something inspiring every day.** When you get up in the morning, before you do anything else, spend 15 minutes reading something motivational, something enlightening. Do the same thing at night for 15 minutes before you go to bed.

2. **Find a quote that really means something to you (maybe one in this book).** Copy it or cut it out and hang it on your wall where you can see it every day. A short quote can take you a million miles.

3. **Take an honest look at the people around you.** What kinds of attitude do they bring to the table? Do they pump you up or bring you down? Everyone is entitled to a bad attitude now and again—but if the people you know are constantly angry, bitter, or scared—it might be time to find yourself a new crowd. Here's an idea I heard from one of my seminar attendees. Every 30 days he makes a list of the people with whom he's spent the most time over the past month. Next to each name he puts a plus (+) if the person has been a mentor, role model, or has uplifted him in any way. Others on the list may not have much of an influence, either positive or negative, and beside those names he puts a 0. Then there are people who have negative attitudes, people he feels pull him down. He puts a minus (–) sign beside those names. After the list is made, he stops spending time with anyone who is in the "negative" category. Think about the people in your life, and make a positive, neutral, or negative list for yourself. It may be difficult to stop spending time with some of the negative people on your list, especially if they're family members. However, the less time you spend with them, the better off you'll be.

4. **When you're going through a bad time, think about others who have gone through adversity and made it out the other side.** Count your blessings, and think about others who have turned bad attitudes around. I love to watch inspiring movies about people who did not give up even though they had to fight against heavy odds. Those people claimed their right to own a positive attitude no matter what the circumstance, and in the end were able to reap their rewards.

5. **Be selective about the books and magazines you read, the shows and movies you watch, and the tapes you listen to.** We live in a world of high content; information comes at us from every possible medium. Remember, though, that just as inspiring movies can improve your

attitude, too much negative content can have the opposite impact. Nothing determines your attitude—for good or bad—more than the environment with which you choose to surround yourself.

6. **Find attitude mentors, people you can call for an infusion of excitement and enthusiasm.** One of my attitude mentors is Don Fink, the Iron Man competitor. He is now eight minutes away from the world record Iron Man in his age group. He trains eight hours a day. He energizes me. He definitely teaches me what having a positive attitude can do for you. Find people you know who also exhibit that kind of attitude and catch it from them.

7. **Change your focus.** Stop thinking about yourself and start thinking about those around you. Mark Twain once said, "If you want to cheer yourself up, cheer up everyone around you." Be of service to others. Help somebody else with no expectations of getting anything back. Help move someone else's achievements forward and your attitude will lift itself.

> *We who lived in the concentration camps can remember the men who walked through the huts comforting others, giving away their last piece of bread. They may have been few in number, but they offer sufficient proof that everything can be taken from a man but one thing: The last of his freedoms— to choose one's attitude in any given set of circumstances, to choose one's own way.*
>
> —Victor E. Frankl,
> *Man's Search for Meaning*

I Dare You...

When you're feeling that your attitude can use some pumping up, take action using these five strategies:

1. **Say hello to the next 10 people you see, whether you know them or not.** Give them a cheery, "Hey, how're you doing?" and see what happens. Some people may look at you oddly or not respond at all. But most people will smile and greet you just as cheerfully. Try this with 10 people and use it as proof that your world is a mirror: What you send out, you get back. As Ghandi once said, "Be the change you want to see in the world."

2. **Be yourself.** Whether you're going for a job interview or a blind date, to a business meeting or dinner with friends, forget about what others "might" think, how you "should" act or what you "should" say. If you are intimidated by the person or people you're going to meet, remember that they are people just like everyone else. They have their own faults and deficiencies. The better your attitude, the more comfortable you are with yourself, the greater your chances of making a good impression. Have faith that being yourself is enough.

3. **Turn other people's attitudes around—or turn and walk away.** If someone you know is exhibiting a negative attitude, see what you can do to change it. Try using humor. Tell a joke or a funny story. Recommend a tape or CD of a comedian you like. It might be enough just to listen to what the other person has to say without being critical or judgmental. If none of these strategies work, it may be time for you to walk away. Some people enjoy the drama they create for themselves by being constantly negative. If that's the case, hang on to your own positive attitude and don't let the other person drag you down. Keep in mind these words of George Washington, the founding father of the United States, "Associate yourself with men of good quality if you esteem your own reputation, for 'tis better to be alone than to be in bad company."

Any fact facing us is not as important as our attitude toward it, for that determines our success or failure.

—Norman Vincent Peale,
clergyman and writer

4. **Approach each day creatively.** Try something new at least once a day. It doesn't have to be anything major. Last Memorial Day I was invited to my cousin's house for a barbecue. The last thing I wanted to do was spend hours in traffic. So I decided to take a different route; I traveled the back roads instead of the highway. My family and I enjoyed the scenery, and there was hardly any traffic. A simple change in route changed our whole day. When we do the same old thing the same old way for too long, we stagnate, and stagnation fosters bad attitudes. Even a small disruption in the routine can create a fresh approach and a new way of looking at things.

5. **Reverse your expectations.** Often our expectations determine the outcome of events before they happen. We think that people will not be friendly, no one will talk to us, or it will be boring. If that's what you think, you will likely close yourself off to the good things that may be happening. So reverse your expectations; tell yourself that you will be the first to make conversation, and that you will find something interesting to talk about with at least two people. All you have to do is ask people about themselves. Everyone loves to talk about things that interest them, and we all love people who will listen to us.

An Attitude of Gratitude

I am of the opinion that my life belongs to the whole community and, as long as I live, it is my privilege to do for it whatever I can. I want to be thoroughly used up when I die. For the harder I work, the more I live. I rejoice in life for its own sake. Life is no brief candle to me. It is a sort of splendid torch which I have got to hold up for the moment and I want to make it burn as brightly as possible before handing it on to future generations.

—George Bernard Shaw,
playwright

There is such a thing in life as serendipity—when we are unexpectedly lucky, when we are in the right place at the right time. This only happens a few times in life. Those people who achieve success recognize that they are in the right place and are willing to take advantage of any opportunity they might find there. They know that they have been given a gift, but it is up to them to use it well.

We don't know when our gifts will run out. Therefore, we have an obligation to appreciate whatever we have. It's a wonderful thing to possess a positive attitude, an attitude of confidence and great expectations. But there is another attitude that is most important to possess, and that is an attitude of gratitude. Sometimes we think that we can only be grateful if we have a certain income or a fast car or a certain position in life. But in every life, there is much to be grateful for.

Look at everything you have right now. You may not yet be where you want to be, but there is always some good in the place you are now. Appreciate the moment, and appreciate the blessings large and small.

When we create something, we always create it first in thought form. If we are basically positive in attitude, expecting and envisioning pleasure, satisfaction, and happiness, we will attract and create people, situations, and events which conform to our positive expectations.

—Shakti Gawain,
author

In nature, if you want to plant an amazing crop, you start with the soil. In human beings, everything, including attitude, starts with the mind. This is where we plant our seeds, our ideas, and watch them grow. When you plant a crop, you don't just drop in the seed and walk away—not if you hope to have any success as a farmer. You think about and plan for all the steps involved in getting the highest yield—when you will have to water the plants, when you will have to fertilize, what you will need when it comes to harvest time. And we make plans about what we will do if there is a storm or a draught. We utilize foresight to keep the crop alive and healthy.

Yet with ideas, we often plant them and "walk away." We fail to picture the steps necessary to keep that idea alive; we somehow expect the idea to grow by itself. We don't make plans for the future of that idea—we don't picture how we will nurture it or what we will do in case of challenges to its growth.

Foresight is a powerful force. It gives us vision, insight, and inspiration to keep moving forward. It provides you with a mental focus and forward drive. That is why it's the next step in the *Diamond Power* process.

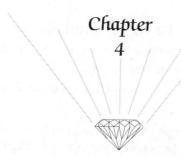

Chapter
4

Foresight:
Applying Your Mental Vision

True wisdom consists not in seeing what is immediately before our eyes, but in foreseeing what is to come.

—Terence,
Roman dramatist

What Is Foresight?

There are some words in the English language that we frequently use without really considering what they mean—or we have a mistaken notion of their meaning. Foresight is one of those words. We think that it's a kind of intuition, an ability to see things ahead of time, things that others can't see—something that either you have or you don't. That isn't what foresight is at all. Foresight is a skill, one that can be developed and used to your benefit.

There are several definitions of foresight in the dictionary, but this is the one I like best: *thoughtful regard or provision for the future.* That is the key. Foresight is taking a realistic look at the many paths that lay ahead and choosing the one that will best lead you to your goals. It gives you the opportunity to prepare for any roadblocks you may come across. It allows you to select and maintain your focus, rather than stumbling blindly forward. It allows you to make necessary changes and adjustments without losing your sense of direction. It simply makes your road easier to follow.

Give to us clear vision that we may know where to stand and what to stand for—because unless we stand for something, we shall fall for anything.

—Peter Marshall,
U.S. religious leader

The Power of Foresight

I would give all the wealth of the world, and all the deeds of all the heroes, for one true vision.

—Henry David Thoreau,
essayist

When the great Michelangelo began as an apprentice sculptor, his teacher made him work in a quarry for several months, just breaking and chipping rocks. He learned how rocks broke apart, how they chipped, what they did under pressure. Then when he began to actually make sculptures, Michelangelo understood how to work with stone. Before he began each new piece, he studied the stone he was going to use. He studied what happened to it when it was cut. He studied where it could be cut and where it would break. Before he ever took chisel in hand, he understood the rock.

Before Michelangelo began to sculpt his great David, he sculpted it in his mind. He knew exactly what he wanted David to look like. He knew David's proportions, his curves, his angles, his stance, his expression. Michelangelo saw it all in his mind's eye.

Then he began to sculpt. He started with a solid block of marble. Because he had studied, he knew the secrets of the stone. He looked at that rough rectangle of solid stone and saw the vision of David he had created in his mind. Then, he said, he chipped away everything that was not David.

Michelangelo saw David so clearly that he made that marble yield to his plan. Was every chip perfect? Probably not. Did he make mistakes or have to make adjustments as he went along? I don't know for sure, but I'm guessing he did. Whatever happened, though, could not erase that vision of David from his mind.

Thid is foresight. It is looking ahead with a clear vision—the ability to have a clear idea of what the future will look like, even before it is reality. It's not magic or fortune telling. It's having a clear concept of what you want your life to look like, directing your actions toward that vision, and then chipping away everything that isn't helping you create that picture.

Be daring, be different, be impractical; be anything that will assert integrity of purpose and imaginative vision against the play-it-safers, the creatures of the commonplace, the slave of the ordinary.

—Cecil Beaton,
photographer

A Vision of Others' Tomorrows

When we think of having foresight, we usually think of being able to see the future for ourselves. But there are some people who have foresight about others. Take, for instance, Angelo Ellerbe—he develops artists in the music industry. Some of his clients include Dionne Warwick, Gladys Knight, rappers DMX and Sisqo, and many others you haven't heard of—yet. Those who are now well-known names started out as unknowns, too. Somewhere along the line, someone like Angelo Ellerbe was able to see their potential, and to help the artists see this potential for themselves.

"My mother told me that you can't judge a book by its cover," says Ellerbe. "I move on from there. I have to make a decision as to whether I will take on a performer or not. I look at the whole person. I base my decision on their honesty, on their sincerity. I look at their energy and their focus, and I can feel where their future is going to be—if they have the ability to apply that energy, if they can think large, if they can claim victory before the battle has begun. Because in claiming victory, half the battle is already won. I help them believe in themselves so they can have a vision of a bigger, brighter tomorrow and a brighter future."

> *No man that does not see visions will ever realize any high hope or undertake any high enterprise.*
>
> —Woodrow Wilson,
> U.S. president

Realize that practicing foresight requires a leap of faith. Earl Nightingale once said, "We need faith strong enough to bear the burden of our doubts." Faith is a critical component of foresight. Stepping out into the future is to be daring and different. You have to believe deep down in your soul that your vision is true and real, otherwise you will let it go too easily. Renew your vision every day as you renew your faith; they will both provide the strong foundation of a better life.

The Virtual Image Video

As a student of martial arts, I became interested in the bo staff. A bo staff is a five- to seven-foot wooden pole that was used as a weapon 500 years ago. It was originally intended for horseback fighting. If you wanted to unseat a rider, the bo staff was the simplest and most effective weapon available.

The competition I wanted to enter was not about fighting a real opponent. It was about certain "forms" or series of strikes, blocks, thrusts, and parries that might be applied in a confrontation, but now the opponent would be invisible.

When I started training with the bo staff, I had only three-and-a-half months until the competition. I would be going up against people who had been training with masters for many years, and I was doing this on my own. I could not train 24 hours a day. My problem was this: *How could I make the most of the limited practice time I had?*

My solution was to use visualization. I bought videotapes of masters teaching the art of the bo staff, and I studied them over and over again. I practiced with the real bo staff every day, and performed every move in my mind hundreds of times, step-by-step. I visualized my form in every spare moment that I had. I visualized every night before I went to sleep. For three-and-a-half months, I lived my "normal" family life and endured the busiest work schedule ever. At the same time, I lived and breathed the bo staff. When it came time for the competition in Atlantic City, New Jersey, I didn't have to think about my form at all. I was able to give my performance everything I had. Ultimately, I took second place in the first national tournament I ever entered.

This is the strength of creating your own virtual reality. Imagine if 95 percent of the visions you create in your head became physical reality! I challenge you to make that happen.

Envisioning the end is enough to set the means in motion.

—Dorothea Brand,
author

I challenge you to practice this skill for yourself. Take an exercise, a sport, or a project—anything that can be broken down into a repeatable sequence of events. See yourself going through each and every step. Every day you should be learning something new, gaining knowledge that will add value to your vision and make it even stronger. Apply your vision to reality and you will be amazed at what you can accomplish.

Don't get frustrated. This kind of visualization doesn't always come naturally. You may fall asleep in the middle of your scenario. You may start to do your steps, and slowly begin to think of other things. This is to be expected. It's difficult to close your eyes and visualize a sequence of events without getting lost. But like any skill, the more you practice, the easier it gets. Have faith that the results you get are worth every bit of effort you have to put in. Your future may depend on it.

A vision is not a vision unless it says yes to some ideas and no to others, inspires people, and is a reason to get out of bed in the morning and come to work.

—Gifford Pinchot III,
management consultant

Dreaming Your Life Away

What is the difference between visualization and daydreaming? Daydreaming is the step between night dreaming and visualization. It is fuzzy, unclear, and unfocused. Daydreaming can be a form of relaxation. It is thinking about the future, but with no strong intent or concentration. There's nothing wrong with that. It's just that it's more of a wish than a plan.

When you daydream or make a wish, you're really asking for a miracle. You want something to happen without having to work for it. It's as if you are standing in the darkness, eyes shut tight, saying, "I wish someone would notice me!" Why would they? It's only when you open your eyes and see what's happening around you, when you step into the light, and when you take action that your "wish" has even a chance of coming true.

Visualization is seeing those steps before you take them. It is very specific. Daydreams help you "think big," while foresight helps you break the big things down into specific steps you can take to accomplish them.

Cherish your visions and your dreams, as they are the children of your soul, the blueprints of your ultimate achievements.

—Napoleon Hill,
author

Don't let your dreams fade away. Sometimes they get pushed aside by the more practical aspects of day-to-day living. That's to be expected. We can't spend every minute planning for the future; we must take care of ourselves and our families today. Just know that your dreams are important, too. You may have to hold onto them for awhile, but the fruit they will eventually bear will be worth the wait.

5 Steps for Developing Foresight

1. **Understand the importance of foresight as a tool for creating a better life.** Of course, you can't always keep everything under control. Life happens. Storms batter us around. But if you have plotted a course,

you can rely on your inner compass to help you reach the shore once again. Otherwise, you might drift at sea, lost and confused. I remember great words of wisdom given by a mother to her children. She told them to nest in the gale. A gale is a strong wind of speeds up to 60 miles per hour. You need to be able to hold steady against such a force. There are birds that pick up mud and dirt in their mouths and mix it with saliva to create a glue to hold their nests together. The structure of these nests enables them to withstand great winds. Foresight—your strong vision of the future—is the nest you create to help you survive when hard times hit. The stronger that vision is, the greater the shelter your nest will provide.

> *Every great work, every big accomplishment, has been*
> *brought into manifestation through holding to the vision,*
> *even though just before the big achievement, comes*
> *apparent failure and discouragement.*
>
> —Florence Scovel Shinn,
> metaphysicist

2. **Create a detailed picture in your mind.** Define your goal clearly. Visualization is a mental exercise; it's a muscle that can be strengthened with constant use. Don't be afraid to add to the picture or reconfigure it. The clearer and brighter you can make the picture, the easier it is for you to be pulled toward it.

3. **Do your research.** Foresight is not based on conjecture. It does not come out of thin air. Foresight comes from gaining knowledge of what has happened in the past and what is important today. That is the only way to gain insight into how to plan for tomorrow. Keep this phrase in mind: People and print. If you're planning ahead in business, for example, find out as much as you can about the industry in which you're interested. Talk to people in the industry. Read books and trade magazines. Surf the Internet. Look for resources that will give you a broader, deeper understanding of your profession. Once you have this knowledge, you can look ahead with confidence. Your foresight becomes stronger when it is cultivated with the richness of your environment.

4. **Don't wait to plan ahead.** There is no special time or place that needs to be set aside for developing foresight. It may help to set aside a quiet time and place to just think, but it's not necessary. Visualization can take place at any time, especially when you're doing "mindless" tasks—when you're stuffing envelopes, doing housework, washing the dishes, listening to music, or traveling from one place to another.

5. **Write down your thoughts, ideas, and plans—anything that pertains to your vision.** Keep a notepad with you at all times so that you can jot down ideas as they occur to you. We all know that the best ideas come when we least expect them. We also know how easily they slip away if we don't give them enough respect and attention.

> *Each eye can have its vision separately; but when we are looking at anything, our vision, which in itself is divided, joins up and unites in order to give itself as a whole to the object that is put before it.*
>
> —John Calvin,
> theologian

Practical Foresight

Foresight is a skill that can be learned like any other skill. The more you practice it, the better you get at it. Successful people often rely on foresight to move themselves forward. They set goals and make monthly and yearly plans, sometimes even five- and 10-year plans. They also know they have to keep reevaluating their plans to make sure they are practical in a real-life scenario.

Here are some questions you can ask to help make sure your plans are within the realm of possibility:

✧ **Will I be able to accomplish this within the time frame I have set up?** Don't give yourself six months to accomplish something that takes two years to accomplish. You will only set yourself up for failure and disappointment. Keep in mind that some of your plans include other people, and you can't always control their time lines. Give yourself limits, but keep them flexible. Don't forget, the tree that bends with the wind does not break.

✧ **Will I be able to create synergy with other things that are going on in my life?** If your plans include something that is far afield from all the other things that are going on in your life, be sure you have a strong reason or passion to pursue it. If you do, then go after it. If not, it will probably take more effort than you'll be willing to devote to it.

✧ **What will I gain by pursuing this course?** What are the rewards—money, status, accomplishment, emotional satisfaction? You are the only one who can measure those rewards and decide if they are worth the required effort.

✧ **What will I lose by not pursuing this course?** How damaging will it be to your self-esteem to give up on this particular dream?

✧ **Realistically, does it make sense?** Does it add value to my life and to those around me? Will it take too much away from current projects?

I think there is something more important than believing: Action! The world is full of dreamers, there aren't enough who will move ahead and begin to take concrete steps to actualize their vision.

—W. Clement Stone,
businessman

When you are focused in one area like a laser beam, you create a depth of vision that is omnipotent. That's what gives it strength.

The Power of the Written Word

I know I said it before, but I'll say it again: *The best way to turn visualization into reality is to write it down.* I have often referred to a book, originally written in 1931 and reprinted many times since, by William H. Danforth called *I Dare You.* It's a simple book, and it's written in a style that is definitely old-fashioned. But the ideas it contains have not aged. In once section, Mr. Danforth includes a workbook page for readers to write out their "dares" or goals for the future.

He says, "The weak ones who are licked or partially licked will stall here. Will you listen to the little imps whispering in your ears that writing down the things you ought to do is merely piffle? Or will you put things down in black and white that need to be done and never quit until you can say, 'Done!'"

I say, don't dismiss Mr. Danforth's ideas as merely piffle. Over the years, they have proven to be true. More than 10 years ago, I filled out his worksheet focusing on the goals I wanted to accomplish. Today, I say that putting my goals on paper helped me focus on them. Here are the categories he suggests:

✧ One habit to change.

✧ One idea to bring to fruition.

✧ One month's thinking in uncharted fields.

✧ One idea to share with others.

✧ One great mental dare for the year ahead.

You can work on all these categories at once, or choose one that is most relevant at this moment. It doesn't matter. As the saying goes, "Just do it!"

> *No one keeps his enthusiasm automatically. Enthusiasm must be nourished with new actions, new aspirations, new efforts, new visions.*
>
> —Papyrus,
> philosopher

You're not born enthusiastic. You don't automatically stay enthusiastic. It must be fed, like the furnace on a train, to keep it going. Instead of coal, you shovel in new information and new actions to keep the fire burning.

Looking Ahead While Living in the Moment

The future begins today. Shakespeare once said, "Every day is a king in disguise." We must plan for the future, but we must live today. Foresight does not involve saying things such as, "I will be happy when I accomplish this," or, "I will be fulfilled when I get a new house (a new car, earn my degree, or whatever else is important to you)." There is a balance that needs to be achieved between looking ahead and getting the most richness out of each day as it comes. The reason we use foresight and visualization is so that we can see where we're going without bumping into ourselves. Find joy in the actions you take today, especially those that are building your future. Someone once said, "Tomorrow's life is too late. Live today."

As much as we plan, we cannot really know what will happen tomorrow. Each day, we are lucky to be alive. So we must count each day as a gift that has been given to us, and show our appreciation by using that gift well.

> *Hold fast to dreams, for if dreams die, life is a broken-winged bird that cannot fly.*
>
> —Langston Hughes,
> poet and writer

I Dare You...

Spend time every day practicing the art of foresight. Find time, no matter what mood you're in, to create the future in your mind's eye.

Based on where you are now, what would your future look like? How would you like your life to be different than it is now? What actions can I take today to move toward that different life? What do I have in my life now that I can use to create that future? What don't I have in my life that I can work toward getting?

> *Go within every day and find the inner strength so that the*
> *world will not blow your candle out.*
> —Katharine Dunham,
> dancer

Create a virtual reality that can become a physical reality. Your mind is the most potent, powerful tool a human has. And we have all been given that tool, free and clear. Use it to your best ability.

> *Every situation—nay, every moment—is of infinite worth;*
> *for it is the representative of a whole eternity.*
> —Johann Wolfgang von Goethe,
> author

Foresight is what enables you to move forward. But in order to be effective and successful, you can't just move forward from here to there and back again. You have to be aiming at something in order to hit a target. In the next chapter, you'll learn that what separates a vision from reality is having a clear, purposeful goal on which to set your sights.

Chapter 5

Goals:
Setting Them and Reaching Them

It must be borne in mind that the tragedy of life doesn't lie in not reaching your goal. The tragedy lies in having no goal to reach. It isn't a calamity to die with dreams unfulfilled, but it is a calamity not to dream. It is not a disaster to be unable to capture your ideal, but it is a disaster to have no ideal to capture. It is not a disgrace not to reach the stars, but it is a disgrace to have no stars to reach for. Not failure, but low aim is a sin.

—Dr. Benjamin E. Mayes,
president, Morehouse University

What Are Goals?

The most glorious part of having a goal is the journey toward it. It's the ability to go after something, get knocked down, come back up, struggle, strive, move forward, accomplish one goal—and then go beyond it. Getting to the goal is only part of the reward; the rest comes from what you've learned and how you've grown along the way.

It's been said that when the astronauts who went to the moon came back to Earth, they suffered from anxiety, depression, and other emotional problems. Why? Because they spent years preparing for their mission—and what do you do after you've gone to the moon? They had reached their ultimate goal and no longer had anything to strive toward. It's a lesson to remember: No objective is so great that it is the be-all and the end-all. We must always be setting the bar a little higher, reaching for another goal.

Goals can be defined in many ways. There are dozens of synonyms for the word: target, purpose, objective, destination, intent, aim. Dreams and wishes become reality when we set goals for ourselves. The great motivator Napolean Hill said that "a goal is a dream with a deadline." Goals give us direction and focus. They make the impossible achievable. They help us keep our vision clear and our footing steady. A goal accomplished is not just another step toward a destination; it's a building block in the foundation of our self-esteem.

The Power of Goals

If you're bored with life—if you don't get up every morning with a burning desire to do things—you don't have enough goals.

—Lou Holtz,
football coach

Just as there are many ways to express the word "goal," there are many ways to get to one (some of which you'll find as you read on). But none of the things you read here, or in any other book or magazine, will work without one main ingredient. That ingredient is hunger—a burning desire—an intense longing to get to a certain place or do a particular thing.

I believe that human beings are born with a need to achieve. I believe that we are at our best when we're on our way to achieving a worthy goal. A worthy goal is something that you believe in, something that is challenging for you. It is the best way to get through the tough times in life. The easiest way to avoid depression is to always have some goal you're working towards that keeps you excited.

Success is always built on a strong sense of purpose—on the faith, belief, and passion we have for the goals we set. We need goals that are set high. Whoever said that we should set realistic goals is unrealistic. We don't need to set impossible goals, but we do need to amaze ourselves—and we have the capacity to do that every single day.

The most successful people keep asking themselves, "Where am I now, and where do I have to go?" They keep working toward their goal. They live for it. And once they achieve it, they set new, higher goals. Think of yourself 25 years from now. Will you look back and think, "I could have done more"? Or will you recognize your hunger and desire and let it lead you to a goal you thought was beyond your abilities? As Kramer on Seinfeld once said, "Wouldn't it be hell if someday God showed you what you could have done with your life?"

We need passion to drive us forward. It's something that we look for in ourselves, but that others also look for in us. When managers, especially sales managers, are looking for new people, they look for attitude, effort, and passion. You can teach almost anyone the skills of a job, but you can't teach passion. Managers are not only looking for people who can sell, they are looking for people who can open up new business. It's a difficult thing to do.

When I first went into sales, I wasn't passionate about what I was selling, so it took great effort to open new accounts. Later on, I looked for jobs where I had a great belief in the product I was selling. I was passionate about the product and passionate about selling, and suddenly I found that it was 10 times easier to gain access to key people.

What had changed? Were my sales skills so much better at the later jobs? Of course, experience taught me some things about how to sell, but it was that burning desire that kept the momentum going later on. It's not so hard to figure out: If you hate what you're doing, you'll stop at the first sign of difficulty. If you love what you're doing, nothing can stop you. You must have that inner desire to cope with the obstacles to reaching your goal.

> *When we are motivated by goals that have deep meaning,*
> *by dreams that need completion, by pure love that needs*
> *expressing, then we truly live.*
>
> —Greg Anderson,
> basketball player

The Wake-up Calls of Life

It was 1969. Israel and Egypt were at war, and a young Israeli officer named Jack Lehav was assigned to serve at the Suez Canal. There was one day of fighting Lehav will never forget.

"We were shooting at each other in an absolutely crazy battle. All that separated us from the Egyptians was 200 to 250 yards of water. You could look through a periscope from the bunkers and see into the canal. All of a sudden, I saw two huge whales, calmly swimming. I said to my guys, 'Stop shooting.' And apparently the Egyptians did the same, because the shooting stopped.

"All of us raised our heads and looked into the water. For 10 minutes, everybody stopped what they were doing, which was fighting and killing and shooting and bombing, and watched this miracle of nature going by. I thought, 'Look what two whales can do to two nations!'

"As the whales headed south and disappeared from view, we slowly headed back to the bunkers. A very good friend of mine, another young officer, stood out there and kept on looking. I screamed to him, 'Get down!' but I was too late. Within a tenth of a second, which is all it takes in a war, a bullet went through his head and he was dead.

"Something very strong happens to you in life at that moment. In wartime you make close friendships with people, then in one second a close friend is in your arms and he's dead. I realized we all come to this planet for a short visit. It could be 10, 20 years, or 80 or 100. And you get a chance to contribute, to do, to set yourself goals, and you never know when it could end. It could end for you tomorrow.

"I realized then and there, 'Hey, mister, you have a chance. You don't know what this chance is like. Go and get the most out of it.'"

There are moments in life that are so shocking, that make such an impact that they make us realize just how vulnerable we are. They make us want to 'get the most' out of whatever time we have, to set goals, and to accomplish them. They are the wake-up calls of life.

The good news is that we don't have to wait for a life-changing incident to set goals for ourselves. Sometimes we need reminders, like Jack Lehav's story. We need an emotional kick to jump-start our resolve and commitment—a neon sign that says, "Life is precious; don't waste the time you've got." We need to invest as much as we can in life so that we can get the most out of it. That's what goals are all about. They're about setting a course and remaining true to it, not stopping when things become too difficult or too easy. They're about pushing on in the face of adversity and constantly reminding ourselves of the basic elements of life: who we are, what we're here for, and whom we can serve.

He who has a why to live for can bear almost any how.

—Friedrich Nietzsche,
German philosopher

How to Go After Your G•O•A•L•S

Here is an acronym for the word "goals" that may explain just how goals work:

G: Gather information. Look at all possible sources. Read books and listen to tapes on the subject. Find someone who has accomplished a similar goal to yours. Don't think that your goal has to be something that has never been accomplished before. Stanley Mason is president and founder of Simco Incorporated Product Development Support Services. Mason holds more than 65 patents for his inventions and has been called the modern day Thomas Edison. Many of his inventions are improvements to products that are already on the market. Often, he goes to a store, buys a bunch of different products, and then thinks about how he can improve them. "You've got to get totally immersed in your goals and ideas," says Mason.

Collect as much data as you can. If your goal is to open a restaurant, for instance, talk to people in the restaurant business. Visit some of your favorite eateries and analyze what they do well and what they don't. Take these ideas as a starting point, then add your own creativity to the mix.

O: Organize. After you've gathered as much information as you can, sift through the data, then prioritize your information. Successful people know that nothing is ever achieved in one giant leap. It's the tiny steps you take, one by one, that help you reach your destination. In order to transform your dreams and visions into reality, begin by putting your goals down in writing. Write them down in the present tense. For instance, instead of writing, "I will get 10 new clients next month," write, "I have 10 new clients in February." Putting it in the present gives the goal a better sense of reality. There is energy that comes from setting goals and writing them down. They literally propel you into action. A goal can be the spark that ignites the fire within and the fuel you need to keep that fire burning.

A: Action. Just do it. Even if you're not totally prepared, take the first step. This is the most important step because we learn the best lessons from experience. Some people get so caught up in writing down their goals, they never take the steps to achieve them. No matter how far away your goal may seem, the only way to get there is to take the first step.

L: Look back at your plan. Ask yourself a few questions: Am I on track? Am I going about this efficiently? Are there other ways to do it? Be sure you're flexible enough to make adjustments along the way. You might find that a step you planned to take is no longer available to you or is not the best path to take. Use the lessons you learn from this to help you move on and try again with new information. Look at the big picture, then go back and fix the details.

S: Set new goals. We are at our best when we are climbing, stretching, and challenging ourselves. Don't settle for what you now know you can do—reach for the next star. Success, once reached, can make you complacent. There are people who reach a certain level of success and begin to lose their hunger. The passion is gone. It's like the astronauts coming back from the moon. The only way to keep going and remain successful is to set a new goal and start a new journey.

Keep the Momentum Going

My son, Jordan (who was four at the time) and I were bicycling in the park on a beautiful path that goes up and down some rather steep hills (at least for a 4-year-old). I looked at Jordan, who had a familiar determined look. His tongue was sticking out of the corner of his mouth and he was pedaling like crazy, even as we were going down a hill. I called out to him. "Jordan, relax," I said. "We're going downhill. You can coast a little bit."

"But Daddy," he said wisely, "Look at the hill coming up."

You might see your goal as reaching a summit and then coasting downhill from there so you can enjoy the ride. It's wonderful to enjoy the road, but don't forget that there's always another hill ahead. So many times in my life, when things are going well, that's when I have got to pour the momentum on. Success breeds success. My son reminded me that coasting is only downhill. So enjoy the ride, but keep pedaling, and keep the momentum going.

> *What you get by reaching your destination is not as important as what you become by reaching your destination.*
>
> —Dr. Robert Anthony,
> writer

It's as Easy as 1, 2, 3...

DO THIS EXERCISE RIGHT NOW. Go get a pen and a piece of paper and come back. If you don't do it now, if you delay even for a couple of hours, the likelihood is that you won't do it at all. So get up and get that pen and paper.

This is the most powerful goal-setting technique I've ever used. There are two reasons for this: one, it's easy to do; and two, it commits you to take action.

1. **On your piece of paper, write down 10 goals for the next 12 months.** Seven of the goals should be related to your business or profession. Three should be personal. Out of the first seven, one should be such a stretch that other people might even laugh at it. As businesswoman Mary Kay Ash once said, "A good goal is like a strenuous exercise—it makes you stretch." If it's that hard, if it's that challenging, there will be great reward that comes with it.

2. **Choose the most important goal on your list.** Ask yourself, "Which of these goals, if I were to achieve it, would have the greatest positive impact on my life?" Write that goal on top of your piece of paper. Write it in the form of a question. For example: "How can I make salesperson of the year by next January?" Make the question specific, including deadlines if possible.

3. **Write down 20 answers to the question.** Force yourself to list 20. The first few will be easy; the rest will get progressively more difficult. At the end of the exercise, choose one of the items on your list of 20 answers. Do it immediately. Pick up the phone. Write that letter. Redo your resume. Buy what you need. Don't hesitate—just do it.

If you take these three steps, your life will be totally different one year from now. You'll be accomplishing more. You'll be more confident. You'll be a better salesperson—whatever it is you set out to do. All you have to do is write down 10 goals, pick the one that will have the most positive impact on your life, write down 20 ways to achieve that goal, and take one immediate action. Repeat the process for the next goal on your list, and so on, until you've completed the list. If you can do that, the world is yours.

Keep the Oak in Sight

You must have long-range goals to keep you from being frustrated by short-range failures.

—Charles C. Noble,
writer

Not long ago, I met a man who is a multimillionaire. His name is Don Storms. Several years ago, he was a very successful television personality who was fired when new management came into his organization.

He went through an agonizing period of depression and an I-just-don't-care-anymore attitude. But he was able to turn himself around and become incredibly successful in an entirely new field.

How did he do it? "It was a sense of purpose," he says, "having a goal, and a new dream to strive toward." It was having this goal—making a success of his new business venture—that enabled Storms to turn his life around. When I met him, I asked him about the secret to his success. He told me it was because he kept his eye on the oak tree.

"The oak tree?" I asked. I had no idea what he was talking about.

"When I was growing up in the country," Storms told me, "we used to plow the fields. We would never look down at the ground we were plowing. We'd look at the oak tree, shoot for that, and plow a straighter furrow. If you look at the adversities—oh, there's a rock, or a tree stump, or a small ravine—you'll be wandering all over the place. But if you've got an oak tree in your sight and you're heading right for it, you'll get past the rocks and stumps and accomplish your goal."

It doesn't matter if you're plowing a field, or plowing a trail to a new business. You want to get to the other side. If your goal is fuzzy and you're not sure where you want to go, you'll bump into every stone and stump in your path. If, however, you have that goal in front of you, firmly planted in your mind, it will act like a magnet and draw you straight to it.

> *The most pathetic person in the world is someone who has sight but has no vision.*
>
> —Helen Keller,
> writer and lecturer

Straightening Out Your Ss

There are many ways to think about reaching your goals. One way has to do with bicycle riding. I started thinking about ways I could improve my own bicycle-racing capabilities. When you're setting goals—in life, in work, or in bicycle racing—the point is not just to ride toward the goal; it's constantly thinking of ways to make minute improvements in everything you do to make it easier to accomplish your goal.

What happens when you're riding your bike and you start to get tired or you lose your concentration? Your bike begins to waggle all over the road. Instead of going straight forward, which is your intention, you slow down and start to swerve your way down the street in an "S" motion. Not only do you reduce your speed, you're riding a longer distance. This means that if I take the "S" and straighten it out, I could be decreasing the distance I'm traveling by 50 percent. In order to stop taking those unnecessary curves, you have to sharpen your focus and regain your concentration.

The same thing happens many times in life. You're riding along straight towards your goals when you begin to get tired or distracted. Obstacles take you off course. Before you know it, those things cause you to start to S your way through life. That's when you have to straighten out your S and keep focused on the path ahead.

Just take the ball and throw it where you want to...
Home plate don't move.

—Satchel Paige,
baseball pitcher

Jumping Steps

Not too long ago, I was playing with two of my children. They were standing at the top of the steps leading into the house; I was standing at the bottom landing. I said, "I'm going to jump from here to the fourth step. Do you think I can make it?" Looking down from the top it didn't seem difficult at all, so they both said "Sure you can." Then I told them to come down to the bottom and look up. It looked much steeper from that angle. So I asked again, "Do you still think I can make it?" This time they both said, "No."

So then I said, "Now look up at the fifth step. Do you think I can make that one?" They both said, "No way!" So I leapt with all my might—and landed on the fourth step.

I asked my kids, "What's the lesson here?" They said, "You didn't make it." I said, "That's true, but what did I learn? The lesson is that when you shoot for something, aim even higher than you think you can go. What's the worst that can happen? You miss by one step and you land where you wanted to go in the first place! Don't be afraid to set your sights a little higher each time you set a goal."

Do not let what you cannot do interfere with what you
can do.

—John Wooden,
basketball coach

7 Great Ways to Achieve Your Goals

1. **Write down your goals on a small piece of paper you can keep in your wallet.** Most likely, you use your wallet every day, so you'll see your goals before you every day. Goals are often associated with making more money, so the more money you make, the more you'll use your wallet. The more you use your wallet, the more often you'll see your goals in front of you.

2. **Write your goals on a board at home or at work.** Put them up in front of you. I write my goals on whiteboards and bulletin boards on the walls of my office. They're the first thing I see when I walk into my office. They help me stay focused on my larger goals and on the day-to-day things I need to do in order to reach those goals (and having your goals staring you in the face all day also tends to make you feel guilty when you're not working toward them).

3. **Tell everybody about your goals.** Once you say them out loud, you're committed to them. People will ask you how you're progressing toward your goal. They remind you of your commitment. This doesn't mean you can never change a goal, it's just another external reminder to keep you on track. If you do change a goal and people ask you about it, you will have to lay out the reasons for them, which will help you determine whether you made the change for good, sound reasons, or just because the original goal was proving difficult to achieve. As the German writer Goethe once said, "Concerning all acts of creation, there is one elementary truth…that the moment one definitely commits oneself, then providence moves too."

4. **Break down your goals into small chunks so they're easier to handle.** If you pursue a difficult goal and keep failing, you will easily get discouraged. The only way you can get from point A to point B is to take one small step at a time. Often, we don't give ourselves enough credit for the individual steps we take. But it's only by breaking down large, seemingly unattainable goals that we make them attainable. If you break down your goal into small components, you can build your confidence with each step. Remember this ancient African proverb: The best way to eat an elephant standing in your path is to cut it up into little pieces.

5. **Put the goals that you are passionate about on your goal board.** It's difficult to go after a goal because you feel you *have* to. It's much easier to go after something because you *want* to. You've got to want to get to this goal. Otherwise, the smallest obstacle will stop you in your tracks.

6. **Write down all the benefits of your goal being achieved.** Even if your goal is based on something you don't like, find reasons you want to do it. If your boss says, "I need that report done by October 15," make a list of the benefits you'll get by doing a great job on the report and completing it on time (or even earlier). Your boss will be impressed. You can remind your boss about this when it comes time for performance review. You'll have a better chance of getting promoted, which will mean more money for you and your family, which will mean that you can move into a bigger house, for example. Even if you're not excited about the goal itself, you can be passionate about what achieving that goal will do for you.

7. **Talk to people who have achieved the goal you're trying to achieve.** Talk to everyone you can to get feedback. Don't assume that what they say is the only way, but let them give you pieces of information you can put together. You become well-rounded this way.

I Dare You...

There is only one dare here, but it's a big one. I dare you to do more than you think is humanly possible. I dare you to set worthy goals, to set them nobly, and to follow a straight path in their direction. Everyone goes through times when they are coasting along, not sure of where they are going. Everyone goes through periods of confusion and insecurity. It's human nature. Just remember that goals help get us out of confusion, they lead us toward security. Keep the oak tree in sight and you'll be amazed at who you are when you get there.

The ultimate goal of all our lives is to be happy and fulfilled. Goal-setting is simply a tool we can use to help us on our way. There's no need to overwhelm yourself by setting too many goals at once. Work on one at a time; then as soon as you are nearing one destination, you can begin planning for the next journey. Goals should be chosen with great care and concern. Be prepared to get what you go after. Whatever it is that you really want can be achieved if you write it on the page and engrave it in your mind.

*Despite the success cult, men are most deeply moved not
by the reaching of the goal but by the grandness of the
effort involved in getting there.*

—Max Lerner,
educator

It's one thing to set goals; it's another to follow through on them. In this chapter I asked you to set one goal that might make other people laugh. This is not an easy thing to do. It takes guts, fortitude, and courage. Everybody faces a moment of truth at some point in their life, when they have to face the music and dance.

If you look at any successful person, you'll find someone who, like the phoenix, has faced the music many times, has stumbled or fallen, only to rise again. It's that ability to rise up again and again, to be tenacious, to be persistent and never give up on a dream that has gotten them through so many obstacles. We look at them and see the end result—we don't know all the effort that's gone before. But behind the scenes, they've forced themselves to keep on going long after many others have given up. It's amazing that one of the greatest truths of life is one of the first sayings we learn in life: If at first you don't succeed, try, try again.

Chapter 6

Persistence:
Getting Through and Getting It Done

Nothing in this world can take the place of persistence. Talent will not; nothing is more common than unsuccessful people with talent. Genius will not; unrewarded genius is almost a proverb. Education will not; the world is full of educated derelicts. Persistence and determination alone are omnipotent. The slogan 'press on' has solved and always will solve the problems of the human race.

—Calvin Coolidge,
U.S. president

What Is Persistence?

Tenacity and persistence are two of the strongest words in the English language. To be persistent means to continue steadily or firmly in some state, purpose, or course of action; to last or endure. Tenacity means to hold fast, to refuse to let go or quit. The difference in the two words are subtle; I use them interchangeably because they really mean the same thing: To try, try, and try again until you achieve your goal.

People who are tenacious are good at breaking barriers. They do not let other people stop them from achieving their goals. They are able to overcome deficiencies in talent, education, skill, and opportunities. They push ahead against all odds, and, more often than not, surprise themselves with all that they can accomplish.

Patience and tenacity of purpose are worth more than twice their weight in cleverness.

—Thomas Henry Huxley,
biologist

The Power of Persistence

Persistence is the ability to look at incoming information, evaluate it, and either discard it or use it to your advantage. In life, you can't control the outcome but you can control the income. You can control what you do with incoming data. You can change your attitude. You can strengthen your faith. You can fail and fail again, and make smarter decisions each time to start once more. There will always be setbacks and difficulties; you can't stop them from happening. They're part of life. But you can stop them from stopping you.

Persistence means going after your goal with laser-beam focus. Every single action you take is done with precision and purpose. When you give your word, you keep it. When you make promises, you focus on delivering. When you see an opportunity, you go for it. Of course, this is not as easy as it sounds. We all have doubts.

We all have times when we say, "Is it really worth my time and effort to keep going in this direction?" It's not a bad thing to ask questions—you may find that you need to shift your focus somewhat, or try another path. Persistence doesn't mean that you stick to your vision blindly. It means that you consider all paths and keep trying until you find the right one.

Getting things done when there is a lot at stake is difficult. You have to weigh every option: are you going to concentrate your time and effort in this direction, or are you going to move on? If your decision is to keep going, then you have to know that failure is not an option.

Getting through and getting things done can become a way of life, whether it's doing a report, starting a fitness program, getting a job, landing a deal, or starting a company. It's a process that sometimes calls for aggressive persistence and other times calls for quiet confidence. The combination of both will keep you constantly moving forward.

There are no secrets to success: Don't waste time looking for them. Success is the result of perfection, hard work, learning from failure, loyalty to those for whom you work, and persistence.

—Colin Powell,
U.S. Secretary of State

When Is a Failure Not a Failure?

"Tenacity is not something you're born with, it's something you develop," says Bill Phillips, author of *Body for Life: 12 Weeks to Mental and Physical Strength.* "For me, it came from developing the habit of never seeing a failed effort as a failure. I've probably made more mistakes in my business than most people make in a lifetime. I just make them faster. I fail fast and try again. I don't see myself as a failure because something I tried failed. As long as I'm trying, I'm never truly a failure.

"Tenacity is about doing better than what you think your best effort is. So often people say, 'I'm doing the best I can.' In reality, they could do better. A great place to learn about breaking perceived barriers is in the gym. The way people exercise is often the way they approach everything in their life. They get to a certain point, it starts to be a little uncomfortable, and they draw the line right there. But the way to approach every challenge in life is to push yourself beyond what you think you can do, whether it's during a workout or during your workday, or in any aspect of your life.

"You can't worry about other people's perceptions. Sometimes, when others see you breaking out of your comfort zone, it makes them uncomfortable. But if you look around and see that people are putting forward a half-hearted effort, you'll also see that they're getting half-hearted results. Those who succeed are willing to set their mind to something, to go out and get it. They're willing to push themselves to a higher level."

Energy and persistence alter all things.

—Benjamin Franklin,
U.S. statesman

10 Tips on Persistence

1. **Get back up.** If you get knocked down nine times, get up the 10th. That's the key. You can't let the setbacks get to you personally. People may tell you "It can't be done." Sometimes all that means is that *they* couldn't do it. Don't let other people's thoughts make you think differently. When you're knocked down, get back up again no matter how much it hurts you or your pride. You never know what may happen the next time.

2. **Chip away today for success tomorrow.** One step at a time—that is how great things are accomplished. Achieving "overnight success" may take years, but it will come to those who are focused, persistent,

and keep their eyes fixed on their goals. If you lay one brick each day, pretty soon you've built a foundation, then a room, then a whole house. It can only be done one brick at a time.

3. **Can't get through the door? Try the window.** If the window is locked, go down the chimney. Look for every opening, try every single possibility. Don't give up because the one way you've tried is blocked. There are many paths that lead to the same destination. As Henry Wadsworth Longfellow said, "If you only knock long enough and loud enough at the gate, you are sure to wake somebody up."

4. **What doesn't kill you makes you stronger.** Life is full of potholes; you can't avoid them all. The one thing you can count on is that the going is going to get difficult. That's when you find out what you're really made of. That's when you realize that you can do 10 times more than you thought you could. Yes, you'll get worn down. You may have to take a break to rest and recover. But when you come back, you'll be so much stronger and so much wiser about dealing with potholes than you ever were before. Surprise yourself; surpass yourself. That's what creates your inner strength.

> *Steel must endure the forge in order to become strong.*
> *Adversity is the tempering of one's mettle.*
>
> —Anonymous

5. **Get help.** There is a romantic image we all have of the rugged individual, the one who blazes new paths relying only on his or her own stubborn strength. That is a romantic fantasy. There's no reason to do everything yourself. There are lots of people around you who will be more than willing to help. Some may turn you down. Some may not believe in you or your dreams. Ignore them! Find those out there who can lend you support, whether it be physical, financial, or emotional. The tenacity of a team multiplies the tenacity of the individual.

6. **Build fortitude with patient courage.** Keep the body, mind, and heart focused. I've been working on a project for seven years, and it is just now becoming a reality. Of course, this was not the only project I had during these seven years. Still, I never gave up on this particular dream. There are things in life that may take time for you to achieve. Speed is not always of the essence. Sometimes the old adage that "slow and steady wins the race" is the way the world works. It takes both courage and patience to keep going when a goal seems unattainable, but that's how the greatest rewards are gained.

How many a man has thrown up his hands at a time when a little more effort, a little more patience, would have achieved success?

—Elbert Hubbard,
author

7. **Prepare and practice.** There is a method of kung fu called hing kung, which is the art of walking on any substance, including snow, grass, and sand, without leaving footprints. This requires years of intensive practice. There is only one way to become a master of hing kung, and that is by concentrated effort, day in and day out in very small steps. You cannot proceed to the next step of practice until the last one has been mastered. It takes tremendous discipline and patience. The hing kung student is prepared to fail many times. Yet every time he fails, he gets up and begins again. You can become a master of whatever you pursue by practicing your craft over and over, no matter how many times you fall or fail, and by believing that in the end you will be successful.

8. **Keep the faith.** Speechwriter and game show host Ben Stein once said, "It is inevitable that some defeat will enter even the most victorious life. The human spirit is never finished when it is defeated...it is finished when it surrenders." You cannot be persistent unless you believe in what you are doing, unless you have faith even through defeat. To put it another way, when you go after Moby Dick, bring the tartar sauce. Think of the rewards that will come your way once you accomplish your goal. Don't give up. Belief and faith are what make tenacity possible. Your enthusiasm and positive attitude are the momentum that makes the going a little easier.

Flaming enthusiasm, backed by horse sense and persistence, is the quality that most frequently makes for success.

—Dale Carnegie,
teacher and author

9. **Get beat up.** Dive into the action. You can theorize all you want, but there is nothing like being in the thick of it to teach you the lessons you need to learn. You can learn a lot by reading books and magazines, from listening to tapes, from watching what other people do. But experience is the best teacher there ever was. When you go out there, you set yourself up for scrutiny. You're going to get beat up. You don't have to go out looking for a fight, but you have to face the blows when they come. And you have to know, especially when your opponent is

bigger and stronger than you are, that you have it in you to go one more round. You may be defeated, but the next time you step into the ring you'll be a much better fighter.

> *Bulldogs have been known to fall on their swords when confronted by my superior tenacity.*
>
> —Margaret Halsey,
> author

10. **Focus.** Stay in the moment. Think about what you have to accomplish at the moment you're doing it. You can reflect upon the past and dream about the future when the project is completed, but while it's under way, keep your focus sharp and to the point. When your attention drifts, your tenacity falters and you lose sight of your goals. When your concentration is strong, however, you are so focused that nothing can distract you from your task.

> *Even if our efforts of attention seem for years to be producing no result, one day a light that is in exact proportion to them will flood the soul.*
>
> —Simone Weil,
> author

Dialogue With a Tenacious Leader

David D'Alessandro is president and CEO of John Hancock Financial Services—the youngest person to hold both offices for the 139-year-old company. In his view, being persistent is synonymous with being focused.

BARRY FARBER: How did persistence play a part in what you've accomplished so far?

DAVID D'ALESSANDRO: By keeping it focused and keeping it simple. If you surround yourself with good people, it allows you to focus on those things that are most important to be tenacious about. My philosophy about both obstacles and opportunities is the same: I want to fully understand this situation, and I won't be satisfied until I do.

BF: Can you give me an example?

DA: Recently, my financial people came in and told me there was a large problem with one of our businesses. I had a feeling there was something wrong with their report. In any corporation, big or little, the financial people tend to be slaves to the numbers. If a number is spit out of a computer, they think it's gospel.

But I instinctively felt that the numbers were wrong. I spent four solid hours trying to understand the genesis of the problem. I had to go back and back and back to get to the root. Finally, we discovered that it was a simple human error. Four or five months earlier, someone had typed in the wrong number. That number was then used as the base for all future calculations. The accountants were willing to believe what the computer told them. But I knew it was wrong; I knew that if I was persistent, I would find the answer. And I did.

BF: What was the result of your being so persistent?

DA: We saved $2 million that would otherwise have been a loss.

BF: Are you always that persistent?

DA: I have to be. I'm the head of the company. People know that I'm incredibly focused, so it makes them pay more attention to detail. They don't want to make mistakes because they know I'll pursue the truth until I find it.

Success…seems to be connected with action. Successful men keep moving. They make mistakes, but they don't quit.
—Conrad Hilton,
businessman

Girls Can't Do That

For as long as she can remember, Andra Douglas has loved football. Growing up, she played with the boys in the neighborhood. Of course, when she got to school, she was told, "Girls can't play football." But something inside her wouldn't take "no" for an answer.

Andra is currently the promotions designer for *Money Magazine*. But she is also the owner, general manager, and quarterback of the New York Sharks women's professional football team.

"I'd like to say that you develop a thick skin, but that's not true," says Douglas. "I still sometimes go home in tears. You get doors slammed in your face every time you turn around. But it's worth it all. Last year we played our first game. There weren't a lot of people watching, mostly friends and family. But we had 60 women on the roster, and we were all lined up on the field in our uniforms and helmets. This game didn't mean anything to the sports world. But to us, we might as well have just won the Super Bowl—and we hadn't even played the game yet.

"Every time someone told me this couldn't be done, I just thought, 'Well, you're wrong.' Women can be good at this sport and they should have the opportunity. I believe that women are the power of the world. We have to come from so much farther behind to get where we are going. To me, that means we have more tenacity than anyone else.

"You have to be tenacious to get anywhere. You have to believe in yourself when no one else does. You have to keep knocking on doors. You have to show up at every event and make contacts; you have to believe that someday you're going to meet the person who's going to help you make it happen. It sounds so cliché, but it's true. I just kept showing up, believing in my talents and my dreams and my goals."

> *Never give up, for that is just the place and time that the tide will turn.*
>
> —Harriet Beecher Stowe,
> author

I Dare You…

In everything you do, every time you're ready to stop, every time you think that's all you've got, push a little further (as long as there are no health or medical consequences). Every time you do something, look back at the last time you did it and make sure you're doing it that much better, putting that much more effort into it. You want to constantly beat your own effort so that you're opening the threshold for the next time, making it easier to go through.

> *You may have a fresh start any moment you choose, for this thing that we call 'failure' is not the falling down, but the staying down.*
>
> —Mary Pickford,
> actress

Slow and Steady Wins the Race

Things are rarely accomplished by one great burst of energy; success comes through continuing on day after day, long past the time when you think you *should* be successful. Those who persist, who continue steadily in their course of action, will win in the end.

Persistence is well-known in the animal kingdom. David Attenborough, in his book *The Trials of Life: A Natural History of Animal Behavior* tells about the kusimanse, a dwarf mongoose from West Africa. The kusimanse lives on chicken eggs. When it finds an egg it "puts its forelegs over it and with a vigor that would not disgrace an American footballer, hurls it backwards through its splayed hind legs." The animal does this over and over again until the egg cracks.

Then there's the Egyptian vulture, which lives on ostrich eggs. When the vulture finds a nest of eggs, it picks up large stones in its beak and then tosses them toward the nest. What it lacks in aim, it makes up for in persistence until it manages to break open one of the eggs.

Successful people don't give up. They throw their stones over and over again. When they run into obstacles, they find ways around them. When they get tired, they don't quit; they find something to rejuvenate themselves and they start again.

Man may remove all obstacles through quiet perseverance.

—Chinese proverb

Second Wind

There are times in life when we surprise ourselves. It often happens when we're exhausted, when we think we've come to the point of no return. "This is it," you think. "I can't go on any more." This may be the time to take a break and get some needed rest. On the other hand, there's something to be said for pushing forward. Sometimes taking a rest only serves to remind you of how much there is still to be done. So it may be time to persist, to get to the other side of that wall, to experience the second wind phenomenon. That's when—just when you thought you could do no more—your energy returns even stronger than it was before.

I know that when I give myself the chance to keep going, I find myself getting a third, fourth, and fifth wind when I least expect it. Something happens that's difficult to explain. Perhaps that accomplishment has its own energy field. When you are so focused on getting something done, you tap into deep stores of energy that give you the ability you need to keep going.

This is persistence. Persistence is the ability to go past the state of mind that wants to stop us from achieving our goals. The next time you're tempted to give up or give in, reach deep down inside and gather all your strength to keep going. Before you know it, that second wind will come along to keep you aloft.

The Timeless Art of Persistence

Some of the most uniquely capable people in history have been artists. The best artists, of course, have enormous talent, but what they have most in common is their ability and willingness to persist in creating their art.

Take Matisse for instance. He knew the meaning of persistence. He painted and repainted his canvasses many times. He once said, "A masterpiece is never finished, it is just abandoned." Matisse's father wanted him to be a grain merchant and a lawyer. But at the age of 21, Matisse became gravely ill. To help him pass the time, his mother gave him some paper and crayons. From that time on, all he wanted to do was paint.

Matisse could have made a good living from the government, painting church ceilings in the style of the masters, which he did for a time. Then he found he couldn't do that anymore. He had to keep doing what he did best. Even though he had a wife and three children to support, he gave up the government subsidies and persisted working day and night on his own paintings.

When Michelangelo painted the Sistine Chapel, he did almost all of it by himself. And he had to invent the process as he went along. To paint a fresco, you have to have wet paint and wet plaster, and you have a limited time frame in which to work. You have two hours to put down the plaster, two hours to paint, and two hours to guess what will happen to your color as it dries. So there he was—painting, plastering, and inventing 62 feet above the floor of the chapel. And he didn't do it lying on his back, as most people think. He painted reaching up to the ceiling, with the paint and plaster constantly falling in his face.

The world would be a much poorer place without the persistence and hard work of artists like these. The artists did not settle for easy paths in life. They persisted, one brush stroke at a time, until they achieved greatness.

In each age men of genius undertake the ascent. From below, the world follows them with their eyes. These men go up the mountain, enter the clouds, disappear, reappear. People watch them, mark them. They walk by the side of precipices. They daringly pursue their road. See them aloft, see them in the distance; they are but black specks. On they go. The road is uneven, its difficulties constant. At each step a wall, at each step a trap. As they rise the cold increases. They must make their ladder, cut the ice and walk on it, hewing the steps in haste. A storm is raging. Nevertheless they go forward in their madness. The air becomes difficult to breathe. The abyss yawns below them. Some fall. Others stop and retrace their steps; there is a sad weariness.

The bold ones continue. They are eyed by the eagles; the lightening plays about them; the hurricane is furious. No matter, they persevere.

—Victor Hugo,
French novelist

So How Do You Know When to Stop?

A man came up to me once and told me about a project he had been working on for 15 years. Because he had heard me speak about tenacity and persistence, he asked me this "simple" question: "How do I know when to quit?"

The simple answer is "Never!" But, like everything else in life, a simple answer won't always suffice. If you have been truly persistent for a long time and you have gotten nowhere, perhaps you should take time to evaluate your course of action. Is your goal realistic? Are the expected rewards worth the time and effort (and maybe money) you'll need to continue? Are there other people you can bring in to help you get to your goal (if you haven't tried that already)? The bottom line is, you may have to do some deep soul searching and, at some point, say to yourself, "It's time to move on."

On the other hand, don't give up too easily. You need to believe in yourself, to have faith that you can, and will, finish what you start. If you have that deep-seated belief in the value of what you're trying to accomplish, keep your focus and push on. You never know when you will reap what you have been sowing all this time. Things come to us in the strangest ways, in the most unexpected times. It could take a week, it could take a year. There's no way of knowing.

But you're the only one who can keep struggling along the path to get there. It's your inner drive, your unwavering faith, which will likely make the difference between reaching your goal and falling short.

> *The miracle, or the power, that elevates the few is to be*
> *found in their industry, application, and perseverance under*
> *the promptings of a brave, determined spirit.*
>
> —Mark Twain,
> author

No matter how persistent we are, no matter how tenacious and focused we are in getting the job done, we cannot always count on things going smoothly. Things change. The environment changes, the people change, the situation changes. We must be able to adapt. You can't keep doing the same thing over and over again and expect to get different results. You need to focus on the ability to go in a different direction, if need be, to call on different people, to change your methods. You must be able to see change as an ally, as something that will help you deal with current situations and move with events. Persistent doesn't mean stubbornly sticking with a particular routine that just isn't working. Being persistent means that if your way doesn't work, you find another way. Trying not to change simply gets you stuck in place. Everything around us changes constantly. It always does and always will. We have to embrace it, not look away from it.

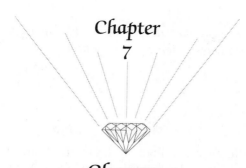

Chapter 7

Change:
How to Benefit From Constant Turbulence

When you're through changing, you're through.

—Bruce Barton,
advertising executive

What Is Change?

What is my definition of change? It's four quarters for a dollar. One thing changes to another. Change means to make the form or content of something different from what it is, or from what it would be if you left it alone; to transform or convert.

For human beings, change means life, and life means change. You can sit still and do what appears to be nothing, but change is still going on. The day changes from morning to night, the seasons change from summer to fall to winter to spring. The body changes all by itself. Blood flows through our veins, the heart beats, and food is digested and turned into fuel. We're living and dying at the same time. Even if we do nothing, nothing ever stays the same.

I, for one, do not want to sit still. If things must inevitably change, I want to be the one who makes change happen. I want to learn more so that I may change wisely. I want to change my body so that I may become stronger. I want to change my environment so that I will be healthier. I want to change my thinking so that I have a better attitude. I want to change my attitude so that I have a meaningful spiritual connection with the universe. I want to embrace change so that I may benefit from the opportunities it constantly presents. I want change to be something that moves me forward, as well as something that I look forward to.

*I can't change the direction of the wind, but I can adjust
my sails to always reach my destination.*

—Jimmy Dean,
entertainer

The Power of Change

If you want to focus on change, look at your children. One day, I took my daughter, who was then 8 years old, out to lunch. As we talked, I couldn't help thinking about going to restaurants with her when she was so small she needed my help for everything. She's changing so fast.

Watching her, I was both happy and sad at the same time. Of course, I love to watch her mature and to be able to have "grown-up" conversations with her. At the same time, I wish I could stop time so that she would stay small enough to always need my help.

What my father-daughter luncheon made me realize is that because things change, we need to get the most out of every moment. When life is good, squeeze it like a sponge to get every drop out of it. Take a mental snapshot of the good times. Then when times are bad, replay that good picture in your mind and know that just as the good times changed to the bad, so the bad will change and good times will come around again.

My hobby is to try and understand how life works and how we can apply its lessons to human potential. One of the most important lessons I've learned is that there is no organism on this planet that can survive without change. From the smallest single-celled ameba to the complex human body, we must always be moving and changing. If there's anything in life we can depend on, it's change.

Change is difficult for many people. But really, it's what makes life exciting—constantly learning, changing our minds, habits, environment, and the people with whom we surround ourselves. It's mixing things up, looking for a better recipe and the best ingredients to make the best cake, and not settling for the same old thing.

The goal of change is not just to make something different, it's to make something better and more efficient. It's easy to do the things you've always done, and to do them the way you've always done them. It's a lot harder—but a lot more rewarding—to be proactive and constantly looking for ways to improve.

The secret of change is to focus on the opportunities, of a new path, not on the comfort of a worn trail.

Change is the law of life. And those who look only to the past or the present are certain to miss the future.
—John F. Kennedy,
U.S. president

Life Changes

"Things change all the time—every day brings something new for all of us," says Dr. Phil Santiago, official chiropractor for the 1992 and 1996 U.S. Olympic track and field teams.

"These are usually small or gradual changes. But there are also two types of major changes that can happen in your life. The first is the change that you elect to make—from moving to a new home, to taking a new job, to separating from your spouse. These are all stressful circumstances, even though they're of your own making. Even good things that happen can create stress in your life.

"In 1992, I was chosen to be on the medical staff of the U.S. Olympic team. This is one of the highest honors you can attain in my field; it's like a lawyer going to the Supreme Court. When I came back, I was like an athlete who is forced to retire. I just kept thinking, 'Where do I go from here? I've hit the heights, now what?'

"I was still dealing with those thoughts when the second kind of change took place—both my parents were killed in a car crash. There are times when change is due to circumstances beyond your control; times when life presents us with something so unexpected and so devastating that you think you will never be the same again.

"The worst part of that kind of change is the fear. You lose your base, you lose your security, you lose your place in the world. Your life is like a nightmare where you're standing at the edge of a tall building and you're afraid of falling. Your comfort zone is gone in an instant. The challenge is that you have to establish a new base and a new comfort zone, and at first it doesn't seem possible.

"Of course, I went through all the stages of mourning, the anger, and the denial. But I knew I had to get back to my base, back to a positive mental attitude. I knew I had to surround myself with positive people. I started reading motivational and inspirational books. When you lose your base, it is possible to get it back again. It may not be exactly as it was before, but keeping positive influences around you helps you get grounded again.

"I had to get back to the positive side of life. I had to find new goals and a new focus. It didn't happen over night; in fact, it took several years. But it's the only way to deal with change. If you stay on a positive note, you can undergo any kind of change."

> *All change is a miracle to contemplate; but it is a miracle which is taking place every second.*
>
> —Henry David Thoreau,
> philosopher and author

9 Great Ways to Benefit From Change

1. **Learn something new every single day.** Read something, meet someone new, take a class, take up a new sport, or start a new hobby. Find at least one thing every day that makes your life (and perhaps the lives of those around you) better.

2. **Take the heat.** A wise man I know has a routine he follows when faced with difficult choices and changes. He sits inside an adobe hut that contains a pit where rocks are piled high and heated to 1500 degrees. The goal is to face forward and take the heat.

   It teaches him that he must come to terms with the difficulties before him and "sweat it out." When he emerges from the hut, he knows what he must do to accept and benefit from the changes before him. The lesson he learns is that when you're confronted with change, embrace it, attack it, understand it, and face it. If you do, you will not only find the opportunities that lie within, but you will also diminish the problems that change presents.

3. **Step away.** The "heat in the hut" scenario accomplishes two things at once. On the one hand, it allows my friend to face his fears. On the other hand, it gives him a chance to better understand the coming changes. Sometimes you need to step outside of your everyday environment. You need to get the big picture.

   You need to take a physical, mental, and/or spiritual break. You need to step back and say, "Does this really make sense? Am I worrying about something that is ultimately irrelevant?" When you're in the middle of a situation, you can't always see the opportunities and advantages. This is when you need to give yourself a little time and another point of view.

*Being willing to change allows you to move from a point
of view to a viewing point—a higher, more expansive
place, from which you can see both sides.*

—Thomas Crum,
writer and speaker

4. **Be adaptable.** Charles Darwin once said, "It is not the strongest of
the species that survive, nor the most intelligent, but the one most
responsive to change." This is a major advantage human beings have
over other animals. We are probably the most adaptable species on
Earth—if we're willing to change.

Human beings can also be very stubborn. There are times when
we see change coming and we think if we adapt, we will be giving in or
conforming. That's a negative way of thinking. Instead, think, "What
would it be like if I tried to get the most out of this situation?" Use the
energy that change provides instead of trying to swim upstream.

*Enjoying success requires the ability to adapt. Only by being
open to change will you have a true opportunity to get the
most from your talent.*

—Nolan Ryan,
baseball great

5. **Get rid of ego.** When we let our ego get in the way of what needs to be
done, when we look at a situation and say, "My way is the only way," we
are edging greatness out. Of course, it's good to have a healthy, confident
ego. But when you get to the point where you think you know best
above all others, when you're so busy pointing fingers that you don't
look at yourself, then you're letting your ego take over. Remember
that when you point a finger at somebody, there are three fingers
pointing back at you.

A wise man changes his mind, a fool never will.

—Spanish proverb

6. **Study outside your profession.** Find people who are the best at what
they do. Study their ideas and methods and figure out how you can
apply them to your trade. Respect your curiosity. If you want to know
how something works, find out. If you see something that interests you,
pursue it. Whatever you learn from these "outside" adventures will
make your life much richer, and help you make beneficial changes in
your present situation.

A person needs at intervals to separate himself from family and companions and go to new places. He must go without his familiars in order to be open to influences, to change.

—Katherine Butler Hathaway,
author

7. **Look to the past and see the benefits of the present to change for the future.** Look back and remember who you were at various times in your life, how you thought, what actions you took, and who you surrounded yourself with. Look at what you've accomplished and what changes you made to get to this present point. Imagine what would have happened if you hadn't made those changes. What would have happened to your business, to your relationships, to your life?

   By looking to the past and seeing how changes improved your present life, think about changes you can make for the future. Do this whenever you're faced with change so that, instead of looking at it in a negative light, you can see the benefits change has brought.

8. **Get rid of what doesn't make you happy.** Remember that if you want to make changes in your life, *you* have to make changes in your life. If you are truly unhappy, it is probably time to make a major change. Say good-bye to negative people in your life. Find a new job, or a new career. Move to a new city. If you make one change in your life, everything else changes, too. If you wallow in your misery, change will come—but probably not the way you want it to.

9. **Take small steps.** It's not always necessary to make the major changes in Step 8. Maybe you don't have to change your job or your career; perhaps you can find a different way to do things that are more productive for you. Maybe you don't need to move clear across the country. A new apartment down the block might be enough to get you out of your rut. A huge change taken quickly might open new opportunities, but it might also add a lot more stress.

   Don't just change for the sake of changing; change in a way that makes sense and gets you closer to your goals.

You Know What They Say About Change...

To attain knowledge, add things every day, to attain wisdom, remove things every day.

—Lao-Tse,
Tao Te Ching

We can, and should, learn something every day—but we should remove something every day, too. Use and apply the knowledge and experience you gain as you learn new things, and realize that what you used before may not work now because the environment is different today from what it was in the past. That's where true wisdom comes in; it's the ability to hone and fine-tune the information you get so that it can be put to the most practical use in the moment.

If you don't like something, change it. If you can't change it, change your attitude. Don't complain.

—Maya Angelou,
poet and author

You have two options. You can either change the situation, or you can change your mind about the situation. How many times do you react negatively to things that happen to you? Is your first thought, "Nothing good can come of this"? If so, you might want to ask yourself some important questions: "How can I change this? What can I do differently? How can I attack it? If I can't change it right now, how can I change my mind and my attitude?"

There are very few things that are as omnipresent as change. Adversity happens often, but not every second. We don't reach our goals every day. We're not always negotiating; we're not always creating. But we are always changing. We all pray for miracles in our lives. Consider change as a miracle and your life will be full of wonder.

Change can either challenge us or threaten us. Your beliefs pave your way to success or block you.

—Marsha Sinetar,
writer

What you believe influences how you deal with change. If you believe that change is difficult to handle, it will be. If you believe that change is exciting, it will be. The mind is, after all, what separates us from other species.

No other living beings, though they contain hearts, lungs, stomachs, eyes, ears, mouths, and even brains, have the power of the human mind.

No other living beings have the ability to change their surroundings and their circumstances based on how they change themselves. Only we have this extraordinary power of transformation. We can start out poor and end up wealthy. We can change ourselves from illiterate to highly educated. We can turn disadvantages into advantages by using this wondrous tool handed out free to each and every one of us.

> *That's the risk you take if you change: that people you've been involved with won't like the new you. But other people who do will come along.*
>
> —Lisa Alther,
> writer

We all know how difficult it can be to make changes. You may decide to make some changes that are not universally approved of. Your friends, your colleagues, even your loved ones may tell you you're making a mistake. But you have to be true to your heart, especially when it involves moving away from people who have been bringing you down.

Although we need to move away from people who pull us down, we are reluctant to do so because we're afraid that we won't have that person to go to in the future. But the unhappiness and the bad energy of the relationship override the benefit. There's no need to be afraid of letting go of this relationship. Instead, you should feel comfortable and realize that as this person moves away, somebody else will come along and see the new you who has decided to take a new path and a better way of life.

> *Consider how hard it is to change yourself and you'll understand what little chance you have in trying to change others.*
>
> —Jacob M. Braude,
> writer

Many a relationship has failed over time because one person was determined to change another. It's an impossible task. People don't make lasting changes unless they want to make them. The best way to help someone change is to lead by example. There's an old saying that goes, "What you're doing speaks so loudly, I can't hear what you're saying."

Actions really do speak louder than words. So the actions you take have much more influence over another person's behavior than any lecture might. Ghandi once said, "Be the change you want to see in the world." If the other person does not or cannot follow your example, it may be time to move on to a better situation.

*Some people change their ways when they see the light,
others when they feel the heat.*

—Caroline Schroeder,
writer

We have all experienced what I call a "light bulb" moment—a moment of truth where an idea suddenly becomes clear to us and we know with uncanny certainty what we need to do next. It can happen in the most unexpected times: when you're in the middle of an ordinary conversation and someone says something to you that just hits home. It can happen when you read a quote whose meaning and importance becomes immediately clear. It can happen during a quiet walk in the woods or in the middle of a game you're playing with your children. These are the quiet moments of change.

Some people just see a good idea and they change...they see one word, one quote. There are other situations, however, that are more like lightning bolts—adverse situations where things happen fast. We lose a job, a spouse, or our home.

It's usually when the heat is on that we see our true selves. That's when you say, "Wait a minute. I've got a choice here. I can die or I can live. The only way to live is to make a change, and make a big one." Adversity often brings on change in difficult times, but there is often great strength that comes with it.

*Nearly all great civilizations that perished did so because
they had crystalized, because they were incapable of
adapting themselves to new conditions, new methods, new
points of view. It is as though people would literally rather
die than change.*

—Eleanor Roosevelt,
U.S. first lady and humanitarian

I Dare You...

Be the first to make a change. Be the first to present a new idea, even if it sounds crazy. Be the first to try something new. Be the first to befriend a newcomer.

Imagine what the "first-timers" of history had to face. Would you have ridiculed Thomas Edison if he told you of his idea to light up the world? Would you have laughed at a horseless carriage or snickered at the idea of a telephone? Would you have been outraged at the thought that the world was round, that you could sail around it without falling off the edge? Or would you have had the courage of Amelia Earhart who accomplished great feats everyone said a woman could not do? Would you have been able to sit at the segregated lunch counter in Alabama in order to break the color lines? Someone has to be the first to do these things—why not you?

> *He who rejects change is the architect of decay. The only*
> *human institution which rejects progress is the cemetery.*
>
> —Harold Wilson,
> British prime minister

Make a small change every day. Look at your desk and your work environment. Sometimes we let papers and other things collect on our desks so that they end up covering over important papers. Every once in a while, move those papers around. Clean out one drawer and you might be surprised at what you find. Change your work environment to make it cleaner, more organized.

You don't need to make radical changes. It's difficult to get the motivation to make a major change. Instead, I dare you to make small, directed changes every day to alter and improve the way you spend your time.

> *Life is made of millions of moments, but we live only one of*
> *these moments at a time. As we begin to change this*
> *moment, we begin to change our lives.*
>
> —Trinidad Hunt,
> writer

One Final Thought...

Have you ever read a book that really "speaks" to you? One that is truly inspirational and motivational? Maybe it's a biography of someone you admire, or a book of quotes, or a novel with a strong message—a book that has real value because it gave you so many wonderful ideas. That is not a book that should be read once and put on a shelf. Go back and read it again. Read it again every month, or every six months, or once a year.

When you do go back to it, you'll find that its original message has increased tenfold. That's because by the next time you read it, you will have changed. You will have taken actions inspired by your first reading, and those actions will have added to your life experience. You've gathered more knowledge from other sources that may now change your understanding of what you read before. You are merging your new knowledge base with the information you previously gathered. The words of the book remain the same, but everything else is now different. You enrich your original reading of the book and get a whole new meaning from it.

> *Change has considerable psychological impact on the human mind. To the fearful it is threatening because it means that things may get worse. To the hopeful it is encouraging because things may get better. To the confident it is inspiring because the challenge exists to make things better. Obviously, then, one's character and frame of mind determine how readily he brings about change and how he reacts to change that is imposed on him.*
>
> —King Whitney, Jr.,
> business executive

One of the things that help us deal with change is having a strong foundation and solid ground to stand on. That way we will not be blown away by the winds of change. In every company I work for as a consultant, they always come back to the reinforcement of the basics that made them successful in the first place. They want me to help their people get back to those fundamentals. Losing those fundamentals leads to the downturn of many companies. In times of turbulence, the one who has the strongest base is the one who is left standing.

Chapter 8

Fundamentals:
Building Foundations for Everything We Do

Each person has inside a basic decency and goodness. If he listens to it and acts on it, he is giving a great deal of what it is the world needs most. It is not complicated, but it takes courage...to listen to his own goodness.

—Pablo Casals,
cellist

What Are Fundamentals?

A fundamental is something that is an essential part of something else—a foundation or basis. Nothing can be achieved without the fundamentals. Because we live in such a hurry-up-I-need-it-yesterday world, we sometimes want to skip over the fundamentals. We don't want to give them the attention they deserve. However, there's a favorite saying of mine that goes, "Stick to the basics and you never have to go back to them." When we get away from fundamentals, our results suffer. The basics keep the foundation strong. When the basics fall, everything else comes down with them.

The more one does and sees and feels, the more one is able to do, and the more genuine may be one's appreciation of fundamental things like home, and love, and understanding companionship.

—Amelia Earhart,
aviatrix

The Power of Fundamentals

Why is it that "fundamentals" has such a negative connotation? Where's the "fun" in fundamentals? When we think of fundamentals, we usually think of words like *tiresome* and *boring*. It's really all in how you look at it. The fun part comes once you understand how to do something and see the rewards you'll get from doing that thing really well. There is a built-in excitement, enthusiasm, and satisfaction that goes along with accomplishing a difficult task. Then, when you're confronted with a similar task, it's possible to stop and say, "Wait a minute. I know how to do this!"

Successful people know how to build strong foundations. They reach such depths of skill and knowledge that they cannot be knocked over by any storm. They understand that the "fun" comes after the fundamentals; once you have the basics down, you know the secret to success. It's hard work, plain and simple.

In order to build a foundation, you have to start digging. You have to take up that shovel and move that dirt around. There's no other way. And when things go wrong, when you feel the walls crumbling around you, you have to go back and shore up the foundation once again.

That's what works for me. When things are hectic, when I'm burnt out, when I have five different projects happening at once, I take a step back and determine what is most important to me at that moment. I have to decide which project needs the most of my time based upon the amount of effort necessary and the rewards to be gained. Once I make that decision, I get down to the fundamentals—writing letters, making phone calls, following up, checking all the details. And when I've completed these fundamental actions to the best of my ability, I know that I will be successful. It's the fundamental process of hard work and determination that gives me the strongest foundation from which to work.

> *Build your empire on the firm foundation of the fundamentals.*
>
> —Lou Holtz,
> football coach

The Fundamental Priorities

Joan Borysenko is a political scientist, a psychologist, and the author of *Inner Peace for Busy People: 52 Strategies for Transforming Your Life.* She spends her life studying how people connect with each other and with the world around them. This study has helped her to understand the "bottom line," the fundamental qualities that go into making us human—even in the midst of the business of our daily lives.

"It doesn't sound very scientific or sexy to say that every human being has basic needs," she says. "We need a balanced diet. We need to be out in nature, in the sunlight, a certain amount of time every day. Everyone needs to move and exercise every day, even if it's a 10 minute walk around the block. Every human being needs touch; touch releases a growth hormone that restores your immune system. Deep conversation raises our serotonin level so that we feel comfortable in our skin and at home in the world. These are such basic things. And yet what happens when people get crazy busy? They forget these incredibly basic fundamentals.

"We all need to ask ourselves, 'What are the fundamental priorities in my life?' My friend Loretta Laroche wrote a book called *Life is Not a Stress Rehearsal*, in which she lists some epitaphs that might be written on a tombstone. One of my favorites is, 'Got it all done. Died anyway.' The things we do are not the fundamentals of life; it's the things we are. The fundamentals of life are *kindness*, *caring*, and *compassion*. No matter what else I'm doing, if I'm not listening to other people, if I'm so wrapped up in myself that I can't see others' pain then I am not being what I was meant to be. I might be writing a brilliant paper, but I'm not being a brilliant human being, because my own moral and ethical fundamentals have been undermined.

"Part of the problem is that we spend too much time looking for peace and happiness outside of ourselves. We think, 'If I get that job then I'll be happy. If I get that car, then I'll be happy.' We need to recognize that happiness is already inside us. We were born with everything we seek, but now that we're adults, we think we need to take workshops to try and figure it out. We have to recognize that we already have what we are seeking—a sense of inner peace. It is the most fundamentally precious thing that we own."

> *The wisest keeps something of the vision of a child.*
> *Though he may understand a thousand things that a child*
> *could not understand, he is always a beginner, close to the*
> *original meaning of life.*
>
> —John Macy,
> author

Acres of Diamonds

There is an old story that was originally told by Russell Conwell, the founder of Temple University. It is a fable about a man named Al Hafed, who lived in ancient Persia. He was a successful farmer, a contented and wealthy man. One day, a priest came by and began to tell Al Hafed all about diamonds, how much they were worth, and all he could buy with just a handful of diamonds. Suddenly, Al Hafed felt poor and discontented; he was determined to become immensely rich. He sold his farm, left a neighbor in charge of his belongings, and went off to search for diamonds.

He wandered all over the world looking for diamonds. He spent all his money. Finally, penniless and dressed in rags, he stood at the ocean's edge, and when the tide came in, he cast himself into the sea, never to arise again.

Meanwhile, the man who bought the farm brought his camel to drink from a brook on the property. As the camel was drinking, the man noticed a curious stone in the stream, which he picked up and put on his mantle. The priest who had first visited Al Hafed happened to stop by, saw the stone and said, "A diamond! Al Hafed must have returned." The farmer said no, that he had found the stone in the stream in his garden. The two men rushed out and found many more beautiful diamonds. And, the legend goes, it was on this spot that one of the greatest diamond mines in the world was found.

This story holds a lesson for us. Why are we willing to travel the world, looking for that which will make us rich, when it is really right in our own backyard? We keep looking for greener pastures. We don't search inside to understand the truest value of who we are, so that when we do venture out there, we're walking on the firmest ground in the world. Nobody can stop us when we know what fundamentals lie within.

The Pain of Discipline Is Easier to Endure Than the Pain of Regret

There is nothing worse than looking back on your life and saying, "I wish I had done this, had taken this risk, or had grabbed that opportunity." The pain of regret can be truly agonizing. The pain of discipline—making yourself do something you don't want to do—is nothing in comparison. It is temporary. When the task is completed, the pain disappears. But we live with regret for the rest of our lives.

Every level of action we achieve serves as the foundation for the new one to follow. If you never take any risks or try anything new, you will stay at the same low level of existence. But every time you put in the effort, you build your foundation higher, move on to the next level, and reap your well-deserved rewards.

In 10 years, you'll be proud of the hard work you're doing now. "Yes," you will say, "it was difficult. I put in long hours. I endured discomfort and inconvenience. But I made it through and reached my goal." So remind yourself as you're putting in those extra hours, when you're taking necessary actions and completing the fundamentals, when you're tempted to give up and go home— remind yourself that you never want to look back 10 years from now and say, "If only..." Those are the two saddest words in the English language.

> *Have regular hours for work and play, make each day both useful and pleasant, and prove that you understand the worth of time by employing it well. Then youth will be delightful, old age will bring few regrets, and life will become a beautiful success...*

—Louisa May Alcott,
author

Fundamentals for Life:
12 Clichés of Achievement and Why They Work

I started out my work life as a salesperson. Now, I do many different things, and one of those things is teaching other people how to be better at selling. In fact, I recently wrote a book on the subject—a book that is based on 12 of the most fundamental truths every salesperson must learn in order to be successful: *The 12 Clichés of Selling (and Why They Work)*. They are so fundamental, in fact, that they have become clichés. But the thing to remember about clichés is that just because an expression is time-worn, just because it may be conventional wisdom or common knowledge, doesn't make it any less true or useful.

I soon realized that although these clichés were originally meant to apply to selling, they can be applied to all of life. They're really the fundamentals of achievement. One reason is that everybody sells something. Even if you're not selling tangible goods, you're selling your ideas, you're selling yourself to those around you. So the clichés of selling are also fundamentals of building a good foundation for life:

Cliché Number 1: It Takes All Kinds. The beauty and wonder of life is that you don't have to be born with a specific set of talents to be able to achieve success or fulfillment. In fact, a deficiency in one area often leads us to make up for it in other areas. It makes us fight even harder to get what we want. Never compare yourself to others and try to get what they have; instead, make the best of your gifts.

Cliché Number 2: Never Take No For an Answer. This cliché does not mean that we should push our way past others with no consideration for anyone else. It's about being persistent, not pushy. It means that you keep on going, no matter how many times you hear the word "no." It's about exploring all avenues to reaching your goal, being creative in your approaches, and being professionally tenacious. It means being confident without being cocky, not letting "naysayers" stop you from pursuing your dreams. What is the fundamental reason, the biggest reason people get ahead? The ability to keep going when others might give up is one of the surest paths to success.

> *Most people give up just when they're about to achieve success. They quit on the one-yard line. They give up at the last minute of the game, one foot from a winning touchdown.*
>
> —H. Ross Perot,
> businessman

Cliché Number 3: The Relationship Is Everything. In sales, the one thing that most often gets you past barriers and through objections is the relationship that is formed between the salesperson and the customer. That is true in life as well. When you're reaching for a goal, ask yourself, "What kind of relationships do I have?" Are you adding value to that other person? People buy from people they like, trust, and respect. Are you earning those things from the people you know? That means you have to keep their needs in mind, as well as your own. Are you nurturing your relationships so that they will blossom for you later on?

> *Personal relationships are the fertile soil from which all advancement, all success, all achievement in real life grows.*
>
> —Ben Stein,
> speechwriter and game show host

Cliché Number 4: Your Attitude Determines Your Altitude. Effective action is 30 percent what you know and 70 percent how you feel about what you know. Attitude is everything. Once, when I was hosting my television show, someone told me about a woman with whom I would be working. "You'll love her," he said. "She's so dynamic and enthusiastic." People never say, "She's so intelligent and has so many degrees." It's not what this woman knows that really impresses people, it's how she gets that knowledge across. She's excited about what she's doing, and that excitement is truly contagious. If you were about to hire a new employee and you had to choose between two people with the same background, the same skills, and the same academic degrees, which would you hire? You'd choose the one with the highest degree of excitement and enthusiasm. It's what makes the difference, hands down.

Cliché Number 5: The Harder You Work, the Luckier You Get. Often, we see the results of someone else's efforts and we don't realize the blood, sweat, and tears they put into their achievement. We think, "How lucky he is." But the truth is we create our own luck through hard work and effort. But the work ethic of one individual is far superior to any luck. People who get rich quick, who inherit large sums of money or win the lottery, never appreciate their wealth. They always feel that they have not earned it. It's only when we have worked hard for something and reached our goals that we can say, "This success is mine. I have truly earned it." Those who have truly earned success are truly lucky.

> *The average person puts only 25 percent of his energy and ability into his work. The world takes off its hat to those who put in more than 50 percent of their capacity, and stands on its head for those few and far between souls who devote 100 percent.*
>
> —Andrew Carnegie,
> financier

Cliché Number 6: Fail to Plan, Plan to Fail. Turning a dream into reality is like turning a rough stone into a beautiful gem. In the diamond industry, the first person to deal with a stone is called a planner. It can take six months to a year for some of the larger diamonds, to decide just how a stone should be cut. If done incorrectly, a valuable stone can shatter into thousands of worthless pieces. Human beings are not always that careful with their own lives. If you study high achievers in any field, you will find that they have clearly articulated goals that they are constantly striving to achieve. What's more, they don't sit back and rest once a goal has been met; instead it inspires them to go on and make the next goal that much more challenging. Not long ago, while walking through the sales department of a client's office, I noticed a huge banner hanging on the wall. This is what it said: "The most important thing about a goal is having one." Talk about simplicity. Most people don't have goals—the kinds that are specific and achievable. We all need not only have goals, but to write them down, to keep them in mind, and to take the daily actions necessary to reach them.

"Would you tell me please, which way I go from here?"
"That depends a good deal on where you want to get to,"
said the Cat.
"I don't much care where—," said Alice.
"Then it doesn't matter which way you go," said the Cat.

—Lewis Carroll,
Alice's Adventures in Wonderland

Cliché Number 7: It's Not What You Know, It's Who You Know. It's all about connections. The relationships you build can give you the ability to springboard into different areas of life and work. One person can introduce you to another, who can introduce you to someone else...and so on. Connections can also come to your aid when you're facing a challenge. It's much easier to solve a problem when you have a network of people you can call on to help you move forward when you're blocked. It's fundamental for success to build relationships that keep your Rolodex full. Remember, the key to networking is to strengthen your relationships. Anybody can take your Rolodex away, but they can't take away your relationships.

Cliché Number 8: Knowledge Is Power. Bobby Fisher was the greatest chess player in the world. This was because from morning to night, from when he woke up to when he went to sleep, all he thought about was chess. It was his obsession. He knew more about chess than anyone else. And it was this knowledge that made him a champion. It's amazing what you can accomplish when you apply that kind of depth of knowledge. That's why it's so important to keep studying, learning, and improving. The more we learn, the more we earn—not just in dollars but in the rich intangible rewards life has to offer.

Cliché Number 9: You Can't Fit a Square Peg into a Round Hole. One of the most difficult things for a salesperson to learn is when to walk away from a sale. There are times when this action makes the most sense; when something just isn't right. Perhaps the other person's values and yours are not the same. Perhaps you realize that pursuing your present course isn't going to get you where you really want to go. Perhaps you are doing something out of habit or because someone else has told you it's what you should be doing. That's when it's time to reevaluate what it is you're trying to accomplish. You always want to end with a win-win situation. There are times in life that we try to force a situation to fit our goals. But to get—and keep—the best footing in life, we have to make sure every step is moving us in the right direction. We need to ask the right questions and listen to and learn from the answers. Only then can we understand if the move we're considering is the right one—in terms of who we should be working with and what type of deals we should make. Sometimes we continue to push in the wrong direction because we don't see another option, or we're too tired to try something else. When that happens, we always end up suffering.

Cliché Number 10: Don't Sell the Steak, Sell the Sizzle. The saying "Don't sell the steak, sell the sizzle" first appeared in 1936, when, according to advertising executive Elmer Wheeler, it was deemed to be "principle number one of salesmanship." In life, the sizzle you sell is yourself at your very best. The pianist Arthur Schnable once said, "The notes I handle no better than many pianists. But the pauses between the notes—ah, that is where the art resides!" A note on a piano is a note on a piano, no matter what you do. What makes you an artist is your own interpretation, the timing and pauses you put in between the notes. Whatever your profession, what makes you unique is what you bring to the table. That's what you must let people know about what you do. That is your sizzle; it's your special value.

Cliché Number 11: You Get What You Pay For. In life, there is no free lunch. If you want to get ahead, you have to pay your dues. And in most cases, those dues are the fundamentals. You must learn the fundamentals before you can go on. People who have paid their dues have an added value. That's why so many owners who want their children to take over their business want them to start from the bottom and work their way up. They want them to spend time in shipping, in customer service, in sales, in management. They want them to pay their dues by building relationships and getting respect in all those different areas and by getting the big picture of how the entire business works. When they do take over the business, they'll have earned the respect and the credibility to run the company. It's only after you've paid your dues that you get what's due you.

Cliché Number 12: Honesty Is the Best Policy. Most people think that this cliché is about telling the truth to others. It is, and that's a fundamental part of life. But it also means being truthful with yourself—truthful about what you're doing and what you believe in. You cannot work passionately and steadfastly toward a goal unless it is something that has real meaning for you. If you're really honest with yourself, you will live with a sense of purpose and choose "a path with heart." You will not become so obsessed with achievement and material possessions that you forget how to enjoy life and appreciate the people who love you, and whom you love.

My crown is in my heart, not on my head,
Not decked with diamonds and Indian stones,
Nor to be seen: my crown is called content;
A crown it is that seldom kings enjoy.

—William Shakespeare,
poet and playwright

I Dare You...

Sweat both mentally and physically, every single day of your life. Fundamentals require hard work, but with hard work comes great rewards. Do something that is mentally challenging; push yourself beyond the limits; push yourself to another level. Think about the bigger picture. Reach for more than you think you can possibly get. You may get discouraged, but you'll be surprised, too.

Break things down to simple steps—the smaller the steps, the easier the climb. Do a little bit toward achieving your goal every day, even if it's five minutes here, five minutes there. Break everything down into its simplest elements.

Remind yourself that the basics are foundations forever. When you're getting bored or frustrated because you're doing something over and over again, remind yourself that you're trying to build a habit. Your goal is to get to the point where the fundamentals are ingrained and you don't have to think about them anymore. When the fun of learning something new has lost its luster, I dare you to keep going until you have built a foundation so strong that nothing can tear it down.

A Final Thought

Everything in life has its roots, which support all present and future efforts. Fundamentals are the roots that will lead you to new heights and greater accomplishments. Because of your dedication to the principles of fundamentals, you'll be amazed at your accomplishments.

Once you have the fundamentals, you can go in almost any direction without veering too far off your course. You can try new ways to achieve your goals, new ways to use your mind and your ability to create new pathways for success. That takes creativity. Some people think that creativity is not an essential element of success—if you have it, great, but if not, you can still get along. However, it takes great creative thinking to differentiate yourself from everyone else out there. It takes great creativity to think "out of the box." It takes great creativity to find new ways to deal with old problems. In fact, when things aren't working as well as they should, creativity is critical.

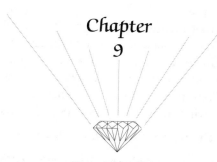

Chapter
9

Creativity:
Unleashing Your Untapped Capabilities

When in doubt, make a fool of yourself. There is a microscopically thin line between being brilliantly creative and acting like the most gigantic idiot on Earth. So what the hell, leap.

—Cynthia Heimel,
writer and humorist

What Is Creativity?

Steven Pinker, author of *How the Mind Works*, says, "All of us are creative. Every time we stick a handy object under the leg of a wobbly table or think of a new way to bribe a child into his pajamas, we have used our faculties to create a novel outcome."

That is what creativity is all about—novel outcomes. It doesn't matter if the outcome is a stable table or a rocket engine, the source of creativity, and the work involved, is the same. One dictionary defines creativity as "having or showing imagination and artistic or intellectual inventiveness." So what does it take to be creative? Does it take unusual talent or exceptional intelligence? Not necessarily.

It's not always the most talented artist who comes up with the most creative result. It's not always the smartest individual who puts forth the best ideas. Charles Darwin was only a mediocre student. Albert Einstein failed algebra. Many famous and obviously creative people never even finished high school. In fact, Steven Pinker also says "there is little or no relationship between IQ and achievement in any sphere of adult endeavor yet studied."

Because it is not that creative people are more intelligent than anyone else, it must be that they use their intelligence differently. They are not content to follow the paths that others have taken; they collect knowledge and then apply their own ideas and uniqueness to the situation. They are in a constant state of incubation. They focus on something, put it to a test, put it aside, then come back with an even stronger focus and put it to another test.

Creativity = Create + Activity

Creativity is merely a plus name for regular activity...any activity becomes creative when the doer cares about doing it right, or better.

—John Updike,
author

Interview With an Inventor

Stanley Mason holds more than 65 patents for his inventions and has been called the modern day Thomas Edison. He has invented such practical items as the contoured disposable diaper, the granola bar, and the squeezable ketchup bottle. He lives on a sprawling farm in Connecticut. Every room is filled with books, and papers are strewn everywhere. Mason is always involved in one invention or another.

BARRY FARBER: How do you go about inventing something?

STANLEY MASON: It's not very complicated. The creative process is simply trying very hard to solve a problem.

BF: Do you spend your life looking for problems?

SM: Always. Since I was a little child.

BF: So problems are really opportunities to stimulate creativity?

SM: Exactly. Who would be interested in a product that nobody wants or can use? If you want to be more creative, walk through life hunting for problems. When I go to a restaurant, I figure out, was this a good meal? Was it served efficiently? What was missing? How can it be made better? It drives my wife crazy, but it's how I view life.

It's the way I come up with all my ideas for inventions. For instance, one day I was reading *Ladies Home Journal*. I read at least one magazine a day. In this magazine, there was a story about a man who produced flowerpots. While doing his market research, the man discovered that 19 million American families have more than 12 plants. He also discovered that there is always at least one sick plant among the 12—not because of under-watering, which was the basic assumption, but because of over-watering.

I read this story and thought, what is the problem here? People are over-watering their plants. So I decided to make a flowerpot that would prevent you from over-watering a plant. I designed it and redesigned it and finally came up with one that worked, and I patented it. That's what it takes to make an invention: find a problem, come up with a solution, test it, retest it, redesign it, retest it—and then if it works, patent it.

BF: Do you have any advice for aspiring inventors?

SM: A school near me asked me to come and talk to first and second graders about inventions. They were coming up with some crazy ideas. I told them to work on solving problems. That's what an invention is. Anybody can think of an idea, but to think of an idea that solves a problem is really terrific. Now every year they have an "invention convention" and the kids come up with some fantastic problem-solvers. So that's my advice for everyone. Be hungry for solving problems.

Creativeness often consists of merely turning up what is already there. Did you know that the right and left shoes were thought up only a little more than a century ago?

—Bernice Fitz-Gibbon,
advertising executive

The Power of Creativity

Stanley Mason is the personification of what we all think an inventor should be. He is part eccentric, part dreamer, and part workaholic. When he gets an idea, he pursues it—not just in his mind, but first on paper and then in tangible form. He can spend hours, days, or weeks researching for just the right screw, hinge, or spring that will make his invention work perfectly. This is how inventors work.

He also has the ability to get lost—to follow his idea down paths that others may deem futile or tangential. When he wanders down these paths, he often comes out with solutions that even he could not have foreseen. That is how creativity works.

You don't have to be an inventor to be creative. Yes, some creative people have had wild, crazy ideas that have changed the world. Others have given us an easier way to get ketchup out of the bottle. Still others have found new ways to manage a business, lead a class, or do housework more efficiently. Many people assume they are not creative because they haven't invented anything "real." The reality is that most of us have to be extremely creative just to survive in today's information and action-packed world.

You can't "think" or "wish" yourself into being more creative. But there are several ways you can help cultivate creativity. Here are three of them:

- ✧ **Visualize.** Turn your idea into a mental picture. The simplest way to make creativity work for you is to see your idea being successful even before you know exactly how it is going to work. Try to picture each step you must go through as being successfully completed. Get a picture of how all the parts will work together. You may have to change some of your plans as they move from your brain to the real world, but this idealized picture will give you a definite place to start.

- ✧ **Put the pen to paper.** Although computers have their uses, there's something about writing things down the old-fashioned way that seems to stimulate the brain. Whether you write your ideas down in a list, a formal outline, or just brainstorm information, putting the pen to paper gives your ideas order and clarity.

- ✧ **Be open to change.** It is hard to be creative when you are in a rut. When you do the same thing every day in the same old way, your ideas are going to come out the same way they always do. If you want to increase your level of creativity, increase your level of activity—physically and mentally. Give yourself a new frame of reference. Try more things, learn more things, get involved in more things. Let yourself be surprised by what you find. It's the element of surprise that gets you excited. It changes your mood, your ideas, even the way you look at life.

Take the approach of martial-arts expert Bruce Lee: You collect information, you discard what is not useful, then you use your own style, personality, and intelligence to create something better.

> *Creativity can solve almost any problem. The creative act,*
> *the defeat of habit by originality, overcomes everything.*
>
> —George Lois,
> author

The Natural Path to Creativity

Imagine that you have been lying in a hospital bed for a year. The only sense you've really used is your sight and your hearing. If you were suddenly taken out of that environment, would you even be able to walk? Probably not; all your other senses would have atrophied.

That is an analogy that comes from Kevin Reeve, director of Tracker School, the largest tracking, nature, and wilderness survival school in the world. Located in the Pine Barrens of New Jersey, the school has taught an estimated 70,000 students for more than 22 years.

"The natural world gives you a chance to use all of your senses to the fullest degree," says Reeve. "Ultimately, you become a better synthesizer. And I believe that synthesis is what makes for great creativity.

"To me, creativity means utilizing your whole brain. So much of our society numbs us to using our brains. It's what we call the "Homer Simpson syndrome"; the typical mental midget who hardly uses his brain at all. At the other end of the spectrum is what we call the "aboriginal brain." When you look at aboriginal or native trackers, they utilize 80 to 100 percent of their brain's potential. They have developed new neuro-pathways in order to be successful trackers.

"The whole idea of becoming a tracker is that it forces your brain to think in new ways. You have to look for details while you're seeing the big picture. You're looking at the ground, but you're hearing all the sounds and 'reading' the landscape. The translation of this is that when I get into the 'regular' world, I'm much better at seeing patterns. Learning to look at interactions in the natural world teaches you how to spot all different levels of connections in your life. You start to see synchronicity between things that are seemingly unrelated. But when you study the patterns and relationships, you realize they're all a part of the same process.

"It's all part of learning to be much more aware of what's going on around you. One of the biggest deterrents to awareness, however, is 'the same old thing.' You get into a rut. You get out of bed and shave your face starting on the same side every day; you brush your teeth in the same way; you have your rituals. We all do. The problem is that you're not aware of what you're doing. You might even drive to work and not remember the drive at all.

"When animals get into that rut, they are extremely vulnerable. The animals that stay alive are the ones that are constantly aware. The oldest buck is the one that figured out how to vary his routine so he wouldn't be preyed upon.

"Too many people live in that rut, in that "Homer Simpson" state where they don't have to use their brains. There is no way to be creative in a rut. One of the things that we tell people is to always be a tourist. Even if you've been in a place 100 times before, look at it through the eyes of a tourist. See it for the first time. Force yourself out of the rut of the routine. Take the time to really look at and experience what is going on around you. Utilize your whole brain your whole life."

> *Sometimes you've got to let everything go—purge yourself.*
> *If you are unhappy with anything…whatever is bringing*
> *you down, get rid of it. Because you'll find that when*
> *you're free, your true creativity, your true self comes out.*
>
> —Tina Turner,
> singer

GET THE IDEA?

IDEA = Innovate, Detach, Escape, Act

Innovate: Change the way you do things. Shake things up. Learn new things. Expand your current boundaries of knowledge. Read everything you can get your hands on. Explore new ways of thinking through new outlets. Look for common threads that link your interests, hobbies, job, family, business. Develop these themes. Make synergy your goal.

As South African scholar William Plomer said, "It is the function of creative men to perceive the relations between thoughts, or things, or forms of expression that may seem utterly different, and to be able to combine them into some new forms—the power to connect the seemingly unconnected."

Detach: Tone down your emotional connection and gear up your objectivity. Detach yourself from the norm, from the way things have always been done. Ask yourself questions: If I had to start from scratch, what would I do? Which way would I go? Which path would I take? Who might be able to help? Whose ideas would work well with mine?

Don't assume that a problem you're handed must be solved the way it has been solved before. Experiment. Pretend that the problem (situation, predicament, product, or puzzle) is made of building blocks that you can build up, tear down, and rebuild in any way you want. Take it apart and put it together in a whole new way and see if it functions well or solves the problem better than before.

Escape: Sometimes there is no better way to improve the quality of our thinking than by taking a break. When we are concentrating intensely for a long period of time (and the length of that period varies from individual to individual), our brain gets overheated. We come to a point where we may be going through the motions, but we are not thinking clearly or productively. That's when we need to rest, relax, and rejuvenate.

Rest comes in many forms. For some people, it's a good night's sleep. For others, it's a 20-minute nap. Still others find the best way to rejuvenate is to stop working, exercise for an hour or so, and then come back to work again. Whatever type of break you take, when you come back to work again, you will feel calmer, more capable, and more creative. You'll be ready to begin again with renewed energy and a fresh attitude.

Act: Do you know a person who always comes up with great ideas, but never does anything about them? An idea in a vacuum is of no use to anyone. It's an exercise in futility. It is only when an idea is combined with action that it becomes valuable. Thomas Edison had an idea of how to make electricity. It was only when he took action—over and over again, until he discovered the way to make his idea work—that he lit up the world.

> *Creativity comes from trust. Trust your instincts. And never hope more than you work.*
>
> —Rita Mae Brown,
> author

How Creativity Won Over Cancer

Grace McGartland is the president of a company called Thunderbolt Thinking and the author of a book by the same name. She teaches corporations how to come up with creative solutions to whatever problems they may be having, for example, how to help their people get through a merger, how to implement a change in procedure, or how to get employees to work in teams.

Several years ago, McGartland was diagnosed with cancer. "I had to make a choice," says McGartland. "I could choose to shrivel up and die, or I could find a way to get through this illness. I chose to find a creative way to live. I knew this was going to be a tough ordeal. So I drew a picture of a huge wave sweeping over the shore. I made copies of the picture and sent it to everyone I knew, along with a letter asking that whenever I went in for chemotherapy, everyone visualize that wave sweeping over me and pulling the cancer cells out.

"I also drew a picture of a woman with hair. I envisioned how my hair would look when it all grew back in. I put that picture on a bulletin board in front of my desk and I looked at it every day. And you know what? I just turned 49 and I'm the only one in my family who doesn't have grey hair!"

> *It is the creative potential itself in human beings that is the image of God.*
>
> —Mary Daly,
> theologian

How Creativity Helped a Corporate Merger

Recently, a bank in Chicago was undergoing a merger. Bank officials were concerned that their customers were going to suffer. They hired Grace McGartland and her company, Thunderbolt Thinking, to show their employees how to keep their customer service on target.

McGartland started off the day by asking the seminar participants to reflect on the best personal experience they ever had with customer service. Then she asked them to draw a picture of that experience.

"The first thing that does," says McGartland, "is to put everyone on the same level. Here's the senior vice president, all dressed prim and proper in his grey suit, and he's pulling out crayons and paper along with everyone else. The second thing is, it's fun. People get loose and let their minds go. One man drew a picture of his favorite Chinese restaurant, how he gets takeout there all the time, and how well they package the food. A woman drew a picture of her favorite dry cleaner and how the people behind the counter greeted her. We posted all the drawings on the wall and looked at where the similarities were. Lo and behold, when we started talking about the key elements that were present in all the drawings, we were able to come up with a seven-point customer service strategy for the bank. All from silly stick drawings of Chinese restaurants and dry cleaners.

"One of the reasons this approach works so well is that it creates a shift in people's behavior. They may come in with a certain attitude about their job, or about the problem at hand. I can't change their attitude. But I can influence their behavior. So if I ask them to draw pictures, I'm helping them to look at the problem from a different perspective.

"You can do this all by yourself. If you're sitting behind your desk all day, struggling to solve a problem, try standing up for awhile. Just this small shift in perspective can set you on a whole new and creative path."

The things we fear most in organizations—fluctuations, disturbances, imbalances—are the primary sources of creativity.

—Mary Wheatley,
Leadership and the New Science

Creativity can be described as letting go of certainties.
—Gail Sheehy,
writer

Patrick Mulcahy's 5 Steps to Creativity

Patrick Mulcahy is CEO of Energizer Holdings, Inc. You recognize his company from that pink bunny you see in all the commercials; you know, the one that keeps going, and going, and going...

As CEO, Mulcahy is often asked to come up with creative solutions to all sorts of problems. Although it may sound like an oxymoron, he has a logical, linear, five-step approach for creative problem solving:

Step 1: **Backgrounding.** This step involves gathering any and all information necessary to help you solve the problem.

Step 2: **Define the problem or the opportunity.** A lot of people waste time solving something that is not the core problem at all. Mulcahy adds that it may be necessary to go through steps one and two several times until you get a good definition of what the problem is and you have all the data you need.

Step 3: **Developing creative solutions.** This is the one that everyone likes to focus on. You can start with logical, obvious solutions and then push the limits all the way to the outlandish. This is also the part of the process that can often benefit from bringing in other people. Lay out the problem or the opportunity for them, debate, brainstorm, and use the collective energy to come up with a solution. (There is also one option that people don't always consider, and that is to do nothing. Sometimes the best solution is to take a "wait and see" attitude.)

Step 4: **Laying out all the possible solutions you have come up with and choosing one.**

Step 5: **Executing your idea.**

"A lot of people get caught up in the loop of steps one, two, and three," says Mulcahy. "They don't pick a solution and they don't execute an idea. You can be very creative and have wonderful ideas, but if you don't move to action, you really aren't going to get anyplace.

"You can use these five steps for any kind of problem, whether it's business or personal. It can be as simple as where you want to go on vacation. The first thing to think about is what you want to do. In my case, I know what I want to do (I want to learn how to sail), but my problem is how I can carve a couple of weeks out of my schedule to do it. So I'm going to have to sit down and go through this five-step process.

"To me, creativity is hard work. I don't think you just get these light bulbs and these insightful ideas out of the air. I also think it's a misguided idea that there are those people who are extremely creative, and those who are not. There are simply those people who work very hard in a disciplined process to come up with ideas that enable them to eliminate a problem or take advantage of an opportunity."

Creativity represents a miraculous coming together of the uninhibited energy of the child with its apparent opposite and enemy—the sense of order imposed on the disciplined adult intelligence.

—Norman Podhoretz,
writer

Creativity and the Competition

I'm often asked this question: "How do I deal with the competition?" My answer: "You don't." At least not directly. In business, in any situation where people are doing things similar to what you are doing, you have to be aware of the competition. There are many people who others might describe as my competition, but I don't compete with them. I can't try to be like them, nor do I want to. And they can never be like me.

This is because we are all unique. We have different things to offer. We let outside influences (for example, the alleged competition) get us down instead of using our creative resources to look inside ourselves and see what we have to offer in order to differentiate ourselves. We can all use our own creativity to add value to every situation in which we find ourselves.

When we're competing, we're comparing. But when we're creating, we're using what we have as unique individuals to create something that has never been done before. How can you be effective trying to do something someone else is already doing?

Competing with others is uncreative effort. If you spend your energy constantly improving yourself, you'll exceed beyond the competition.

> *While we have the gift of life, it seems to me the only tragedy is to allow part of us to die—whether it is our spirit, our creativity or our glorious uniqueness.*
>
> —Gilda Radner,
> comedienne

Laughter and Creativity

Ritch Davidson has an unusual title for a businessman. He is the senior vice emperor of Playfair, Inc. He is a creativity consultant to major corporations. When asked for his take on creativity, he sites a study by Dr. Alice Isen of Cornell University. In her study, Dr. Isen gave three groups of people matchboxes, candles, and thumbtacks. Each group was to come up with ways to attach the candle to the wall.

The first group was shown a funny movie before they started their assignment. The second group was shown a film about Mother Theresa. The third group was not shown anything, and told to begin the task immediately. The first group, the group that started their assignment by laughing at a funny movie, came up with more creative solutions and a broader range of possibilities than either of the other groups.

"That shows there is clearly a connection between having fun and creativity," says Davidson. "In my company, we stress that fun and play are valuable in the workplace (and everywhere else, too). It supports creativity. When people are in the middle of an intense problem or facing the kind of crisis that comes up all the time, the best thing they can do is take a break and have some fun. It allows people to get into a looser frame of mind, which actually opens up creative channels.

"Your brain keeps working all the time. Everyone has experienced this situation: you're faced with a seemingly unsolvable problem. You scrutinize it from every angle and come up with nothing. At the end of the day, you're home playing with your kids or your pet, thinking about what to have for dinner, when suddenly the solution, or at least part of the solution, pops right into your mind. Without even knowing it, your brain has made an association with something going on around you, and suddenly creativity breaks the wall you've been hitting your head against, and you're on your way to solving the problem. When you take a break from a problem to have some fun, it may seem as if you're avoiding your responsibilities. What's actually going on is that you're giving your brain time to process information and put it together in a new and unexpected way."

> *There is a fountain of youth: it is your mind, your talents,*
> *the creativity you bring to your life and the lives of the people*
> *you love. When you learn to tap this source, you will have*
> *truly defeated age.*
>
>   —Sophia Loren,
>   actress

> *Creativity is not the finding of a thing, but the making*
> *something out of it after it is found.*
>
>   —James Russell Lowell,
>   U.S. diplomat and writer

Nothing is easy. Even the creative process. It's hard work in action. Sometimes, however, we try too hard and get burnt out. How do we recharge our batteries and get the energy we need? The next chapter will explain what energy is, why we need it, and how we get it.

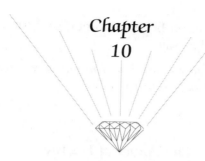

Chapter
10

Energy:
How to Recharge Your Battery Every Day

I found that I could find the energy...that I could find the determination to keep on going. I learned that your mind can amaze your body, if you just keep telling yourself, I can do it...I can do it...I can do it!

—Jon Erickson,
writer

What Is Energy?

You may be surprised, as I was, to find out that energy is defined simply as "the capacity to do work." It comes from the Greek work *enérgeia*, meaning activity, which stems from the Greek word *érg*, meaning work. What it boils down to is that the amount of energy you have determines your ability to do work. It could be the kind of work you do in an office every day, or it could be the kind of work it takes to pedal a bicycle or chop some wood.

Here's the good news about action and energy: The more action you take, the more energy you have; the more energy you create, the more actions you can take. The two feed off each other. This has to do with inertia and momentum. Inertia is when "matter retains its state of rest as long as it is not acted upon by an outside force." In other words, once you take an action, you start the ball rolling. That's when momentum (the "force with which a moving body tends to maintain its velocity and overcome resistance") comes in. Once the motion begins, momentum takes over to keep it moving. One action begets another, and the energy of motion builds upon itself. As they say,

> *Chop your own wood and it warms you twice: once when you chop it and once when you burn it.*

> —Proverb

The Power of Energy

Energy is one of most valuable and most coveted resources in the world. Wars have been fought, businesses built, and personal fortunes made and lost over sources of energy worldwide. Why, then, don't we pay more attention to our own individual energy sources? How do we make our best natural resource work for us? We do it one step at a time.

You don't have to "put in" a whole lot to make a major difference. All you need to do is to change your FRAME of reference. If you want to put more energy into your life, you need to look at these five areas:

F	R	A	M	E
O	E	I	I	X
O	S	R	N	E
D	T		D	R
				C
				I
				S
				E

FRAME is "framed" by food and exercise because those are foundations on which energy is built. It is within this foundation that we take in and utilize all our energy: what we eat and drink, how we relax and enjoy life, how we breathe, how we think, and how we build the body.

If you just exert a little more energy in each of these areas every day, your energy will increase tenfold. Don't try to overhaul your whole life at once; that's an impossible task. Start slowly. It doesn't take major changes to change for the better. You can add in one new food a week. Give yourself an extra five minutes of peaceful relaxation. Start exercising by stretching the muscles and slowly work your way up to a more strenuous routine. Remember, the smaller the steps, the easier the climb.

The Energy Frame: FOOD

There is a drug each and every one of us takes every day that affects our mental alertness, our emotional stability, and our overall physical well-being. It's a drug that causes us to experience sudden mood swings and to be alternately hyperactive and exhausted. It's a drug that can be found in every home, every day of the year. That drug is food.

There is no perfect diet for everyone, and you should always consult a physician or nutritionist before making changes in the way you eat. But scientists now know that the particular foods we eat cause changes in the chemicals in our brains, which in turn affect energy levels and mood. Dr. Judith Wurtman of McLean Hospital (a Harvard Medical School teaching hospital) and Dr. Richard Wurtman of MIT were pioneers in studying the effects of food on mood and energy.

They discovered that food affects two key neurotransmitters (chemical messengers) in the body. One is dopamine, which improves energy and alertness. An amino acid called tyrosine, found in protein, is the building block of dopamine. So eating protein actually helps us remain alert and energized. The second key neurotransmitter is serotonin. Serotonin has a calming effect and helps us feel relaxed and more in control. An amino acid called tryptophan, found in carbohydrates, is the building block of serotonin. Too many carbohydrates, and we become so calm, we fall asleep.

The Food Frame

The idea is to find the balance, and find the way of eating that is best for you. No food is intrinsically good or bad. Its value depends on how the food affects you. But there are certain common sense choices we can make:

- Lean proteins.
- Fish.
- Tomatoes.
- Carrots.
- Nuts.
- Salads.
- Leafy green vegetables.
- Fruits high in vitamin C and antioxidants.
- Grains that are high in fiber.
- Beans.
- Eight to 10 glasses of water a day.

Many people treat their bodies as if they were rented from Hertz. They are something they are using to get around in, but nothing they genuinely care about understanding.

—Chungliang Al Huang,
philosopher and tai chi master

The Energy Frame: REST

In many respects, the body is like a luxury automobile. Treat it well, give it the right fuel, and keep up the maintenance and it will take you on a fabulous ride. Treat it poorly and it will need constant repairs and it will not get you where you want to go. Food may be the body's energy fuel, but rest is what keeps it from wearing down prematurely.

There are different kinds of rest. There's the kind we get from a good night's sleep, from a lazy afternoon lying in a hammock, or simply from staring out into space for a couple of minutes every now and again. Then there's the kind of rest that I get from building a stone wall in my garden or that a Fortune 500 CEO gets from yacht racing. It's the kind of rest that is not an end unto itself, but that is used for refueling and rejuvenation to give you the energy you need to actively participate in life.

Even though these "rest" activities expend energy, they also give the mind a chance to see things from a different perspective. When a CEO races a yacht, he's pursuing an activity that he finds restful. At the same time, he learns about teamwork, leadership, and adapting to changes in weather. He takes this information back to his company and improves the way he runs his business. Engaging in hobbies and interests that are so relaxing gives us time to clear our minds and think of other things.

The Rest Frame

There are as many ways to rest as there are people in the world. Here are a few:

✦ Take a 20-minute power nap in the middle of the day. Studies have shown that napping for about 20 minutes gives us much-needed rest without making us overtired. More than 30 minutes will make you groggy.

✦ Take a short (no more than 10 minutes), brisk shower in *warm* water to get reenergized. Falling water has a powerful energizing reaction owing to "negative ions" or molecules that have adopted an extra electron. This increases the release of seratonin in the brain.

✦ Change your activity. One friend of mine takes a break from work by making phone calls to raise funds for his favorite charity. While that may not seem like rest to most of us, it gives him a change from his usual routine and supplies him with positive energy. Whatever type of break you take, when you come back to work again, you will feel calmer and more capable. You'll be ready to begin again with renewed energy and a fresh attitude.

The Energy Frame: AIR

The one activity in which the body is always engaged, whether we're eating, resting, or involved in any activity, is breathing. Because it's regulated by the autonomic nervous system (which controls basic body functions like heart rate and respiration), we hardly ever think about how we breathe. Breathing is one of the best tools we have to calm the nerves and release stress. And most doctors agree that although stress is one of the greatest "energy zappers," a good breathing technique is one of the best ways to get rid of its harmful effects.

The Air Frame

Human beings breathe 21,600 times a day. Most of the time we're not even aware of it. Here is a breathing technique to help you learn to control your breathing for relaxation:

1. Pick a comfortable, quiet place where no one will bother you.

2. Put on soothing music that will play quietly in the background.

3. Sit in a comfortable position with your back straight, giving your lungs plenty of room to expand. (Some people like to sit in the lotus position or with their legs gently crossed because it helps keep the back in the best position).

4. Close your eyes.

5. Take a deep breath through the nostrils all the way into the pit of your stomach. Think about the air coming in and filling your lungs.

6. Hold the air in for at least 5 seconds (this is not recommended for pregnant women).

7. Slowly breathe out through your mouth.

8. Release your stress and tension along with your breath. Relax your body step by step, first the head, then the neck, the shoulders, the arms, the back, the legs, and the feet. This can also be done lying down at night if you have trouble falling asleep.

9. Relax for 10 to 15 seconds and begin again.

10. Do this for five minutes each day. As you get more comfortable with the process, increase it to 10 or 15 minutes. Each time you do the exercise, try to take in and blow out more air so that you're getting more oxygen and releasing more stress.

Life is hard. It's breathe, breathe, breathe, all the time.
—Anonymous

The Energy Frame: MIND

The "I can do it" attitude is everything in life. Your accomplishments multiply a thousandfold when you infuse them with a sincere belief in a positive outcome, and steep them in energy, excitement, and enthusiasm.

We all want that kind of energy. It comes naturally to some people; most of us have to work at it. Each of us is a unique instrument. We have different backgrounds, different experiences, different metabolisms, and different ways of working. There is no one way to get more energy. You have to constantly test yourself to discover what works best for you. However, one sure way to get more energy is to throw yourself off balance every once in a while. Make a change. Any kind of change will throw you off balance for a time. But it's in that space, that area of limbo when you're out of your comfort zone and you're not quite sure where you'll end up, that you learn the most. It's in that space between where they are now and where they want to be that most people give up. That's when they give up on their diet, stop going to the gym, give up on that project, let go of their dreams. It just takes too much energy.

Understand that you have to go past the energy drain to get to the energy gain. If you want to make changes in your life, *you have to make changes in your life*. Realize that it takes time, that energy is created slowly and builds. And remember the words of author Germaine Greer: "Energy is the power that drives every human being. It is not lost by exertion but maintained by it."

The Mind Frame

Here are some ways to increase your mental energy:

✦ Read everything that interests you. You never know when something you have read will inspire you. Inventor Stanley Mason says he reads every book, magazine, and journal he can find. He believes that he's storing all this information in his mind, and that "it comes back to him" when he needs it most. He gets energy from learning new things every day.

✦ Engage your senses. Take a walk in the woods and observe the environment. Listen to the variety of sounds from the birds and animals, from the wind rustling through the leaves, from your footsteps breaking new ground. Notice what happens to your body when your energy is directed toward a particular sense, and what happens when you concentrate all the senses at once.

✦ Capitalize on your personal energy schedule. Some people have more energy in the morning; others have a difficult time getting started, but are raring to go at night. If you're an evening person, use the morning to organize and focus yourself; whenever possible make appointments for later in the day. Do the opposite if you're a morning person. See what you can do to change your daily routine so that the times you need to be most productive coincide with your peak energy hours. You'll be amazed at how much more you can get done.

Many ordinary people have harnessed the power of a positive mental attitude to help them achieve extraordinary success. They exhibit an enthusiasm for life that buoys their spirit, gives them energy, and carries them beyond any skill or talent they may have.

> *The Greeks have given us one of the most beautiful words in our language, the word enthusiasm—a god within. The grandeur of the acts of men are measured from the inspiration from which they spring. Happy is he who bears a god within.*
>
> —Muriel James and John James,
> *Passion for Life*

The Energy Frame: EXERCISE

With our busy 21st-century lives, it's hard to find the time or the energy for exercise. But research has shown that exercise can actually increase your feelings of energy. In fact, it can restore your energy so that you have enough to get all your daily tasks accomplished, and still have some left over to enjoy life.

Scientists are not exactly sure why exercise makes us feel better. One theory is that exercise increases our brain's production of hormones called endorphins, which help to elevate mood and decrease feelings of fatigue. Another theory says that exercise increases the amount of neurotransmitter activity in the brain, also believed to regulate mood and emotions.

And a third theory says that it is simply the fact that exercise increases the amount of oxygen that is transported to the brain that gives us those elevated feelings. Whatever the cause, the result is the same. Exercise increases our feelings of health, well-being, self-esteem, and energy.

Regular exercise can make a big difference in your overall energy levels and in how you feel about yourself. This is something Joe Bourdow, president of Val-Pak, recently discovered. Not too long ago he was driving home after work and passed a sign advertising the services of a personal trainer. "I thought, 'Should I? Can I?'" says Bourdow. "I hadn't exercised since I was cut from the baseball team at TC Williams High School in 1968." Intimidated by the thought of starting an exercise program, Bourdow nonetheless decided to talk to the trainer, who then put him on a program of 45 minutes of exercise three days a week.

"I found a trainer who knows how to take care of the body of a middle-aged, not particularly in-shape person. And it's made a tremendous difference in terms of energy and health," adds Bourdow. "And, if you've had a bad day and you're frustrated about work, you just stop by the gym, hit the punching bag and think about all those people who annoyed you so much. After about half an hour, you forget what you were so mad about. It's certainly a reasonable investment for what you get back."

> *Why is it so important to exercise? You need to oxygenate your tired cells. You're feeding more oxygen-carrying hemoglobin to your red blood cells. Your heart will release more blood with each beat so it works less to circulate it through your body. Physical activity will help your skeletal muscles use oxygen. Your muscle cells become more fit in burning fats and fuel. Your breathing rate is balanced so that you are not winded so easily. The bottom line is you will have more energy to expend.*
>
> —Carlson Wade,
> *Natural Energy Boosters*

The Exercise Frame

Here are a few simple hints about exercise:

✦ Get some rhythm. Music can actually help you exercise. According to Dr. Bob Arnot in his book, *The Biology of Success,* you will work out harder and longer when you use the correct tempo music to exercise. Energizing music is a big reason that spin and aerobics classes are so popular.

✦ Exercise relieves PMS. In his book, *The Balance,* nutritionist Oz Garcia states, "It has been scientifically proven that exercise can help reduce the symptoms of PMS. Aerobic conditioning produces endorphins, neurotransmitter-like compounds that work as both a pain reliever and an anti-depressant. I suggest to my clients who suffer from PMS that they walk, run, or work out in a health club when symptoms arise."

✦ Use common sense. If you haven't exercised for a while, don't try to run a marathon tomorrow. Even moderate exercise has been shown to lower insulin levels, raise good cholesterol HDL levels, and lower blood pressure. You don't have to be an exercise fanatic to get the benefits of higher energy levels.

"Pedaling" Your Ideas

"If you want to know when I get the greatest mental energy and best ideas, they come when I mountain bike," says Bruce Jenner, Olympic gold medal winner and entrepreneur. "I go up into the mountains and ride for an hour or two. I'm huffing and puffing, my heart is beating at 160, I'm really working. At the same time, it's quiet and peaceful. The scenery is incredible. No phone calls, nobody's bugging me.

"That's when my mind starts going. I go over speeches in my head, I think about what's going on with my business, I come up with marketing ideas. My head is filled with ideas. I've been biking for so many years, I don't have to think about what I'm doing unless I hit some really rough terrain. The blood is pumping, the heart is working. I'm alive—and my mind is working.

"Even though I'm putting a lot of physical energy into biking, my mental energy is increasing. To me, having energy means being physically fit. If you're in good physical shape, you can handle a lot more intellectually and emotionally as well. But the physical comes first. All you have to do is lose your health, and all the other things you're doing in life become trivial."

Bruce Jenner may be an Olympic athlete, but he is no different than the rest of us when it comes to needing energy to stimulate his thinking and accomplish his goals. Energy determines how you move forward physically, mentally, and emotionally. It governs what you do and how you do it. Most of the time we take energy for granted. We think of it when we're running low on fuel, when we haven't taken proper care of ourselves and we feel we are not up to the tasks ahead.

We are all living organisms here on this planet. Life is too short and precious not to have our minds and bodies function at the optimal performance levels. We must be aware of what we eat, what we drink, who we're with, and how we think. We can harness our mental, physical and spiritual energy to keep us motivated and inspired, allow us to take more actions, and to make those actions more powerful and vibrant.

> *The most important weapon on Earth is the human soul on fire.*
>
> —Ferdinand Foch,
> French marshal

Top 10 Things to Do to Get More Energy

1. **Exercise at every opportunity.** Try some deep knee bends and stretching from side to side while you're brushing your teeth, for instance. Or when you get out of the shower, grab the one end of the towel with your right hand behind your head, and the other end with your left hand behind your back. Gently pull the towel downward until you feel the stretch in your shoulders and triceps. Hold for 15 to 30 seconds, then reverse hand positions.

2. **Take power naps.** A 15 to 20 minute nap is great for refueling. Many of the busiest high achievers are masters at taking naps in odd places in order to refuel and refresh themselves during a long day at work.

3. **Get involved with your community.** Often, meeting new people, especially a diverse group of people, can add new energies into your life.

4. **Find hobbies and interests that are fun, that engage your mind, body, and/or spirit, and that give you something to look forward to.** Having things to look forward to creates enthusiasm, which gives you more energy.

5. **Get back to nature.** There's nothing like a day outdoors to refresh your energy and give you a renewed outlook on life. Spend a day (or more) at the beach or hiking in the mountains by yourself or with your friends or family with no cell phones, radio, or television. If you can't do that, spend a few hours in the park. Allow the energy of nature to help you feel calmer and more capable when you return to work again.

6. **Have a massage.** It's great for the circulation and pushes the toxins out of your body. Go for a professional massage, or exchange body rubs with your spouse or partner.

7. **Visualize the benefits of a project or exercise.** Think about what will be accomplished or how good you'll feel when the job is completed. If you imagine the results of the effort you're expending, you're more likely to start the task with more energy and enthusiasm.

8. **Write down your goals.** Keep track of them. Check them off when they have been completed. When we start to accomplish things, we feel better about ourselves and our energy naturally increases. Success breeds success just as energy breeds energy.

9. **Avoid refined sugar.** Although it might give you a quick energy boost, it actually depletes energy in the long run. If you feel the need for a sweetener, replace it with a natural substance like honey.

10. **Surround yourself with energy.** It's contagious. Find high energy mentors and learn what they do to keep up their energy.

I Dare You...

When you're feeling stressed out or low on energy, take action using these four strategies:

1. Commit yourself to exercise at least once a day for the next 30 days. Consult your physician or trainer about what exercises are best for you. Do some stretching and toning workouts, and some cardiovascular routines to get your heart pumping. You'll be amazed at how your energy increases when you make exercise part of your daily routine.

2. Commit to eating one more fruit a day, and one extra vegetable. Replace those unnecessary carbohydrates you snack on in the evening with fruits and vegetables. Try not to eat after 8:00 p.m. so that the body has time to start digesting your food before you go to sleep.

3. Drink at least eight glasses of water a day.

4. Do breathing exercises three times a day. Take a deep breath in through your nose and hold it for five seconds. Let the oxygen fill your lungs. Then breathe out slowly through your mouth. Let your muscles relax. This is one of the best things you can do to reach your peak performance level, especially when you're stressed, nervous, or angry. Then when you come back to the situation, you'll be better able to deal with it logically rather than emotionally.

*The longer I live, the more I am certain that the great
difference between the great and insignificant is energy—
invincible determination—a purpose once fixed, and then
death or victory.*

—Sir Thomas Fowell Buxton,
English philanthropist

If you look at successful people, you'll find they are all energy-filled and action-oriented. They don't wait for things to happen to them, they are always the ones who start—and keep—the momentum going. They don't let inertia set in. Taking action and having high energy doesn't only lead to success in business.

Not long ago, there was a study done of approximately 40,000 people in the world who are now over 100 years old. What they have most in common is not that they stayed on a particular diet, or did any special exercise routines. The trait they all share is that they continue to be engaged in and energized by life. They interact with other high-energy people, they have hobbies, they work in their gardens, and they take an interest in the world around them. They laugh and cry often.

Even at 70, 80, and 90 years old, when you keep your mind active and energized, there is definitely an impact on your physical being. If you are excited about living life, your body will follow. You may not move with the full force and energy of your earlier years, but you will not sit back and vegetate. Instead of bemoaning the fact that you only have a short time left to live, you will enjoy the energy of every precious moment.

*Life begets life. Energy creates energy. It is by spending
oneself that one becomes rich.*

—Sarah Bernhardt,
actress

The study of people who live to be 100 is very interesting. Another interesting study concluded that people who have pets live longer than those who don't. What do these two studies have in common? The people who live the longest are involved in strong relationships—with their loved ones, their communities, even their pets. Apparently, strong relationships keep us going. They help keep our minds intact and keep us feeling connected. We need connections to get through the tough times. But not just any connections. Your energy is strongest when you surround yourself with people with high energy. That's why it's important to pick and choose the relationships you make and the relationships you keep.

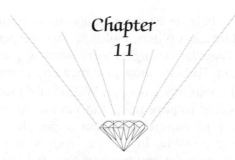

Chapter 11

Relationships:
Connecting With the People Around You

The quality of your life is the quality of your relationships.
—Anthony Robbins,
motivational speaker

What Is a Relationship?

Whenever you have more than one thing, you have a relationship. There is nothing in this world that is not related to something else. A person alone has a relationship with his or her environment. Two people, who are otherwise strangers, have a relationship if they are in the same room. There are all types of relationships in this world, and all degrees of relationships. Some are short-lived, but intense. Others are casual, but long-lasting. Some are of our own choosing, others are forced upon us. Some are positive, and some negative. Relationships are associations, connections, and they are, in the end, what life is really all about.

The Power of Relationships

No man is an island, entire of itself; every man is a piece
of the continent, a part of the main.

—John Donne,
poet

When the World Trade Center was attacked, many of those who perished realized that they were in grave danger and might not make it out alive. What did they do with the precious seconds they had left? They reached out to connect with their loved ones. They made phone calls to their spouses, mothers, fathers, siblings, children—to the people who meant the most to them. Their last thoughts were about those they loved, and those who loved them. Relationships give meaning to our lives.

This world is all about other people. We are not meant to be solitary creatures. We are meant to have people around us to love, care for, and support. We all know that there are negative people around. We must avoid them whenever possible. Instead, actively seek out those people who enjoy living, who support creative thinking and bold ideas, who are actively pursuing dreams of their own. These are the people from whom we get our greatest inspiration.

At the end of your life, it won't matter what your profession was or how much money you made. It won't matter where you went to school (or whether you went to school), what kind of clothes you wore, or how much your car cost. What does matter is how you dealt with people in your life. Did you love them? Did you accept love from them? Did you learn from them? Did you teach them?

> *Treasure the love you receive above all. It will survive long after your gold and good health have vanished.*
>
> —Og Mandino,
> motivational speaker

Looking at Things in a Different Way

John Gray is a relationship counselor, and author of the *Men are from Mars, Women are from Venus* books. His philosophy is based on the premise that in any relationship, the most important thing we can do is accept and acknowledge each other's differences. In most cases, that means learning to look at things differently. The strength of this concept was brought home to Gray under tragic circumstances.

"Several years ago, my father was found dead in the trunk of his car," he says. "He had picked up a hitchhiker who robbed him and left him in the trunk. He died of heat asphyxiation. For some reason, even though the police had been notified three times about an abandoned car on the highway, the message was not clear and they arrived too late to save him.

"My brothers and I went to Texas where it happened. I was completely devastated; I felt that in order to fully understand what happened to my father, I needed to get inside the trunk myself. I did, and my brothers closed the lid. I could see how my father had struggled to escape. I could see the marks where he had banged on the roof of the trunk. He found a screwdriver and tried to pry the lid open, but he couldn't. He was able to pry the back light free to let in some air.

"While I was in the trunk, I stuck my hand out through the hole where the back light had been. When I pulled my hand back in, one of my brothers said, 'Why don't you see if you can reach your arm through and push the release button?' And I did. I pushed the button and the trunk opened. Everything stopped in that moment. I had never thought to try that. Obviously, my father had not thought of it either. If he had, he could have gotten out of the trunk.

"I realized later that neither he nor I thought of it because when we were in the trunk, we were thinking about how to get *out* of the trunk, not how to get *in*. There can be no clearer example of the value of looking for a different point of view. So many people are stuck in their trunks—stuck in their ways of thinking and their ways of doing things. We need to hear other people's points of view, and we need to give our own. Because sometimes, just by looking at something in a different way, we can unlock that trunk so that we can come out and open our hearts."

> *The biggest mistake is believing there is one right way to listen, to talk, to have a conversation—or a relationship.*
>
> —Deborah Tannen,
> writer

Reach Out Your Hand

Sometimes we don't even realize that there are many people around us who are willing to give support. Take a good, hard look at the people in your life. There are probably many folks who have been reaching to you over the years, saying, "Try it, come on, go for it. Here, let me give you a hand." Even in tough times, even in poverty and in pain, there are always people around you who are willing to walk at least partway down the road with you.

We have thousands of opportunities to be kind to others, to reach out to strangers. We've always got that ability within us, regardless of our environment or our position. And when we utilize that ability, the energy that is released is truly unbelievable.

> *Here is a basic rule for winning success. Let's mark it in the mind and remember it. The rule is: Success depends on the support of other people. The only hurdle between you and what you want to be is the support of others.*
>
> —David Joseph Schwartz,
> writer

Symbiosis

There are many books you can read to find out how life works—books on relationships, philosophy, and biology. One of the richest books I've ever read on how life works is about ecology. It's called *The Hidden Forest: The Biography of an Ecosystem,* by Jon R. Luoma. It is about a parcel of land in Oregon called The Andrews Experimental Forest. This is a pristine piece of land that has survived unchanged for thousands of years. It has not been developed by man and is being preserved so that it can be studied by a variety of scientists.

What Mr. Luoma writes about is how every event, good or bad, and every bit of life—from a fungus to an animal—is crucial to the forest's existence. His book is a study of "the delicate balances of the relationships of the natural world." And in this natural world, Luoma describes many instances of symbiosis.

According to *Webster's Collegiate Dictionary*, symbiosis is "the living together of two dissimilar organisms, especially when this association is mutually beneficial." Luoma described one instance where scientists were trying to figure out the relationship between a fungus and the cells of a certain type of pine needle in which it lived. The fungi were "stealing" food from the pine needle that would help the fungi photosynthesize, which they couldn't do on their own. But why then didn't the pine needles show signs of damage? It turned out that "In exchange for the energy-rich sugars and starches fed to them by the tree, the fungi return the favor by forming alkaloid compounds, poisons that act against defoliating insects, a sort of chemical warfare conducted on behalf of their hosts... ." In other words, they discouraged insects from eating these particular pine needles.

If the fungi took too many nutrients from the pine needles, they would kill their host. If the pine needle didn't give up some of it's food, the fungi wouldn't be able to save the needles from predatory insects. Together they both survive and thrive.

It's important to understand that human beings, as part of the natural world, also survive and thrive in symbiotic relationships. There are times when we don't live by this concept, when we take more than we give and we end up destroying that which we need most. Or we give everything we've got and end up destroying ourselves. It's the "delicate balance" that we seek, the perfect give-and-take.

Of course, being human, we cannot expect perfection. But we can take time when relationships are not working to think about symbiosis. What is it that you need from this relationship that you are not getting?

And what does the other person need that he or she is not getting? If you can answer those questions truthfully, you can live again in harmony.

The world basically and fundamentally is constituted on the basis of harmony. Everything works in cooperation with something else.

—Rev. Preston Bradley,
theologian

Don't Take Your Loved Ones for Granted

Of course, fungi and pine needles aren't the only instances of symbiotic relationships. The old saying, "opposites attract" is based on the premise that one person looks for someone who has what he or she lacks. You'll often find business partnerships where one person has the creative imagination, for instance, and the other the financial or administrative skills. In personal relationships, you may find one partner who is described as "spacey," while the other is a logical realist.

Problems arise, however, when you take for granted, or fail to appreciate, those qualities that drew you together in the first place. The "administrator" may begin to rely too heavily on the "creator" to come up with new ideas. The creator may give up fiscal responsibility, assuming that the administrator will always take care of the details. The administrator may become angry with the creator for not paying attention to details, or the creator may start to get annoyed with the administrator for not being imaginative enough.

That's when it's time to step back and reevaluate. You have to go back and rediscover the mutual benefits that have been keeping you together. Think about how you complement each other. Look at the big picture. Construct a mental image of your life, what it is like with the other person, and what it would be like with that person gone.

There are things that we take for granted because they're always there. There are people in our lives we take for granted because we assume they will stay forever. Take them for granted long enough, and your assumptions will be shattered.

"Taking It for Granted"
When nature shows its beauty
All independents blend in so fine.
Only when one looks at the details
Will they see the divine.

—Barry Farber

Advice From John Gray on First Dates

Here's a tip from John Gray about what to do when you first meet someone:

"The first and most important step is to take into consideration what that person wants, what that person is thinking and feeling. Step out of your own shoes for a moment. Men and women approach situations differently, right from the first date.

"The man wants to impress the woman; he wants to put his best foot forward. So he does what he would do at a job interview, where he wants to impress the boss. He gives his resume. He talks about himself. At a job interview, they want to hear all about you, and that's how you try to impress them. But on a date that doesn't work.

"Meanwhile, she's trying to impress him. And the way women impress men is by being a good listener. He's talking about himself; she's being a good listener and asking lots of questions. The result is that by the end of the date, she's thinking, 'This guy only thinks about himself. He talked about himself all night, and never asked anything about me!' And the man is thinking, 'She didn't say anything at all. I thought she was interesting, but she didn't have anything to say!'"

So, in order to make this date successful, both the man and the woman have to change their behavior a bit. He's got to stop talking and do some more listening; she's got to stop asking so many questions and offer up some information about herself.

Hopping On (and Off) the Bandwagon

True relationships are true no matter what the circumstances. Be wary of friends who are around only when times are good. I have a personal friend who is very successful. He is often in the limelight and attends high profile events and functions. Over the years, he has made many friends. Not too long ago, he went through a bad spell. His fortunes dipped, and he was not as social as he had previously been. Some of those "friends" turned out to be people who had jumped on his bandwagon. As soon as he went through rough times, they jumped right off. Although this was painful for my friend, he was grateful for the opportunity to find that many of his friends stayed around and offered him needed support. He now had a much clearer picture of who his true friends were. Now that he is on the upswing again, some of those who had deserted him are trying to get back into his good graces—with no luck. As Benjamin Franklin once said, "A false friend and a shadow attends only when the sun shines."

You Never Get a Second Chance to Make a First Impression
All great business is based on friendship.

—J.C. Penney,
businessman

The success of every business depends on its ability to form strong relationships with customers. Salespeople, especially, must learn to build relationships if they want to get new customers and keep the ones they have. Because becoming a successful salesperson depends on earning the trust and respect of potential buyers, this is a process that must be continually practiced. You're not only selling your product, you're selling yourself.

First impressions can help you build the kinds of relationships you need to build your business. Here are six keys to help you sell yourself to customers and make a powerful first impression:

1. **Begin on a high note.** All emotions are catching. If you walk into a meeting and you are in a bad mood, depressed, anxious, or exhausted—and you show it—your prospective customer will slide right down to your level. On the other hand, if you are upbeat and enthusiastic, your customer will want to ride that wave along with you. It's especially important that you be in an upbeat mood the first time you meet someone. A prospect who is having a hard day doesn't want to know that you feel that way too. He wants to feel that your visit with him is a high spot in your day, and that you've been looking forward to meeting him.

   There are times when, for whatever reason, you're not really looking forward to meeting a new prospect. You may have to psyche yourself up, pump up the adrenaline, and make that call as if it was your best day ever; in other words, "fake it to make it."

2. **The eyes have it.** Twelve years ago, when I was about to go into business for myself, I asked a good friend if he had any advice. His simple words of wisdom? "Make eye contact." There's no substitute for looking a person in the eye, smiling sincerely, and saying, "Hey, it's nice to meet you." When you're making a sales presentation, or any time that you're making an important point, be sure to look right into the eyes of the other person. If you're explaining the benefits of your product to a prospect while you're looking down at the floor or over your shoulder, your words may be telling the prospect one thing, but your eyes will communicate a lack of confidence.

3. **Have a firm grip**. A handshake is second only to eye contact in conveying or betraying an air of confidence. It may be a cliché to recommend a firm handshake, but many a good impression has been ruined by an ineffectual handshake or one that is overly vigorous. The physical contact of the two hands meeting gives you an unparalleled degree of bonding. But you've got to do it right, you've got to practice. Extend your arm early as a display of eagerness and friendliness to break the ice. Concentrate on allowing your hands to grasp fully and firmly, and adjust your grip to the other person's, making sure it is equally firm.

4. **Have some questions ready.** The way to get those potentially awkward first few moments flowing is to go in prepared with several opening questions. Asking questions provokes conversation and immediately creates a more relaxed environment. These are simple, general questions used to engage a prospect. If you meet a prospect who doesn't know you or your company, try to get the person talking while you spend your time listening. Ask them questions like "What have you heard about me or my company?" "What are your perceptions?" "What do you think is good about my company and what do you think is bad?" When you get their information, you can support the correct perceptions and correct the wrong ones.

5. **To serve, not to sell.** Whenever you go in to see a client, but especially when you meet someone for the first time, you have to go in wearing your problem-solving hat. Your objective is to help this prospect find solutions and to increase his business and his profits. If you're going in with the purpose of pushing your product, you're going to have to work very, very hard to make that sale. You might not have solutions at the tip of your fingers at the first meeting, but the prospect needs to know that you've got his problems and concerns firmly in your mind, and that you can come back with ways you (and your product or service) might be able to help.

6. **Lighten up.** Over the years, the sales profession has earned itself a shady reputation. Although most salespeople are honest and hardworking, customers are understandably guarded when dealing with people they don't know. Customers erect a wall of caution. One of the best ways to break through that wall is with humor. I learned this years ago when I started cold calling door-to-door. There was often a sign on the door that said, "No Soliciting." I would walk in and

tell the receptionist, "Hi. I'm with Non Soliciting Incorporated. I wonder if I could speak to the person in charge of buying signs." Once I got the receptionist to smile, I could go on to say, "I wonder if you could help me out…" Most of the time, the answer would then be, "Yes."

If I had gone in instantly pitching myself and my product, I probably would have been shown the door instead of a friendly face. I once read a saying on the bottom of a shampoo bottle, of all places, that said, "Those who blow their own horn never play a good tune." If you're meeting someone for the first time and you talk about yourself the whole time, what impression are you making? We usually think that to make a good impression we've got to immediately let people know how good we are. But a good impression is more often made by making the other person feel comfortable, recognized, and important. Let them know you're serious about your profession, but that you don't take yourself so seriously.

Everything Is Connected

Everything in this world is connected. Everyone is connected. It is valuable to nurture connections that seek continuous improvement with strong ethical values. Not every connection is worth nurturing. There are negative, potentially harmful relationships. That is why you must constantly evaluate your relationships. Ask yourself, is this someone I want to be around? Is this someone who is uplifting, inspiring, or fun? Professionally, is this someone I want to work with? You have to make choices. The bottom line is that you want to form strong bonds with people you like, trust, and respect. You want these bonds to be strong enough to withstand the ups and downs of life, to be there when you need them most.

And most important, you must be willing to do the same—to be there for people who need you, especially when they are going through difficulties. You don't have to solve everyone else's problems. You might just need to offer a shoulder to cry on, or a few words of encouragement. You never know what small gesture might be the greatest gift. As baseball legend Jackie Robinson once said, "A life is not important except for the impact it has on other lives."

> *How strange is the lot of us mortals! Each of us is here for*
> *a brief sojourn; for what purpose he knows not, though he*
> *senses it. But without deeper reflection one knows from*
> *daily life that one exists for other people.*
>
> —Albert Einstein

Use Relationships to Create a Tidal Wave of Support

Building relationships is one of the most powerful tools you possess for realizing your dreams. It's almost impossible to reach your goals alone. There are many people along the way who can help. It's important to build as many solid relationships as you can with people at all levels, from receptionists to CEOs. Treat everyone you speak to with respect and good humor and they will support you when it counts. Know that each person with whom you establish rapport is a link in the chain that will eventually lead you right to your goals.

What goes around comes around. If your actions benefit others, they will benefit you as well. It's impossible to be of service to everyone, so choose people and places where you will have the greatest impact. In that way, the greatest payback will come to you. When you input so much value into a relationship, you earn the right to ask for the support.

> *He is the richest man who enriches his country most; in whom the people feel the richest and the proudest; who gives himself with his money, who opens the doors of opportunity widest to those about him; who is ears to the deaf, eyes to the blind, and feet to the lame. Such a man makes every acre of land in his community worth more, and makes richer every man who lives near him.*
>
> —Orison Swett Marden,
> founder of *Success Magazine*

When you hear of someone's relationship not going well, you usually hear that there's been a breakdown of communication between the parties. This is as true in negotiation as it is in personal relationships. In business or in life, we need to understand how to communicate. Everybody needs help in this area. I can't tell you how many times my wife says, "Do you actually listen to your customers, because you're not listening to me right now." That's when I have to regroup and realize what my priorities should be. Sometimes it's the people who are most important that we take for granted. We have to remind ourselves of the basic things that keep us connected and keep our relationships strong. It all begins with communication, and that's what the next chapter is all about.

Chapter 12

Communication:
Think With the Mind, Say It From the Heart

It seems rather incongruous that in a society of super-sophisticated communication, we often suffer from a shortage of listeners.

—Erma Bombeck,
humorist

What Is Communication?

There are many ways to define communication. The simplest definition is simply to "make known." Another definition is "to give or interchange thoughts, feelings, information, or the like, by writing, speaking, signs, etc." To me, communication is making connections. Take Helen Keller for instance. She wasn't able to communicate until she learned to connect objects with words. But she didn't stop there. Despite the fact that her physical senses may have been limited, she used her whole self to make connections with others.

Those are the connections that are the foundation for effective communication. It is part of a cycle: The more you connect with people, the stronger your communication becomes; the stronger your communication, the better you connect with people. So how do you go about strengthening those connections? By spreading value and by concentrating on what you can add to a situation, as opposed to what you can get from it. When you do this, you find that people are more receptive to you, they want to listen to you, be with you, and work with you because of the value you're adding.

Good communication is as stimulating as black coffee,
and just as hard to sleep after.

—Anne Morrow Lindbergh,
author

The Power of Communication

Most of the time, we think of communication as talking. I talk to you, you talk back to me—we're communicating. But to me, there is a larger definition of communication that has to do with seeing your place in the world. To me, communication is a threefold process.

It begins with a deep and rich understanding of the environment in which we live—an open, ongoing awareness of everything around you so that you are able to take advantage of every situation in which you find yourself. Second, it is a deep and rich understanding of the people around you, your contacts and connections, so that you may bring value to them. And third, it is delivering that value.

Step 1: **Understand your environment.** Communication is most effective when undertaken from a strong vantage point, when you have the highest awareness of what is going on around you. As Ming-Dao Deng says in his book, *365 Tao: Daily Meditations*, "…a wise person who lives high in the mountains and who is not blinded by…intellectuality, poor health or greed, will be better able to see events in the distance than one who lives in a closed room, eyes on some obscure project. A storm does not happen abruptly, it takes hours, sometimes days to develop. Travelers do not arrive suddenly. They can be seen in the distance. Knowing things in advance is possible with a high vantage point." A practical interpretation of that passage means that it's critical to "work from the mountaintop."

Here's an example of how this works. I have a product that I'm marketing. I want to connect with a particular company even though I don't know anyone there. I start at the top, and call CEO of that company first. I explain my reason for calling, and she likes what she hears.

She says, "I want you to call my vice president of product development. I give the green light, but I want him to look into this." I say I would, but first I ask her, "What are some of the challenges your company is going through, and what is your overall goal?" She tells me what her company is trying to accomplish, and what challenges they face.

Now that this vision is communicated to me, I can speak to the vice president of product development with a focused understanding of the company's vision and how my product can help them reach their goals. My communication becomes much stronger when the link comes from people who have a bigger picture of what's going on. Obviously, the CEO has the clearest view of how the company works. By starting from that position, I am working from the strongest vantage point.

Step 2: **Understand the people around you.** Focus on other people's goals and challenges. You'll be amazed at the many ways you find you can be of service to others. Simply by really listening to the other person, you are strengthening your connection and building rapport. It creates a comfort level that enables communication to be relaxed and natural. That caring and connection will always come back to you in the circle of things, without you having to ask.

Step 3: **Deliver the value.** Follow through on actions you said you'd take. If you promised to introduce someone to another person in your circle, do so. If you find a magazine article or book that might be of interest, recommend it (or send it directly to them). Write thank you notes. Do whatever you can to be true to your word and your purpose.

Man's greatest powers of thinking, remembering, and communicating are responsible for the evolution of civilization.

—Linus Pauling,
scientist

The Miracle of Communication

Even though she could not read, speak, or talk, Helen Keller could communicate like any other toddler—until she was 19 months old. That's when a devastating fever sealed her in a dark, soundless world devoid of human communication. She might have remained in that world were it not for the "miracle worker," her teacher, Annie Sullivan.

Annie spent several weeks spelling words into Helen's hand. Helen quickly learned to make the letters, but she did not know what they were or what they meant. She didn't know that letters made words, or even what words were. One day, however, Annie held one of Helen's hands under a water pump and spelled out the word "water" into her other hand. Suddenly, Helen understood that the letters stood for the name of the liquid she felt on her skin. She had learned to connect objects with words.

In 1904, Helen Keller became the first blind-deaf person to graduate from college. She went on to become an author, a champion of women's rights, and a crusader for the underprivileged and handicapped. She brought hope and courage to millions around the world, with astounding wisdom and optimism:

> *I am only one; but I am still one. I cannot do everything, but still I can do something. I will not refuse to do the something I can do.*

> *It is for us to pray not for tasks equal to our powers, but for powers equal to our tasks, to go forward with a great desire forever beating at the door of our hearts as we travel towards our distant goal.*

> *Everything has its wonders, even darkness and silence, and I learn, whatever state I may be in, therein to be content.*

All this, and so much more, from the woman most people thought could never learn to communicate.

Learn From the Masters

"I know people who are very bright, very knowledgeable," says Steve Adubato, communications coach and author of *Speak from the Heart.* "They can give you lots of statistics, data, and logic. But they never make a connection with people. What I teach my clients, and what I try to live, is a philosophy that says that we have to try to make a human connection. When you're speaking, that means knowing your audience, knowing what will move them, and knowing what will motivate them.

"I once interviewed Colin Powell about the subject of leadership and communication, and I watched him connect with his audience. Powell was asked to give a speech on the subject of volunteerism and community service. At the cocktail party before his speech, he talked to people in a very casual, relaxed way. He listened to people. Then he took out this little folded-over piece of paper and jotted down a few notes.

"Later, Powell started his speech by saying that although he had come to talk about community service and volunteerism, he wasn't going to preach about it or tell people why they needed to do it. He was just going to talk about some of the people in the audience and how they live it every day.

"He took out the piece of paper on which he had been jotting down notes and he said, 'I was talking to Mary at the cocktail party and she told me that she volunteers two days a week at an AIDS clinic. She said she wanted to give something back. The funny thing is, Mary told me that she gets way more from being there than she could ever give back. It makes her feel good about herself and sends a message to her children and her family about what we owe to other people. And Jim…Jim has been his son's Little League coach for the past couple of years. Jim gives up his time on a consistent basis to kids who need a mentor, a leader, a father figure, a coach. He makes a difference in the lives of kids every day.'

"Powell went on to mention three or four other people. I watched the audience watch Powell. I watched them feel a connection to him that I had rarely seen in any other situation. He tapped into a side of us that wants to give and wants to share. He used concrete examples of people in that audience.

"When I talked to Powell later and asked him about his approach to communicating, he said that even if he has a prepared speech, he makes it his business to spend time talking to people who are going to be in the audience. He finds out information that's representative of the larger audience—and this gives him a tremendous edge in being able to connect on the human and personal level.

"When you ask people why they feel nervous about public speaking, the answer you often get is 'I don't know the audience. They're strangers to me.' However, if you spent a few minutes with some people in that audience before you started to speak, you would actually have friendly faces in the audience. You would feel a connection to them instead of just saying, 'Five more minutes till I have to speak…Three more minutes till I have to speak.' You build a crescendo of anxiety that doesn't have to exist if you think of it instead as having a conversation with some friendly people you just met."

Common Sense Isn't So Common, Is It?

Everything we're talking about in this issue is common sense. But we need reminding, sometimes with a twist of information that we've heard before, but we now hear in a different way. That's what communication is really all about—leaving yourself open to hear things in a new and different way.

10 Tips Toward Better Communication

1. **Throw it back.** Have you ever noticed—or even participated in—verbal vomiting? It happens a lot at parties. Here's an example: Person A sees Person B (someone she hasn't seen in a while) and thinks, "I have to tell him what I've been going through, all the things that have been going on in my life." And Person A begins to spew forth all her news. As Person A is speaking, she is leaning forward. Person B is leaning back, listening to this, all the while thinking about all the "stuff" he wants to talk about too. So the verbal vomiting continues.

   We've all seen this happen, and most of us have participated in it at one time or another. Sometimes, however, it's better to take yourself out of the equation. Stop talking about yourself. Make brief statements and then throw the conversation back to the other person. It's difficult because we all like to talk about ourselves. But once in a while, it's good to explore what other people have to say, to get beneath the surface. Then when you decide to really say something, you've had more time to digest what the other person has said. Based on that information, you may find mutually interesting topics of conversation, rather than the competition of verbal vomiting.

2. **Parroting.** Often, just giving someone your undivided attention will make him or her feel important. Concentrate on discovering what concerns them most at this moment, and then let them know you understand those concerns and that you'll do your best to help alleviate them. You can do this by using a technique I call parroting. It's a subtle way of getting people to expand their thoughts. For instance, in a sales situation, a conversation might go like this:

   CUSTOMER: Our biggest concern right now is getting into new markets.

   REP: New markets?

   CUSTOMER: Yes. We're going into two new areas, one where we've never had a rep before, and one where we've had problems in the past.

   REP: Problems in the past?

   CUSTOMER: When we went out there last time...

Of course, you don't use this technique after every sentence, but it is a signal to the other person that you're really listening to what he or she is saying and that you're interested to know more. The goal is to show that you're interested in expanding on something the person is interested in or challenged by, so that you get depth and understanding of what they are dealing with. The more you know about them, the more value you can add to your relationship.

3. **Expand and rephrase.** Have you ever noticed that someone is speaking to you, and you can't remember what they've just said? There are times when we hear no more than two words out of a sentence, or two sentences out of a story. It might be because we're preoccupied with our own thoughts, or it might be because we don't really understand what the other person is saying.

Keep yourself on track by rephrasing what the other person just tried to communicate to you. You might say, "Let me see if I understand what you're saying..." Then you rephrase or paraphrase what they've just said. This accomplishes two things. First, it shows that you've been listening. Second, it guards against communication breakdown. Many sales have been lost and relationships severed because of miscommunication. You said this, she said that, and neither really understood what the other one meant. Restating the information you have just heard can be a powerful way to make sure you're both on the same page.

4. **Listen to other people's goals and challenges.** Recently, I was at business meeting trying to help two groups of people connect with each other. For some reason, they could not seem to find common ground. Finally, I asked one of the parties, "What are the three most important goals for your company right now?" He told us his three goals. The other parties questions were now totally focused on that criteria. Communication is so much stronger when you make a connection to other people's needs and to what's important to them. When someone sees the effort you have made to understand the criteria to elevate their success, you elevate your own at the same time.

5. **Add passion to the equation.** Passion and enthusiasm are contagious. You can't communicate if no one is paying attention, and nothing grabs attention so much as someone who is truly excited about something. Let your passion come through in your voice and your gestures. Find other people who are passionate about what they do, and who communicate that passion to others. Study their methods of communication, and emulate their positive approach to life.

Effective communication is 20 percent what you know and 80 percent how you feel about what you know.

            —Jim Rohn,
            author

6. **Communicate with yourself.** I carry a tape recorder with me wherever I go. When I have a thought, see something interesting, or want to remind myself about a task I need to do, I record it on tape. It not only reminds me of the things I have to do, it reminds me of what I was thinking at the time. So if I think, "Call Jack to set up a lunch date. Be sure to tell him the idea about a television series for his client," I record it, and then add more details and ideas I have. Then, when I play back the tape, I have a strong purpose and some good ideas that might have 'escaped' my consciousness if I didn't record it immediately. It helps make my communication even stronger.

> *Every waking moment we talk to ourselves about things we experience. Our self-talk, the thoughts we communicate to ourselves, in turn control the way we feel and act.*
>
>   —John Lembo,
>   author

7. **Clear your mind and be in the moment.** We make mistakes when we lose concentration, when we let our minds drift away and stop paying attention. You can reflect upon the past and dream about the future when you're out of your current situation, but while you're in it, keep your focus sharp and to the point. This is not always easy to accomplish; we've got a lot on our minds. When your attention drifts, you stop listening to people, you make errors in judgment, and you lose sight of your goals. When your concentration is strong, however, you are so focused that nothing can distract you from communicating clearly and effectively.

8. **Be yourself.** In one of my earlier incarnations as a sales manager, I would often travel around with a rep to see how he was doing. It always amazed me when a rep with a dynamic personality and a good sense of humor would get in front of a customer—I'd wonder what happened to the person I saw just outside the door. The personality and the humor seemed to disappear because the rep thought he had to talk or behave in a particular way. The truth is, he would have been much more successful just being himself. If you're not comfortable with who you are, other people won't be either.

9. **Make eye contact.** The eyes, as you know, are the windows to the soul. There's no better way to tell what a person is feeling than by looking into that person's eyes. Do it when you're listening, and when you're speaking as well, especially when you want to make an important point. If you're speaking to a group, pick someone in the audience and make eye contact with that one person. Then move to another person, and another so that you're making a broad connection with everyone there.

10. **Listen to others as if you had to present their ideas to a group.** When Colin Powell spoke to people at the cocktail party before his speech, he had to pay attention to what they were telling him so that he could use their information at the podium. What if you had to use the information someone was presenting in a speech of your own? Are you paying attention? Do you understand what they're saying and what they really mean? Just see how your ability to focus and listen effectively changes when you imagine yourself in this situation.

> *The most desperate need of men today is not a new vaccine*
> *for any disease, or a new religion, or a new 'way of life.' Man*
> *does not need to go to the moon or other solar systems. He*
> *does not require bigger and better bombs and missiles...His*
> *real need, his most terrible need, is for someone to listen to*
> *him, not as a 'patient,' but as a human soul.*
>
> —Taylor Caldwell,
> *Listener*

I Dare You...

Go to your next event, party, or business dinner, and listen 90 percent of the time. See what you can learn about the people around you. Pay attention. Play detective. Have fun. Throw it back to them. Practice parroting. At the end of the evening, ask yourself what you learned and how much fun you had just by listening.

Think about the two types of people you meet at parties. The first comes up and introduces himself, and begins to tell you all about his life. Then he leaves and says, "Enjoy the party. See you later." What kind of comments do you think you'll make about that person later?

Then there's the other person, who comes up, introduces himself, and asks you questions about your life. He answers your questions, but always comes back to finding out about you. He leaves and says, "Enjoy the party. See you later." What are the comments you'll make about this person? Dare to be the second kind of person.

For 24 hours, no matter who you talk to— a gas station attendant, your spouse, your children, business associates, or friends—get them talking. Say as little as possible about yourself. Whenever you're about to explain something or tell a long-winded story, get them talking.

If your children ask about something, for instance, it's very easy to give an answer. Instead,they will learn more if you ask questions such as, "How would *you* do it?" or "What do *you* think the answer is?" You not only get them to find the answer for themselves, you begin to understand how they think. The same technique can work in business. The mark of a good manager is someone who does not have all the answers, but gets the staff to find their own solutions.

When Is a Question the Answer?

"One of the biggest disappointments in life is an unmet expectation," says communications consultant and 'guru of questions' (author of *The 7 Powers of Questions*) Dorothy Leeds. "So if you want to know what others expect of you, you have to ask.

"For instance, if your boss says, 'I hope that you do a better job on your next report,' ask a clarifying question. You might say, 'Can you explain specifically what you mean by 'better'?' That way you both agree on what is expected of you. The better you clarify what the expectations are, the greater your chances are of meeting them successfully."

There are three important points to remember when asking questions and they are actually questions to ask yourself:

   ✧ **What do I hope to accomplish with this question?** If you stop to think a little before you ask a question, you're more likely to get the information you really want or need. A question such as, "How was work today?" will probably get you this answer, "Fine." Think about the answer you might get to a question such as, "What was the most annoying thing that happened at work today?"

   ✧ **Who am I asking?** Is this someone who gets annoyed if you press for information? Is it someone who needs to be 'schmoozed' a bit before they open up? Or is it someone who prefers to get right to the point, with no unnecessary conversation? If you ask a coworker for help and start off with "How was your weekend?" you probably won't get what you want.

✧ **How can I word the question to my best advantage?** The other night, for instance, someone asked me briskly, "Why did you do that?" Immediately, I was taken aback. If that person had said, "Can you explain how you came to that conclusion?" or if she had softened her tone and changed the words, I wouldn't have felt so defensive.

"Relationships are based on the ways we communicate, verbally and non-verbally," says Leeds. "You're attracted to someone by what they give off, how they look at you, how they speak. That's all part of communication. When building a relationship, you should be focused on learning about the other person. And you do that by questioning and listening."

> *I never learn anything talking. I only learn things when I ask questions.*
>
> —Lou Holtz,
> former Notre Dame football coach

Use Humor to Connect

"The best way to communicate with people is with humor," says comedian Bobby Collins. "I have a special needs child and even when doing sign language, the way I get her to [pay attention] to me is through humor. People will listen to you if you can get them to smile at you.

"So many times issues seem to be black and white. But humor can get past that all or nothing attitude. Even people who have an opposing point of view to yours will be more willing to listen if you approach them with a laugh and a smile. Suppose you want to do business with someone who is from the South and you're from New York. If you just approach it from the point of view of 'this is who you think I am, this is who I think you are,' you both have to laugh about it. Then when you come to the table, it's just two people doing business.

"Laughter breaks down all barriers. People with a lot of money have a lot of ego. People who have no money are fearful and insecure. But you can start on a level playing field when humor is the basis of the relationship. It's the best form of communication I found in life."

> *A person without a sense of humor is like a wagon without springs—jolted by every pebble in the road.*
>
> —Henry Ward Beecher,
> clergyman

There is another reason why communication is so important. Obviously, when we can communicate well, we can share our experiences and our knowledge with others. Communication skills allow us to transfer information to people around us, to become mentors to those who can learn from what we have learned. What's important in life is not only what we do while we're here, but what we leave to others when we're gone and how we live on in the spirit of those we've left behind. In my own life, I constantly think about people who passed on, and yet I remember their words and their actions. They remind me of the simple things in life, of the values that I want to be able to pass on to people I may touch in life. We need to seek out mentors, and to be mentors to others as well. The next chapter focuses on what it means to be a mentor and why we should make being a mentor a priority in our lives.

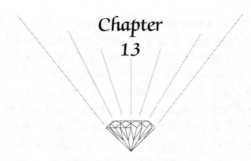

Chapter 13

Mentoring:
How to Find One and Be One

If I have been able to see farther than others, it is because I have stood on the shoulders of giants.

—Sir Isaac Newton,
physicist

What Is a Mentor?

A featured character in Homer's *Odyssey* is a man called Mentor, a loyal advisor of Odysseus who was entrusted with the care and education of Odysseus' son, Telemachus. The word "mentor" has since come to mean a wise and loyal advisor, teacher, or coach. Most of us think of a mentor as one person who takes another person under his or her wing, shares knowledge and skills, and helps that person advance in business. But the truth is, there are mentors everywhere.

I've had dozens of mentors throughout my life. They come and go over the years. Right now, one of my cousins is a mentor, although he would tell you that I am his. In many ways, my cousin is just starting out in life. He's been married just a few years, he just had his first child, and he's starting out in a new profession. He comes to me for advice, and I've helped him out in a number of ways.

During our time together, however, I learn from him as well. He's got a great outlook on life. He's investigated many different cultures and has taken many paths I might not think to explore. He's introduced me to some different ways of thinking and has given me a quest for learning in fresh new areas I might not have found on my own. So we have, in the best sense, been mentoring each other.

A mentor can be a family member, teacher, or boss. A mentor can be a person from history whom you admire and wish to emulate. A mentor can be an author whose ideas speak to you in a special way. The world is full of raw materials that we can use as mirrors to reflect positive images back on ourselves. Humankind has produced thousands of wise, intelligent, caring, energetic, motivated, generous, successful men and women, living and dead, who have given us a fabulous legacy from which to learn and prosper.

It is up to us to listen to what they have to say, to choose from the best and the brightest, to follow what they have achieved, and then to pass on what we have learned to those who come after us. That is the best way to live in the world today and to leave the world a better place for tomorrow.

> *A teacher affects eternity. You can never tell when his influence stops.*
>
> —Henry Brooke Adams,
> U.S. historian

The Power of Mentoring

When Tom Brown was 7 years old, he met an Apache Indian named Stalking Wolf in the Pine Barrens of New Jersey. This Apache, whom Brown learned to call Grandfather, was looking for someone to pass along the knowledge that he had. He was a member of a clan of trackers, Indians who can silently and efficiently track anything in the wilderness, right down to whether a person or animal has walked by on a full or an empty stomach.

Tom Brown now runs the largest survival school in the United States. He has taught thousands of people the lessons Grandfather taught him. So even though Grandfather died many years ago, all those thousands of students have had the benefit of this one person who came unexpectedly into a young boy's life.

In his book, *The Way of the Scout* Tom Brown wrote: "Grandfather told us that we should always hold one question in our minds at all times. And that is, 'What is this telling me?'...All around us were secrets that had to be unraveled, mysteries that had to be understood, and countless questions that had to be answered. Thus we were always searching, seeking and asking questions of the environment, whether of nature or of man."

This is the best lesson a mentor can ever teach—to constantly question what we see around us. When we read a book or a news story, we should ask, "What is this telling me?" When we meet a 'wise advisor' who shares his or her life's experience, we should ask, "What is this telling me?" The answers will bring us to places we never knew we could reach.

The teacher is one who makes two ideas grow where only one grew before.

—Elbert Hubbard,
writer

Follow the Follower

Years ago, in a small store on Main Street, a shopkeeper placed a large grandfather clock in his front window. The next morning, he saw a man walk by, take out his pocket watch, adjust the watch, put it back in his pocket and walk away. Every single morning for the next four years, the shopkeeper observed this morning ritual. Then one morning the shopkeeper was out sweeping the sidewalk when the man passed by, took out his watch, adjusted it, and put it back in his pocket.

"Excuse me," said the shopkeeper, "but I've been watching you do this every morning for four years now. Can you tell me why?"

"Certainly," said the man. "I'm the foreman down at the mill. I blow the quitting whistle at five o'clock every day, and I want to be sure my people get out on time."

"You're kidding," said the shopkeeper. "I've been setting my grandfather clock to your five o'clock whistle all these years!"

The shopkeeper and the mill foreman, like many of us in today's society, were caught up in a game called "follow the follower." Instead of conducting our own investigation or finding someone who truly has the qualities we wish to emulate, we take on the group mentality. We want to be ourselves, but we're afraid to be "different."

There's nothing inherently wrong with following. It's one of the best ways to learn. High achievers are constantly studying other people and their methods of accomplishment. The difference is that they are very particular about the people they choose to learn from. They look for people whose values match their own and who have achieved excellence in their field. They surround themselves with models of success.

You can have unbelievable intelligence, you can have connections, you can have opportunities fall out of the sky. But in the end, hard work is the true, enduring characteristic of successful people.

—Marsha Evans,
writer

Dialogue With a Mentor

Alan Schonberg, the founder of Management Recruiters International (MRI), expanded his company to 1,100 offices in 23 countries around the world and has mentored hundreds of people along the way. In the following interview, he shares his thoughts on mentoring:

BARRY FARBER: How did you first become a mentor?

ALAN SCHONBERG: As I progressed through life and was fortunate enough to achieve some success in my business, I found that a number of younger people would seek me out and want to have me as their mentor. This appealed not only to my ego, but also to my desire to make this a better world. It was something I found I enjoyed, and I enjoy to this day. As a result, I probably have a stable of about 10 'mentees' at any given time. Some come and go, others are on an ongoing basis.

BF: When you are mentoring people, do you learn something yourself?

AS: Anytime you do something in life to help somebody, anytime you participate in an endeavor that is beneficial to someone else, you learn just as much, if not more, as they do. There's something to be learned from everything that happens to you.

BF: Some people say they are afraid to ask a successful person to be their mentor. They think, "He won't have time for me." What do you say to that?

AS: I say that fear keeps people away from doing many things. Get rid of that fear. You're not going to die from asking; it's not going to be a catastrophe in your life. So what if you strike out? So you keep trying.

BF: Have you ever turned anyone down who wanted you to be his or her mentor?

AS: I'm always willing to have an initial meeting with someone. Usually it's a lunch meeting. For some people, that's the only time we meet. Others I see for a short while, still others for an extended period of time. It depends on what they do after our first meeting. How do they then go about putting their life together, changing it, or in some way attempt to benefit themselves? A lot of people just expect things to happen to them or for them. And of course, those things don't happen. If you don't change your behavior, your life isn't going to change.

Teachers open the door, but you must enter by yourself.
                                                        —Chinese proverb

Finding Mentors of Your Own

In order to reach any destination, you've got to take the steps yourself. You can't sit around and wait for others to help you—take action and you will find the help you need. Finding a mentor is about asking for help, advice and guidance. Most of us are afraid to ask for help. We seem to feel that asking for help is a sign of weakness. Actually, it is a sign of intelligence and awareness. Successful people know what their strengths are, and they know they have to depend on others to bolster their weaknesses. They are not shy about asking for help when they need it.

So how do you go about cultivating mentors? Here are a few hints:

❖ **Be selective.** Study the people around you and find someone you like, admire, trust, and respect. Look for someone who has skill or experience you would like to have.

❖ **Be persistent.** High achievers are often available, but they're always busy. It may take many tries before you ever reach the person. On the other hand, most will be enthusiastic about giving back to someone who doesn't give up. After all, that's how they made it.

❖ **Be specific about what you want to know.** Write down any questions you might have. Don't just sit back and wait for words of wisdom to change your life; let your perspective mentor know how you think he or she might be able to help.

❖ **Be willing and eager to work.** Ask your potential mentor how you can be of help. Volunteer to work on a special project. Join trade associations, get on committees, do your fair share. Come up with specific plans of action and ask your mentor for advice and suggestions.

You create your opportunities by asking for them.

—Patty Hansen,
writer

"All I Did Was Pick up the Phone..."

"I was looking at a catalog from Quill office supplies," says Larry Gaynor, CEO and president of the Nailco Group, the number one beauty supply company in the world, "when I realized that they do just what we wanted to do. The only difference was that they sold office supplies and we sold beauty supplies. I thought I could be successful by modeling my business after theirs.

"So I picked up the phone and I called Jack Miller, the company president. I didn't know him at all. I just explained who I was and said, 'We buy all our office products from you. We like your products, we like your service. We need to learn from you so that we can take our company to the level of success that you now enjoy. Can you help us out?'

"He said sure. I flew out there. He brought me into the boardroom, and helped me figure out the next step for my business. That's how our relationship started. It helps to find someone who is in a noncompetitive industry, so that there is less friction. Do your homework to find a company or an individual who mirrors your standards, your ideals, your strategies, and your ways of thinking. Because if they don't have the same values, it's not going to work out.

"But the biggest lesson here is, don't be afraid to call. Find somebody who is better than you, who is smarter than you—but who is willing to spend time with you, either in person or on the phone. Then pick their brains as much as you can."

We are more than 50 percent of the models we choose.
Therefore, it is vital we carefully choose the right models.

—Lord Chesterfield,
statesman

10 Points to Remember About Mentoring

1. **Plan to surpass your mentor.** Don't put your mentor on a pedestal—remember that mentors are human beings, with flaws and faults of their own. So even though you may look up to your mentors, don't let them hold you down. Don't let them argue that theirs is the only way; take

the best they have to offer and make it your own. As you grow and learn and expose yourself to new experiences, you may see beyond your mentor's vision.

2. **Find mentors in different areas.** Most people think there is only room for one "great" mentor in their lives. The truth is, there is room for many wise advisors. Some may apply to your business or career, some to your personal life. Find people who are different from each other so that the knowledge you get is not skewed only in one direction.

3. **Find one great person to emulate.** This is not really a contradiction to point number two, although it seems like it. Amongst the many mentors you cultivate, find one who is the most respected, the ultimate authority, or a genius in his or her field. Find someone who has broken the mold in your industry and has come up with amazing and innovative ideas.

> *He that walketh with wise men shall be wise...*
> —Bible, Proverbs 13:20

Walk with people who are thirsty for knowledge. Those are the people you want to be around. Search out that person who has a passionate interest in something that interests you. In college, people do internships to learn from experienced elders. This is a practice we should continue throughout life.

4. **Read biographies.** Role models don't necessarily need to be people we see around us every day. Go back into history and look for those men and women who have achieved greatness. Study their lives. Take notes. If something they have said or done inspires you, write it down and put it somewhere you will see frequently.

5. **Get rid of "anti-mentors."** Mark Twain once said, "Keep away from people who try to belittle your ambition. Small people always do that, but the really great people make you feel that you, too, can become great." There are some people who are anxious to tell you not what you can do, but what you cannot do. Every time you think of a new idea or new way to go, they tell you you're going in the wrong direction. They try to push you toward their own solution and make you feel that your solution was wrong. They say they want to see you grow, but their actions belie their words. Don't let them pull you down—get rid of them. Don't let anyone undermine your enthusiasm for growth.

Explore the truth. Test and retest what people tell you. Find out for yourself how much merit and relevance their ideas have for your life.

> *Do not believe what your teacher tells you merely out of respect for the teacher.*
>
> —Buddha

6. **Eliminate your own anger, envy, jealousy, and ego.** Sometimes, instead of looking up to those who have more than we do (at the moment), we are jealous of their accomplishments. It's human nature to feel this way. Just don't get stuck on these feelings because they will get in the way of learning. Our own ego puts up barriers to listening to what others have to say. Letting go of that ego allows us to open up and admit that others may have much to contribute. What someone else has will never takes away from what you can achieve.

> *There is a time in every man's education when he arrives at the conviction that envy is ignorance; that imitation is suicide; that he must take himself for better, for worse, as his portion; that though the wide universe is full of good, no kernel of nourishing corn can come to him but through his toil bestowed on that plot of ground which is given to him to till. The power which resides in him is new in nature, and none but he knows what that is which he can do, nor does he know until he has tried... Trust thyself: every heart vibrates to that iron string.*
>
> —Ralph Waldo Emerson,
> philosopher and poet

7. **Emulate, don't imitate.** You want be *like* your mentors, you do not want to *be* your mentors. Take what they have to give—collect the information they have to pass on and use it to your benefit. But use it in your own way. Learn from the best, but hold onto your individual uniqueness and style.

8. **Revisit greatness.** When you find something or someone that has a message for you—a quote, a book, a special person who infuses you with excitement—return to it again and again. Don't throw away a great book after you've read it. Don't disregard a mentor after you think you've learned it all. Experience and age make many things new again. You are a different person than you were five years ago. Go back to your sources and see what they have to say to you now. Once you come back to a source, it sings to you in a different way. What was valuable before is now even richer and more salient.

9. **Become a mentor yourself.** Find one person or a group of people who can benefit from your skill and knowledge, and teach them. You'll be amazed at how much you learn. Every time I do a seminar, I realize how much I learn when teaching others. Not only do I share my knowledge with others, but, more importantly, I refresh and remind myself of the basics I sometimes forget. Being a mentor is when you truly learn the most.

> *I talk in order to understand; I teach in order to learn.*
> —Robert Frost,
> poet

10. **Mentor by your actions.** What you do can have a lasting impact long after your words disappear. In the words of Ralph Waldo Emerson (who said so many great things), "Who you are speaks so loudly I can't hear what you're saying." Children, for instance, will imitate their parents' actions.

Winifred Barnes Conley is a psychotherapist and CEO of the National Learning Laboratory in Bethesda, Maryland. Conley tells of one family that came to her because the children would not do their homework. It turned out that the father insisted on watching television from the moment he came home from work until the moment he went to bed. So the children were constantly sneaking away to watch television instead of doing their homework. It wasn't until the father gave up some of his television time that the children began to improve their study habits.

I Dare You...

Outline a lifelong program on growth of the mind and experience. Take a piece of paper and start by looking one year ahead. What books am I going to read in the next year? What people am I going to contact to impact my learning and my growth in my business? Who will I turn to for advice in my personal life? With whom can I share the knowledge and experience I have gained over the past year? Every 30 days, go over this list and make sure you have made progress toward accomplishing these goals.

Do research before you ask a mentor for help. Joseph Culligan, licensed private investigator and author of *You Can Find Anybody*, suggests going to the library and looking up the *Book of Associations*. There are more than 94,000 associations listed—there is an association for every profession you could possibly imagine. When you find an association that's relevant to your interest, go to their Website or call their media relations department. Get a sense of what's going on within that association (which will tell you what's going on in that industry). You'll learn a lot about the hot topics of the day. Then when you approach a mentor, you can talk about some of these hot topics and your mentor will be impressed with the knowledge you already have.

Read every single day. Even if it's only two or three pages, find a book about something that interests you and feed your brain. Otherwise, it will feed upon itself and shrink.

> *Treat a man as he appears to be and you make him worse.*
> *But treat a man as if he were already what he potentially*
> *could be and you make him what he should be.*
> —Johann Wolfgang von Goethe,
> writer

The Greatest Mentor of All

A Hindu legend says that once upon the Earth, all people were gods. However, they abused their powers. Brahma, who was the god of all gods, decided that the divine spirit should be taken away from mankind and hidden away where no one would ever find it and abuse it again.

One of Brahma's gods advised that it be hidden deep beneath the earth. Brahma said no, man would eventually dig deep enough. Another god said they should sink it to the bottom of the ocean. "No," said Brahma, "eventually man would learn to dive deep enough." Another god suggested taking it up to the highest mountaintop. "No," said Brahma again, "for someday man will learn to climb to the highest peak." The gods were now at a loss and had no more suggestions. "There is nowhere to hide it where man cannot find it," they said.

"Yes, there is," said Brahma. "We will hide it deep within man himself. He will never think to look for it there."

And ever since then, man has been digging beneath the earth, diving into the ocean, and climbing the highest mountains, looking for what is hidden deep within himself.

We can, and should, look to others for aid, advice, and encouragement. But in the end, we must look inside, for it is only there that we will find the spirit of the true achiever. Inside ourselves, in our thoughts and our hearts, we hold the belief that we can achieve our greatest dreams. We only have to look deep enough.

Short-term Mentors, Long-term Effects

"Many of the CEOs I interviewed for my book had traditional mentoring relationships when they started out," says Lucinda Watson, author of *How They Achieved: Stories of Personal Achievement and Business Success.* "That's what happens in a corporate hierarchy. You come to a company as a young person and you find somebody who is going to lead you up the ranks, and you get groomed for success that way.

"But that's definitely not the only kind of mentor there is. I taught communications in the business school at Berkeley for many years. Part of my job was to speak with the students and talk with them about their futures and what they wanted to do. So I was a mentor to them for the time that they were in my school.

"I used to organize luncheons with CEOs in the San Francisco area. I'd invite them to come and speak to 10 young MBA students and share their thoughts and experiences for an afternoon. No one ever turned me down.

"You can be a mentor to someone for a matter of minutes. My grandfather was the founder of IBM. He wanted my father to take over the business. But when my Dad went into the army, he wanted to be a pilot, and he thought he would be an airline pilot when he got out.

"One day, my grandfather had a conversation with General Omar Bradley about what my father would do when he left the armed forces. My dad expressed his doubts about being able to run IBM. General Bradley told him, 'You can do it. I've seen what you can do here, and I know you can run that company.' My dad believed in himself because the General believed in him. That one conversation changed my father's whole direction in life, and he always considered General Bradley his mentor.

"It's amazing that one individual can have such an extraordinary effect on another individual. We usually don't believe that we can really effect change. But if you see someone and you discover what his strengths are, then a chord resonates between the two of you. That person has faith in you because you recognize the best in that person. And you are able to provide the support that a person needs, even if it lasts for no more than one conversation.

"Once you've made your success in life, you look around for what's going to you reward you next. If it's not money, it's developing a mentoring relationship with a younger person. There's nothing like helping someone and having that person say, 'Thank you. You helped me believe in myself.'

"How exciting is that?"

It wasn't the actual information my mentors gave me that made them essential to my career and personal growth. What they did for me was to pay attention, to listen to me, and to give me the kind of confidence that says, 'Yes, of course you can do it.' They believed in me. That's very important.

—Dr. Rhoda Dorsey,
president, Goucher College

If you are a mentor, you are also a leader, even if you're only leading one other person. We are put on this Earth to find out what we do best, do it to the best of our ability, and share our experiences with others so that they can carry on afterward. This is leadership. Some people are quiet leaders, others are more obvious about it. The best leaders are those who are passionate about what they do. Great leaders are people who are so excited about their visions and goals that people are inspired to walk with them and follow in their footsteps. Chapter 14 explores the real meaning of leadership and the role it plays in all of our lives.

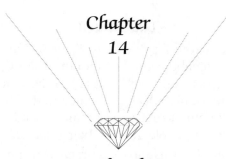

Chapter
14

Leadership:
Creating Powerful Pathways for Those Who Follow

Leadership is a potent combination of strategy and character. But if you must be without one, be without the strategy.

—Norman Schwarzkopf,
U.S. military leader

Who Is a Leader?

The dictionary defines a leader as a "guiding or directing head." A leader can be anyone, and anyone can be a leader. You don't have to be in a position of authority to be a leader. There are many leaders who are in positions of authority, and their leadership is clearly visible. There are others, though, who are leaders by example. They may stay behind the scenes, yet they have great influence over people they meet.

Think about teachers, for example. Do they not "direct" our children? Are they not guides for our future generations? Yet we don't often think of them as leaders. And what about parents? Every parent is a leader, whether he or she wants to be or not. As the old saying goes, "We lead by example." Our children follow what we do, so we must accept that mantle of leadership with great care and responsibility.

And what about each one of us? Can we all be leaders? We can if we have a worthy goal in mind and are not just pursuing selfish ends. We can if we are passionate about what we want to do and pass that passion onto those around us. We can if we care about others and help them achieve their goals, too. We need not look far to find a leader, we need only look inside ourselves.

Undaunted

When Jay Winik wrote his book, *April 1865: The Month That Saved America*, he was writing about the last month of the Civil War. He knew he would be retelling certain events that led to the Union victory, that he would have to do a lot of historical research, and that he had a compelling story to tell. What he didn't realize was that he would also find out a lot about what makes some people good at being leaders.

"What I discovered is this most common trait among great leaders: They can repeatedly suffer failure and be undaunted by it. They adhere to their vision, and they just keep plugging away. Plugging away seems like the simplest explanation you can have, but historically it's very clear. Men who go on to do great things in history often do them against great odds. They do it because they refuse to be defeated by the whirl and sway of events. You see it in Lincoln, you see it in Grant, you see it in Robert E. Lee.

"At the end of my book, I included a panorama of what America would become in the 50 years following the Civil War. I looked at the people who went on to shape the country's destiny. I was shocked by what I found. In 1865, most of these people were failures.

"Mark Twain, for instance, was thinking about going to Hawaii and thinking that perhaps, at some future date, he might be able to write a book. Thomas Edison had just been fired from his fifth job and was working in a telegraph office. Henry Ford's father told him, 'You are a tinkerer and you will never amount to anything.' These men, who all turned out to be great leaders, had the internal drive to keep them going despite repeated failure. The lesson from this? Just when you think things cannot get worse, keep going—and you can make them better."

> *Genius is divine perseverance. Genius I cannot claim nor even extra brightness, but perseverance all can have.*
>
> —Woodrow Wilson,
> U.S. president

23 Traits of Great Leaders

1. **They are realistically positive.** A great leader doesn't have pie-in-the-sky optimism, thinking that everything will always turn out for the best. But great leaders do believe in the great possibility of success and are willing to take the actions necessary to get there. They expect things to turn out well and have confidence in their own abilities to make that happen.

2. **They inspire, they don't dictate.** Great leaders are there to help, but they encourage people to solve their own problems. If someone comes to them with a problem, they say, "What do you think you should do?" They know how to inspire somebody to get motivated so that the person becomes excited about the possibilities that lay ahead.

> *Leadership appears to be the art of getting others to want to do something you are convinced should be done.*
>
> —Vince Packard,
> writer

3. **They surround themselves with success.** They create a very strong environment where they live and where they work. They are focused on keeping things around that elevate their success. They also surround themselves with other successful people. They share ideas with others in their industry and welcome input from their peers and colleagues.

4. **They have a passion for what they do.** Passion means having a deep love, respect, and commitment for what you do personally and professionally. It's possible to be a leader at something you hate, but not for long. Some people find their passion very early in life; others wander from here to there until they discover their life's work.

But all great leaders eventually find vocations they truly love. They are excited and enthusiastic about what they do, and they pass that on to those around them. Once a person discovers his or her passion in life, it becomes like a magnet, drawing them inevitably closer to success, and drawing others along with them.

> *In motivating people, you've got to engage their minds and their hearts. I motivate people, I hope, by example—and perhaps by excitement, by having productive ideas to make others feel involved.*
>
> —Rupert Murdoch,
> publisher

5. **They communicate and speak from the heart.** They are able to connect with people. The greatest leaders are the ones who are spontaneous. They know their overall mission, they know what they want to say, and they can say it without depending solely on a written script. They have a message that they want to share that comes from their passion, and they can share it without preaching or shouting. Their sincerity comes through in their words as well as in their deeds.

6. **They have goals and a vision.** They focus on what they want to achieve, establish priorities, and know what they have to do in order to keep moving forward. They always have a specific destination in mind. Their goals provide them with purpose and allow them to wake up each morning energized and looking forward to the tasks they know must be accomplished that day. Leaders are part of teams, and their goals are tied in with the goals of the team.

In the movie *Any Given Sunday*, Al Pacino, who plays the role of a head coach of a pro football team, tries to encourage a young quarterback by telling him what a former quarterback, who was at the end of his career, said about leading the team: "Do you know what I'll miss the most? I'll miss looking down the field with the team." A great leader not only looks at the goal, but gets the whole team to look at the same goal.

> *[One] characteristic a leader must possess is objectivity. He must be someone who is constantly referring back to his mission when problems come up. Someone who makes all his decisions based not on what he had for breakfast or how he feels or whether he likes the person he's dealing with, but on whether it gets him closer to his vision or backs him off.*
>
> —Warren Bennis,
> writer

7. **They achieve plans through their people, not for them.** There is an old saying that goes, "If you want something done right, do it yourself." That is the mantra of a perfectionist, not a leader. Leaders let their people do what they were hired for, even if it means that they make the occasional mistake. They are grateful for what they have been able to achieve, and are happy to help others do the same. Great leaders are able to see the potential in other people, and to allow them the time and space they need to develop it. As William H. Danforth, the founder of Ralston Purina and author of *I Dare You!* once said, "Catch a passion for helping others and a richer life will come back to you."

> *I start with the premise that the function of leadership is to produce more leaders, not more followers.*
>
> —Ralph Nader,
> consumer advocate

8. **They are bone honest.** They say what they mean and they mean what they say. Jimmy Johnson, coach of the Dallas Cowboys, believes that this is the way to motivate people. Each year, during training camp, he has to encourage nervous, anxious rookies. So at the end of day,

he'll tell each one about the good things they did on the field that day and say, "We think you can play here. We like you." And he means it. Says Johnson, "Sincerity is the most important part of positive treatment. The only thing worse than a coach or CEO who doesn't care about his people is one who pretends to care."

9. **They maintain a sense of humor.** Humor breaks down barriers. I was conducting a seminar recently for a Fortune 500 company. At the company-wide meeting before the seminars began, the CEO took part in a skit in which he made fun of himself. He took a risk doing this, as it might have made him appear foolish. But it had the opposite effect. It took him out of the category of CEO and made him appear human. It made him seem like a real, approachable person and transformed his employees' feelings toward him. Great leaders aren't funny *all* the time (they take their business very seriously). They don't necessarily have a great sense of humor—but they know when a little levity can ease a tense situation and make everyone feel a bit more comfortable.

> *Once you can laugh at your own weaknesses, you can move forward. Comedy breaks down walls. It opens up people. If you're good, you can fill up those openings with something positive. Maybe you can combat some of the ugliness in the world.*
>
> —Goldie Hawn,
> actress

10. **They cultivate awareness.** Leaders concentrate on the big picture, and all their actions are geared towards turning that picture into reality. They are often visionaries, and can see the great possibilities that can come from staying on the path they have undertaken. They see themselves as successful before they ever reach their goals. They are constantly looking out for the opportunities that surround them so that they can steer their ship in the right direction.

11. **Great leaders hire great people.** Great leaders know their own weaknesses, and hire people whose strengths fill in the gaps. They're not interested in "yes men" or people who do nothing but make the leader look good. They want people who fill in any gaps and make the strongest team possible.

> *One measure of leadership is the caliber of people who choose to follow you.*
>
> —Dennis A. Peer,
> writer

12. **Leaders are mentors and leaders have mentors.** When leaders have problems, they have a core group of people the can call upon for help and advice. Every leader has to make difficult decisions. It's always good to consult someone who's been there before, someone who's wiser and more experienced than you. Leaders are also mentors to others. They are as generous with their wisdom as others are with theirs.

13. **They have a commitment to service.** A few years ago, I saw a book with the title, *The Customer Comes Second*. In business, you're always taught that the customer comes first. Who could come before the customer? According to this book, your employees come first. If they feel valued and respected, they will value and respect your customers in turn. Great leaders take care of their employees, and their customers get taken care of in the long run.

> *Leadership should be born out of the understanding of the needs of those who would be affected by it.*
> —Marian Anderson,
> singer

14. **They are constantly learning.** Leaders are readers. They read about their industry. They read about current events. They read about history. They read biographies of men and women who have accomplished much in their lives. They learn by taking action. Nothing teaches better than experience, and great leaders are constantly open to new experiences. They explore new interests. They learn new skills for business and for pleasure. They practice the fundamentals of their business so that once learned, they have a skill for life.

Vincent van Gogh once wrote: "If you study Japanese art, you see a man who is undoubtedly wise, philosophic, and intelligent, who spends his time how? In studying the distance between the Earth and the moon? No. In studying the policy of Bismark? No. He studies a single blade of grass. But the blade of grass leads him to draw every plant and then the seasons, the wide aspects of the countryside, then the animals, then the human figure. So he passes his life, and life is too short to do the whole."

The point is not that you paint the same blade of grass over and over again. The point is that by learning the art of painting the grass, you learn the whole art of painting. Great leaders are willing to put in the time necessary to draw the blade of grass before they try and learn the whole art of painting.

15. **They have faith in themselves first.** Mark Twain once said, "Fear came knocking at the door, faith answered, and no one was there." Great

leaders have to have faith in themselves and in their abilities because they communicate this faith to those around them. Of course, they have moments of doubt and fear just like everyone else. But they don't dwell on them. They acknowledge those moments and let them pass. They exude confidence, and their belief in their vision is so strong that other people can't help but believe as well.

> *The easiest thing to be in the world is you. The most difficult thing to be is what other people want you to be. Don't let them put you in that position.*
>
> —Leo Buscaglia,
> educator and writer

16. **They deliver on promises, or they don't make them.** Great leaders do not make promises lightly. They know that they will remain leaders only as long as they have the trust and loyalty of their "followers." If they break their word, they break that trust. They destroy their own integrity, and once destroyed, it is difficult to regain.

17. **They are flexible.** Great leaders know that there are always many ways to accomplish a task or reach a goal. If one way doesn't work, they will try another. They adapt to changing markets, products, and competition. They understand that their way isn't the only way, nor necessarily the best way. They are open to new ideas and input, and listen to all suggestions even if those suggestions come from unexpected sources.

> *The best way to have a good idea is to have a lot of ideas.*
>
> —Linus Pauling,
> chemist

18. **They are focused.** Leaders get things done. They are people of action. Other people may say about a leader, "Sure, he can be abrasive (or whatever flaw he may have)—but he gets things done." Leaders don't just jump into action without thought; they evaluate situations and take calculated risks. They know that failure is always a possibility, but they aim straight for success.

> *Leadership, like swimming, cannot be learned by reading about it.*
>
> —Henry Mintzberg,
> writer

19. **They are flawed, but they have diamond potential.** They know themselves. They gain respect by admitting their weaknesses, and they work toward improving those areas. Leaders who think they are perfect soon learn otherwise.

20. They understand that recognition is a powerful motivator. Everyone needs praise and recognition. Leaders, like good parents, know that paying attention to their "children," and giving out praise—when it is deserved—is the most effective way to build confidence.

> *Management is about arranging and telling. Leadership is about nurturing and enhancing.*
>
> —Tom Peters,
> management expert

21. They expect excellence and push beyond. They expect the best from their people, and gently push them toward it. We don't always recognize our own capabilities. A great leader has the ability to see what others can't see in themselves and helps them cultivate those abilities.

22. They turn adversity into opportunity. When things go wrong—and they do—they look for the lessons that can be learned. Some people see the difficulties in every opportunity, but great leaders see the opportunities in every difficulty. They experience depression and disappointment like everyone else, but they don't let those feelings overwhelm their desire to succeed. They may be down, but they'll be up again.

> *People seldom see the halting and painful steps by which the most insignificant success is achieved.*
>
> —Annie Sullivan,
> teacher and mentor

23. They have fun. They know that life is short, and they are determined to live life to its fullest. They enjoy playing the game, and they know that means that sometimes you win, sometimes you lose. They thrive on the exhilaration of life's ups and downs, whether they're at work or at play.

The Leaders People Hate...

- ✧ Have no energy and low enthusiasm.
- ✧ Have no vision.
- ✧ Are willing to settle for average performance.
- ✧ Take credit for everything.
- ✧ Are blame-assigners.
- ✧ Are glued to their desks.

❖ Care more about their commission than about their people.

❖ Lack communication skills.

❖ Let their friends stop pulling their weight.

❖ Don't stand behind their team.

Be a Leader, Not a Manipulator

It's amazing what we sometimes do to manipulate other people. Often we're not even aware of what we're doing. What we want is help from other people, and what we end up doing is alienating them.

If you want someone's help, you must let him know you respect and admire his abilities. You want him to become your partner, not your adversary. You can say, "I've seen your work and I think it's terrific. I'm sure I can learn a lot from you. This is what I need to have done. Is there anything I can do to help you do your job?"

You can take this attitude no matter who you're speaking to—your employees, spouse, or children. When something is very important to you, when you're excited about something and want to make sure it comes out well, it's only natural to want to retain control of the situation. But there are times when in order to lead well, you have to let go of the reins. When that happens, those around you feel that you care about them. They will want to prove to you that you were right to place your faith in them, and they, too, will want the best possible results.

> *Leadership has a harder job to do than just choose sides. It must bring sides together.*
>
> —Jesse Jackson,
> civil rights leader

Listening to Yourself

"Some people have a false impression of leadership," says Charlene Costanzo, author of *The Twelve Gifts of Birth*. "They think of it as someone who gets up in front of others and tells them what to do. But the people who have always inspired me most are those who seem to listen to their own inner guides, and who are being true to themselves. Those people lead by example. And they're more effective than those who are consciously trying to lead others.

"Being a leader is important, but you can never forget you are one with those whom you lead. My favorite example comes from nature. When geese fly in formation, there is always one goose who is at the head of the V.

That lead bird is the one who faces the most resistance, and therefore tires fastest. But I recently learned that the geese take turns being in the lead position. When one bird tires, another bird moves into the head of the V. And all the birds behind continue to honk and honk, as if they were urging the leader on, saying, 'Go! Go! Go!'

"I believe we all have opportunities—and a responsibility—to take the leadership position once in a while. Sometimes we look at people in the news, people we perceive to be leaders, and we think, 'I couldn't do that.' Maybe you can't do exactly what that person has done. But we can all listen to our own inner guidance and find the unique abilities we have to make a difference in life. Often when we have big dreams, we say, 'Who am I to think I can do this? Why me?' The question really is, 'Why not me?'"

Those Who Use the Gift Lead the Way

The most complicated material object has been given to each and every one of us. That is our brain. It seems almost sacrilegious not to take advantage of its wondrous abilities. It doesn't take genius to tap into its powers. We all do it every day.

You may not think you have the capability to be a leader. But there's no use comparing yourself with others around you and thinking they are better than you because they can do some things you cannot. Particular people may have skills and abilities you do not; we each have our individual gifts. It's up to you to find and appreciate the gifts that have been bestowed upon you. Your gifts are unlike any others' and you are the only one who can uncover them, develop them, and use them to lead yourself and others to a better way of life.

> *If you don't have a plan for yourself, you'll be part of someone else's.*
>
> —Anonymous

There is one more trait that makes a great leader: a love of learning. Great leaders always want to grow and move forward, and you can't do that by relying only on what you once knew. You must constantly reinforce your view of the world with new sources of learning so that you may teach others. There's an old saying that goes, "Those who dare to teach must never cease to learn." Those who dare to lead must do the same. The next chapter brings learning into focus.

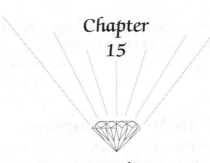

Chapter 15

Learning:
Strategies for Continuous Improvement

Learning is finding out what we already know. Doing is demonstrating that you know it. Teaching is reminding others that they know just as well as you. You are all learners, doers and teachers.

—Richard Bach,
writer

What Is Learning?

To learn means to acquire knowledge, skill, or information. You can learn by study, by example, and most of all, by experience. In some respects, we can't stop ourselves from learning. We learn simply by living. All of our senses provide us with information. We are not all intellectually equal, but we are all able to take in new information, to form ideas, to change our lives. Learning is an equal opportunity employer.

Learning enriches our environment. When a person who can't read learns to do so, for example, he doesn't just learn to put letters together to make words. He opens up whole new worlds. He increases tremendously not only his opportunities to succeed in the world, but also his ability to make a contribution to it. It's the snowball effect at work. You never know where the one thing you learn today will lead you tomorrow. As the famous orator Frederick Douglass said, "A little learning, indeed, may be a dangerous thing, but the want of learning is a calamity to any people."

Learning is not attained by chance. It must be sought for with ardor and attended to with diligence.

—Abigail Adams,
U.S. first lady

The Power of Learning

I was an average student in high school. Although my parents always wanted me to study, I rarely did; I could never get excited about learning. I took a year off after high school and then went to college. It wasn't until I took one particular course that I realized how important learning would become to my future. This time I studied, and this time I made the dean's list.

The course was called Learning Techniques and it was taught by a wonderful man named Adolph Capriolo. He taught us how to read more effectively and the best ways to take a test. He taught us how to think and how to understand situations more clearly. What he taught me and what really got me excited about learning was that I had something to offer— I had the ability to learn, to achieve, and to learn some more. This is what this book is about—that learning is a continuous adventure. And it is an adventure that starts in childhood.

I have interviewed many famous doctors, and they have all agreed on one point—that it is important to establish learning patterns early, when the brain is most receptive. The brain is maximally plastic up until the age of eight. Up until then, it is possible, for instance, for one portion of the brain to take over for another injured part. After the age of eight, this becomes increasingly difficult.

There are two important things you can do to instill the love of learning in children:

✧ **Communicate with them.** Read to them *all the time*. Take them places out of the ordinary, such as petting zoos, hands-on museums, and parks. Spend time with your children, and answer their questions (even if they seem silly).

✧ **Give them love and recognition.** Praise them for learning new things and for jobs well done. Let them know that you are excited when they learn new things.

A *TIME Magazine* article from 1997 titled "Fertile Minds" claims that studies have shown that babies even as young as two-and-a-half months can learn and remember visual sequences and simple mechanical tasks.

Five-month-olds can grasp the basic concepts of addition and subtraction. Six-month-olds can recognize language, long before they know how to speak. Infants even seem to have an innate understanding of the laws of physics, of how the world is supposed to work (for example, that objects can't hang in midair by themselves or pass through solid barriers). If this is how much we're capable of before we're even 1 year old, imagine what the adult mind can do!

You have one life; you have one chance to learn as much as you can and reach your highest potential. The only way you can discover that potential is to experiment and experience, to use your mind and body fully, and to engage yourself totally in life. You are a perfect instrument for testing what you see, hear, feel, smell, and touch. The more you engage your senses, the more you can experience and understand the world around you. Ask yourself, "Have I explored this subject with every level of understanding I have? Have I gone as deep as I can go? Have I been thinking creatively? Have I remained focused? Do I understand the truth of this experience?"

Always remember that the best way to learn is through action—to fail, to fall, to rise up, and try again. Nothing replaces the understanding you get through experience, through totally immersing yourself in an activity so that all your senses are involved. As author John Holt said:

"Not long ago I began to play the cello. Most people would say that what I am doing is 'learning to play' the cello. But these words carry into our minds the strange idea that there exist two very different processes: one, learning to play the cello; and two, playing the cello. They imply that I will do the first until I have completed it, at which point I will stop the first process and begin the second. In short, I will go on 'learning to play' until I have 'learned to play' and then I will begin to play. Of course, this is nonsense. There are not two processes, but one. We learn to do something by doing it. There is no other way."

Or, as science fiction author Ray Bradbury put it, "First you jump off the cliff, and you build your wings on the way down."

What We Learn From Teaching Children

Tracy Caldera is a kindergarten teacher in Livingston, New Jersey, who has learned many lessons from teaching her young students.

"Learning is a relative term," she says. "I had a student once who had a terrible home situation. He was barely able to communicate at all. He couldn't perform many of the basic tasks most children can perform. He couldn't say my maiden name, which was Tenacia—he called me Natno the whole year. But by the end of the year he had learned to speak up and to organize his thoughts. While the other children were beginning to read and write, he was finally able to sit and color and to put a puzzle together. What he learned may have been on a smaller scale than what the other children learned, but it was a huge accomplishment for him. It taught me to appreciate what it took for him to accomplish what might seem like a small goal, but was actually a huge goal for him.

"I've learned two important things from teaching children. One is that there are many different ways to look at things. An adult can look at a tree and say, 'Oh, that's pretty.' A child will look at the tree and say, 'That's a beautiful home for squirrels.' Children always have a fresh way of looking at things, a refreshing point of view. The second thing I've learned is to have enthusiasm for the simple things in life. I'm now teaching my class about duckling eggs. It's amazing to watch how excited they get, how curious they are. You see that they can learn the terminology we know, and they can use the vocabulary we use. They get excited about the smallest things. They have such great enthusiasm for learning. We get so caught up in our daily lives and worries; children take you back to the simple enjoyments that are out there for all of us."

> *The excitement of learning separates youth from old age.*
> *As long as you're learning, you're not old.*
> —Rosalyn Sussman Yalow,
> physicist

You cannot talk about learning without talking about children. They come into the world with open minds, with no preconceived notions of how the world should work. I learn from my own children. After a big snowstorm one winter, I was building an igloo with two of my kids. We hollowed out a big dome of snow. My son, Jordan (who was 5 at the time) began breaking up pieces of ice and putting them onto the floor of the igloo. Without thinking, I said, "Jordan, that's not a good idea."

"But Daddy," said my daughter Hallie (who was then seven), "you said any idea you have is a good idea." She was right. That's what I said, and that's what I meant. Although my perception was that Jordan was just throwing chunks of ice around, he was really fitting the broken pieces of ice together like a puzzle. He explained that he was making a bed out of ice on top of snow so that it wouldn't melt as fast and would make a comfortable home for the igloo dwellers. Hallie was right—it was a great idea!

I also teach my children not to say the word "can't." It makes me think about what I say to them. If they ask me if they can run across the road to play hide-and-seek, I can't just say, "You can't do that." I have to say, "You're not allowed to do that."

Children teach us how to learn. They have no barriers, no rules set in stone. All their ideas are fresh and fascinating. It reminds of the old saying I heard years ago, "I'll never be young enough to know it all." Our minds are never again as clear and uncluttered as they are when we are children, primed for learning. If we only learn to listen to the children, they teach us how to live.

The Legend of Learning

Learn by doing. Take action. Do not pass up opportunities when they are presented to you because you think you haven't prepared enough, or you don't understand 100 percent. Don't reject an opportunity to learn because you don't want to seem like a beginner, or you think you are beyond what is being asked of you. If you find your thoughts headed in that direction, keep this story from *It Begins With a Dream* by Peter Legge in mind:

One night, a group of travelers were preparing to retire for the evening when they were surrounded by a brilliant light and heard a great voice speak. With great anticipation, they waited to hear what important message would be imparted to them. The voice spoke. "Gather as many pebbles as you can," it said. "Put them in your saddlebags, travel a day's journey, and tomorrow night will find you glad and it will find you sad."

The travelers were angry and disappointed. They had expected a great universal truth. Instead they were given a menial task that made no sense to them at all. However, they each decided to pick up a few pebbles and deposit them in their saddlebags. They traveled a day's journey. That night, while making camp, they reached into their bags and discovered that every pebble gathered had become a diamond. They were glad they were diamonds; they were sad that they had not gathered more.

Every day you are presented with opportunities to learn. You must gather information when you can, for you never know when one simple thing you learn today will turn into a gem of an idea tomorrow. If you don't pick up these "pebbles" every day, they won't be there when you really need them.

The illiterate of the future will not be the person who cannot read. It will be the person who does not know how to learn.

—Alvin Toffler,
writer

How the Martial Arts Has Influenced My Life

Cold crisp leaves
Dancing in the sun...

Clear thoughts
Inspirational vision.

That is how the martial arts has influenced me.

The great oak with strength of root will break if it does
   not bend.

Foundations too ridged will crack.

I have learned not to be blind on new paths.
Strength does not guarantee the richness of flexibility.

Through calmness one merges the two.

Stillness leads to concentration of focus,
Opening of the mind.

It is then you see the potentiality of ones life.

That is what the martial arts has taught me.

But I must not forget that
All learning must be accompanied by action.
Constant learning.
Constant action.
Both are equal,
Both are necessary.
We learn from our actions,
We act from our learning.
One without the other suffers.
Both together provide depth and clarity in truth.

Use It or Lose It

The person who does not know how to learn will suffer for it all of his life. Even though our brains are mostly plastic until the age of eight, we continue to grow and learn throughout our adult lives. Dr. Russell L. Blaylock of the University of Mississippi Medical Center says that "The process by which the brain is 'wired' and 'rewired' is referred to as plasticity. This means that the brain is always changing and repairing itself… We now know that even the brains of adults are constantly changing and being rewired." This means that we never lose the ability to learn new things.

Even more exciting is the fact that science is now telling us that continuous learning keeps us living longer and healthier lives! In her book, *Your Miracle Brain*, author Jean Carper explains that women with college degrees live several years longer and retain better mental and physical abilities at age 75 than their "less educated sisters," and that Alzheimer's is more likely to strike people who are less educated as well. "The idea is that exerting your brain intellectually starting in childhood," says Carper, "spurs brain cells to explode with new branches, creating millions of new connections, or synapses, between neurons. This means consistent mental stimulation actually builds more brain tissue, giving you a 'bigger memory board,' so you can think more quickly."

The best thing you can do for yourself is to keep on learning. Invest in yourself and your future health every day by taking a half an hour to learn something new. Study a new language. Take up a new hobby or interest. Go back to school. Keep going, keep growing, and keep learning.

And Then, When You Think You Have Learned Everything…

It's what you learn after you know it all that counts.

—John Wooden,
author

The most successful people in every field know that they can never fully master their craft. There is always something new to learn. Life does not come in a neat little package tied up in a bow. There is never a time when you can say, "Ah, now I know everything about this subject."

One man who is a perfect example of continuous learning was master violinmaker Richard Menzel. He spent more than 30 years as an engineer at the Lockheed Corporation. Yet he always made time for his love of music. He played the violin and studied it from both a musical and engineering point of view. When he left Lockheed to open his shop, he continued his quest for knowledge.

Menzel used the standard tools of his trade, but often created new tools to fix the standard ones. He invented new tools to study areas of violin engineering no one else had explored. He created an instrument to measure the angle of your arm when you're moving the bow from string to string so that you can gauge and improve your form. He invented a machine to study the properties of horsehair used in making bows. "How much pressure does it take to break this hair?" he asked. "How much does it stretch? How much does it expand over time? Nobody knows, but I want to find out."

He invented a tool to measure the amount of pressure it takes to bring a string down to make contact with the wood. Ideally, he could have used that knowledge to construct a violin so that it would take equal pressure all along the length of the string, which would make a better sound. Such a violin may be impossible to construct, but Menzel continued his study with the hope that someday he would find the solution.

In fact, he admitted to being frustrated at the lack of closure in his learning.

"There is no end to studying," he said. "When you solve one problem, it just leads to other questions to be answered." But it is the pursuit of those answers that gives us energy and enthusiasm for life and makes us look forward to endless possibilities that lay ahead. To say, "I have learned enough" is to stop living.

5 Great Ways to Learn

Follow this acronym for "LEARN" to help you learn how to learn:

L: **Look for levels beneath the surface.** The best way to reach the deepest level of understanding of any subject matter is to gather as much information as you can. Multiply your resources. Read books, listen to audio tapes, research the Internet, study biographies of people who have previously attained success in this particular field, and find mentors who can help. The more varied your sources of information, the more levels you'll uncover about the subject. You pick up one idea from one source, and that helps you understand the information from another source, which gives you an idea of how to apply what you've learned, which makes you want to learn even more. As you utilize these valuable resources, they will build upon each other to give you a better answer.

E: **Explore new skills and hobbies.** Don't shy away because you say, "I could never do that." If you just give yourself a chance, you'll be surprised at the things you can learn to do—and learn to do well. The more organizations you join, the more people you meet, the more risks you take, the more your horizons open up, and the more you learn about yourself and the world in which we live.

A: **Act.** There are two courses of action: step by step, and diving in. Both are valid. If a project is large and seemingly overwhelming, then the best way to do it is to break it down into individual steps, learn how to do one step at a time, and then put the project all together at the end. As a fortune cookie once pronounced, "By the mile it's a trial, by the yard it's hard, but by the inch it's a cinch."

On the other hand, there are times when diving into a project, even if you're not 100 percent prepared, makes more sense. Sometimes problems loom large in front of us. We delay taking action because we want to understand the problem thoroughly and know that we have analyzed every possible solution. By that time, however, the problem has totally engulfed us. That's when it's time to get a "gun" and just point and fire, adjust and fire, adjust and fire. It's as if Godzilla was about to destroy your town. It's a big, clear target and you've got to take him down. Your best bet is to start firing and keep firing until you come up with a better solution—constant learning, constant action. Both are equal, both are necessary. We learn from our actions, we act from our learning. One without the other suffers. Both together provide invincible truth.

R: **Repetition.** In order to perfect a skill, we must practice. We must repeat an action over and over until it becomes second nature. The more we practice, the deeper the skill becomes embedded in us. When that happens, it becomes the foundation on which to build other skills. Michael Caine once said, "It's only when a man isn't thinking what he's doing that he's doing what he's thinking." Once you get to the point where you can take an action without thinking, you're ready to learn the next step.

N: **Neutral state.** The philosopher Francis Bacon once said, "If a man will begin with certainties, he shall end in doubts, but if he will be content to begin with doubts, he shall end in certainties." The only way to learn is with an open mind, from a neutral point of view. Listen to what other people have to say—but don't assume that what they tell you is the only way. Keep an open mind. Don't let stereotypes or preconceived notions stop you from letting new information in. Look at all sides of a topic before you make up your mind. Don't assume one person is right before you've heard what others have to say.

> *Two quarreling men came to a judge. The first man told his story. The judge said, "That's right." His adversary, upset at the opinion said, "You haven't heard my side of the story." He told his side and the judge said, "That's right." A third person said, "How can they both be right?" The judge thought about it and said, "That's right."*
>
> —Ellen J. Langer,
> *The Power of Mindful Learning*

I Dare You...

Try these next four strategies for becoming a perpetual student of life:

1. **The next time you're studying something, go all out.** Push yourself. When you feel like stopping, go another hour. Do some more research. Find someone who knows about this subject. Prepare more than you've ever prepared before, and see what kind of results you get.

2. **Every day, do one thing that involves risk, and study what you learn from making this effort.** Step out of your comfort zone. Try a new hobby or interest that will bring value to your life. You don't have to jump out of a plane or go bungee jumping. Risk and effort are relative terms. It can be risky to make a phone call that might end in rejection. For some people, it may take a major effort to cook a healthy meal and get out and exercise. However you define it, set yourself a task that is beyond your usual boundaries, then accomplish it and use what you learn to take the next risk.

3. **Look for things that amaze you, excite you, interest you, and intrigue you.** These are things that will motivate you to learn more about them. Don't worry about how what you're learning will fit into the rest of your life. Serendipity abounds. You never know when something you learn, just because it brings you pleasure, will be just the thing you need to know.

4. **Go back to school.** Sometimes it is difficult to put yourself back in the role of student, but the truth is you are never too old to learn. In fact, research has shown that although some mental processes may take

longer as we get older, they don't necessarily diminish. The best way to ensure that you stay at the top of your game as you age is to stay mentally active by reading, doing crossword puzzles and word games, traveling, and learning. Take classes and pursue new challenges. If you want to keep your brain in good shape, you have to exercise it. In other words, use it or lose it.

Learning is how we elevate ourselves toward success. Understanding gives us strength and courage. It gives us the confidence we need to take action. Education is everywhere, in everything we do. Many people think that when school is over, so is the necessity to learn. Most people see graduation, when they have a commencement exercise, as the end of education. But the word commencement actually means the beginning. The end of our years of schooling is really the beginning of learning.

Through the understanding and knowledge we gain over the years, interpretations of new information become magnified. In other words, every new thing we learn stands on the shoulders of everything else we've learned before. The quest for knowledge is part of being human. We want to know how things work, why things happen, what we can do to change things. Knowledge by itself, however, is useless. It's what we do with it that counts. It's up to each one of us to put it to the best possible use.

> *Learn as if you were going to live forever. Live as if you were going to die tomorrow.*
>
> —John Wooden,
> writer

The Greatest Lesson of All

Sometimes the most important lessons we can ever learn have nothing to do with facts and figures. These are lessons about life, and about our purpose here on Earth.

Dr. Fred Epstein, one of the world's most renowned brain surgeons (even though he was not a great student and was terrible in math in high school), often removed brainstem and spinal tumors from children in risky operations that other doctors wouldn't try. But he knew that the only way he could learn how to save any children was to perform risky operations on the ones who needed them most. He could not accept a child's death sentence.

Dr. Epstein not only saved many of the lives of the children on whom he operated, but he saved countless others because of the methods and technologies he invented while performing these risky surgeries.

Several years ago, Dr. Epstein had a 14-year-old patient who had already undergone several operations for brain tumors. Her prognosis was not good. She was scheduled for one more operation, which would not cure her, but might prolong her life. She had to make a choice as to whether she wanted to undergo another grueling operation.

"If you do this operation," she asked Dr. Epstein, "will I live through the summer?"

"Yes," he replied.

"Then do it," she said. "Give me the summer."

Dr. Epstein and his team performed the delicate operation. She lived to see the summer flowers bloom, and she loved every day she had left to her. She died in the fall, but before she did, she thanked the doctor for the time he had given her. Dr. Epstein will never forget the smile she gave him when she said, "Thank you," for at that moment he understood the reason he was put on Earth. It's a lesson we all need. We must keep on learning in life, no matter what the risks. No matter what the possibility of failure. Dr. Epstein never let the risk of failure stop him—and a failure for him could mean the death of a child. But still he took the risk. And so must we, for there is no other way to learn, and there is no greater lesson.

> *The man who is too old to learn was probably always too old to learn.*
>
> —Henry S. Haskins,
> author

A major part of learning, of course, has to do with memory. Studies have shown that although we often lose some ability to remember as we age, we can stop the decline by keeping our minds stimulated and engaged. That's why constant learning is even more important as we get older. In the next chapter, you will find some ideas to make sure your retention and recall are there when you need them.

Chapter 16

Memory:
Increasing Our Retention and Recall

Intelligence is the capacity to learn. Learning is based on the acquisition of new knowledge about the environment. Memory is its retention.

—Arthur Winter,
Build Your Brain Power

What Is Memory?

Memory is a fundamental cognitive process that allows us to acquire and retain information about the world and our experiences within it. There are three stages in how we form memories: encoding, storage, and retrieval. Encoding is processing an event or information as it comes to you, storage is creating a record of that event or information, and retrieval is being able to play that event or information back when you want or need it.

According to current psychological theory, there is a difference between:

✧ Procedural memory—"remembering how."

✧ Declarative memory—"remembering that."

Remembering *how* to ride a bicycle is procedural; remembering *that* something with a seat on a metal frame with two wheels is a bicycle is declarative. Declarative memory can be split into "semantic" and "episodic" memory. Remembering that my birthday is February 12 is semantic; remembering what I did last February 12 *on* my birthday is episodic. It appears that the most vulnerable form of memory is episodic.

God gave us memory that we might have roses in December.

—James Matthew Barrie,
author

The Reminder Principle

Harry Lorayne's television career began with an appearance on *I've Got a Secret* in 1958. He also appeared on *Jack Paar, Ed Sullivan*, and on *The Tonight Show* with Johnny Carson 23 times. His "secret" talent? He didn't dance, sing, or twirl plates. What he did do was memorize the names of all 400 people sitting in the studio audience. Author of many books on memory, including his *Page-a-Minute Memory Book*, Lorayne is one of the country's foremost experts in memory techniques.

"When I was young, I got terrible grades in school. I kept bringing home failing grades, and every time I did, I'd get punished for it. The tests were all for things that required memorization. You either knew the answer or you didn't. For instance, if the question was, 'What's the capital of Maryland?' you either knew it was Annapolis or you didn't. So I set out to learn how to remember the answers. What I discovered was that the trick to memorization boils down to two words: **Pay Attention**. You can't remember anything you haven't noticed in the first place.

"The first step is making the information you want to remember meaningful in your mind. Most names and numbers, for instance, are abstract. Most names do not mean anything. So how do I remember that the capital of Maryland is Annapolis? I know a girl named Mary. I see an apple land on Mary. An apple, land on Mary…Annapolis… Maryland. I lock the silly picture in my mind, and I will never forget it.

"All memory is based on the reminder principle. One thing reminds you of something else. We make subconscious connections all the time. If you want to purposely remember something, you have to consciously and knowingly make the connection."

What we are interested in is what sticks in our consciousness. Everything else we get rid of as quickly as possible.

—William James,
psychiatrist

Memory and Learning

Learning depends on memory, and memory depends on input. Every word you read and everything you see is input to your brain. The role of memory is to interpret that input. Your brain decides what input is worth keeping and where it should be "placed" in relation to previous knowledge that has already been stored.

Memory is not like an alphabetical filing system. If I ask you, "What was the name of the actress who starred in *Gone with the Wind*?" you can't just look under "Names" and pull out the one you need. Memory depends on meaning and association. So your brain might go fishing around for scenes from the movie, or picture the person with whom you saw the film, or think of the game *Clue* that has a character named Miss Scarlett, and all of a sudden it comes to you...*Gone with the Wind*...Scarlett O'Hara... Vivian Leigh!

Learning How to Learn

A man of great memory without learning hath a rock and a spindle and no staff to spin.

—George Herbert,
English poet

The teacher I talked about in Chapter 15, Adolph Capriolo, taught us various memory techniques, including one called mnemonics, using the following exercise, which, when practiced, can enhance your memory by as much as 50 percent.

First, memorize the following 10 words in order:

1. Sun.
2. Shoe.
3. Tree.
4. Door.
5. Hive.
6. Sticks.
7. Heaven.
8. Gate.
9. Vine.
10. Hen.

You'll notice that the words rhyme with the numbers. Now ask a friend to give a list of words off the top of his or her head. Suppose the first word is noodle. Think of *number one: sun*, then create a picture of the sun and noodle. See yourself at a sunny outdoor café in a plaza in Italy, eating a plate piled three stories high with noodles. The sillier the picture, the easier it is to remember. Do the same for each of the 10 words and their corresponding rhyming words and numbers, and you can easily repeat back the list of words!

I practiced this technique for weeks in my class. Then I was able to remember more things than anyone else. For me, the important point was not that I could memorize a random list of words. It enhanced my confidence in my ability to learn, so my grades changed. I was able to say, "If I can beat everyone else in this class, I can do a lot more. I can get Cs and Ds without studying, so imagine what I can do if I apply myself!"

> *Memory is fired by association. When we perceive*
> *something…from that perception we are able to obtain a*
> *notion of some other thing like or unlike which is associated*
> *with it but has been forgotten.*

> —Plato

I Am Not a Tape Recorder!

Dr. Robert Bjork, chairman of Dartmouth College's Department of Psychology, feels that one key reason people don't "realize their capabilities," is because we think of ourselves as some kind of recording device. When someone explains something to us or we sit passively in a classroom, we expect that we're going to record the information through some kind of human video camera.

"We don't work anything like a videotape recorder," says Dr. Bjork. "The way we learn something new is to relate it or fit it in to those things we already know, in contrast to a videotape, where the more you have on tape, the less room you have for something else."

Human beings have a phenomenal capacity to take in new information, providing that we have preexisting knowledge to interpret and store new ideas. Problems sometimes arise when we try to access things that we have learned. "The mistake everyone makes is that we spend way too much time on input and too little time on output," says Dr. Bjork. "A student will read a chapter three times, highlighting in three different colors until the only material that stands out is material that's not highlighted. That kind of process is nonproductive." Dr. Bjork suggests you take a three-step approach to learning new material:

1. Read the material through once.

2. At the end of the section, try to summarize the key points. Rephrase, in your own words, what you've just read.

3. Try to generate another example related to the material or make up your own "test" questions about what you've read.

"Reading something once and then summarizing it may produce twice the recall level of reading it twice," says Dr. Bjork. "It tends to reveal to us what we understand and what we don't understand. The act of retrieving the material from memory is in itself an important learning process—much more potent than simply having something presented to you."

A man's real possession is his memory. In nothing else is he rich, in nothing else is he poor.

—Alexander Smith,
Scottish poet

6 Ways to Increase and Enhance Your Memory

1. **Concentrate.** If you're not focused on something, you won't remember it. Have you ever read a passage in a book and then realized you don't even know what you've just read? It's because your mind has wandered and you weren't concentrating on the material. Focus on what you're doing, and your mind will store it away.

    Curiosity is as much the parent of attention, as attention is of memory.

    —Richard Whately,
    author

2. **Apply associations.** If I have three or four things I have to do first thing in the morning, I do the one-sun, two-shoe exercise with them before I go to bed. Then when I get up in the morning, I can easily recall the tasks I need to accomplish.

3. **Memorize something every day.** The brain is a muscle, just like all the other muscles in the body. Use it or lose it. Exercising your memory keeps it strong.

4. **Stay organized.** Many times when I'm feeling overwhelmed, it's because I have so much "stuff" around that I can't focus on what is most important. Then I know it's time to clear off my desk, file those papers, and do those small tasks I've been putting off until tomorrow. When I'm organized, it's much easier to remember the key things I'm trying to accomplish.

5. **Write things down.** When you go shopping, you're always better off if you make a list and take it with you. You don't necessarily have to write down every item you want to remember. You can write "veggies," for example, and know that you have to buy carrots, broccoli, potatoes, and onions. You can use the same shorthand when you go into a meeting. Write yourself simple notes that will help you remember the main points you want to cover, and the most important questions you want to ask.

6. **Use cadence.** If you're trying to remember a list of items, set it to music or make it into a rhyme and you will remember it much more easily. Or use acronyms, which are words formed out of the first letters of a series of words you are trying to remember. A popular acronym is "Roy G. Biv," which is used to remember the order of the colors of the spectrum (red, orange, yellow, green, blue, indigo, and violet). Another technique is the acrostic—a phrase or sentence in which the first letter of each word functions as a cue to help you recall the words you need. For example, I learned the sentence "**M**ary's **V**elvet **E**yes **M**ake **J**ohnny **S**tay **U**p **N**ights **P**ining" to help remember the order of the planets: Mercury, Venus, Earth, Mars, Jupiter, Saturn, Uranus, Neptune, and Pluto.

Organization Is the Key

Jay Fee is vice president of Woolf Associates. He is a sports lawyer and an agent for hockey players, with 75 clients, 32 of whom are NHL players. Not only does he have to keep track of his players, he has to keep track of their spouses, girlfriends, and family members—not to mention all the teams and team owners and managers. Then there's his schedule, which he creates up to four months in advance. How can he possibly keep up with all of that?

"I'm not big on memory tricks," says Fee. "I do use technology. I have a PalmPilot program on my laptop. Anything I put in there, I can transfer directly to my PalmPilot and vice versa. I enter tasks every day, and it's a constant reminder of the things I have to do on a daily, weekly, and monthly basis.

"But the truth is, I really rely on my old-fashioned yellow legal pad. I go through countless numbers of these pads; I keep them for a year in my office and then I archive them. At the beginning of each month, I take a clean pad and write down everything that needs to get done. I keep that pad on my desk and make notes on conversations I've had, names, and phone numbers.

"Then at the end of the month, I go through the pad. So if I finish July, for instance, I take a new pad for August. If there's anything I haven't done in July, it gets transferred to my August pad. I also go through the July pad and enter any important names and phone numbers into the computer. And if I have notes on the July pad that pertain to particular clients, I'll make a copy of those notes and place them in the individual's file. And I repeat this process each and every month.

"There are a lot of details to keep in mind. But the details are what give my relationships depth. I watch the general managers of all the teams and make notes on how they act and react in certain situations. I put those notes in team files. Then, if I have to deal with those managers, I can go back to my notes and they help me understand how this manager might handle a particular problem.

"I do all these things because they make my job easier, and I love my job. It's a dream job—a combination of my law degree and my love for sports. I have a passion to start work every day. Of course I keep a lot of details in my head because I work with these people every day. But I also know that I have my notes to back me up, to help me remember the most important things I have to deal with every day."

A Passion for Details

Remembering details is what really impresses people because they love the fact that you've taken the time and trouble to remember something about them. It takes work to remember details—but it doesn't seem like work if, like Jay Fee, you have a passion for what you're doing. If you're excited about what you're doing, if you love your business, you want to learn everything you can about it. You don't mind doing research and taking notes if it's exciting to you. And the more you learn, the stronger your foundation, and the greater the likelihood of your success.

That which is bitter to endure may be sweet to remember.

—Thomas Fuller,
writer

Sense Memory

Suppose you want to remember a particular event or experience, but the details are eluding you. How can you stir up your memories and bring them to the surface? You can try an exercise from the world of acting called *sense memory*. This exercise engages the senses to help your ability to recall details.

You can do this exercise by yourself, but it works best with a partner. You begin by getting comfortable and closing your eyes. Then your partner says, "Try and put yourself back in the time and place of this event. I'm going to ask you some questions. Answer as if you are there right now."

Then have your partner ask questions such as:

✧ What year is it?

✧ How old are you?

✧ Where are you? If you're indoors, what is the room like? What is the furniture like? If you're outdoors, what season is it? What's the temperature?

✧ What time of day is it? Is it light outside? Is the sun shining? Is it cloudy or raining? Is it nighttime? Are the lights on, or is the moon out?

✧ Can you describe the clothes you're wearing?

✧ Who else is with you? What do they look like? What are they wearing?

✧ How do you feel? Are you excited? Tired? Hungry? Nervous? Hot? Cold?

✧ Do you smell anything?

✧ Do you hear anything?

✧ What did you do just before this happened? What did you do right after this happened?

Using your sense memory can usually bring back details you think you have forgotten. Have your partner use a tape recorder or take notes so that you now have a record of the event, and you won't forget it again!

Abruptly the poker of memory stirs the ashes of recollection and uncovers a forgotten ember, still smoldering down there, still hot, still glowing, still red as red.

—William Manchester,
U.S. historian

Pass on Your Memories

One of the fastest growing segments in publishing over the past few years has been memoirs. People write down their life stories, and we love to read about them. Many of those people were famous. Some became famous after they wrote their memoirs. Not everyone who writes memoirs will become famous, or needs to be. You don't need to publish your memories, but it can be a wonderful treasure to pass on to your loved ones.

You may think that you have nothing special to write about. But think about this: Wouldn't you love to have a record of your parents' and grandparents' lives? What if they had written down their memories to pass on to you? You'd think their stories were fascinating.

Your children, grandchildren and future generations will think the same of your memories. Remember, your grandchildren will grow up in a very different world than the one we now inhabit. They may be able to read about these times in history books, but that's not the same as learning about what these times meant to their own relatives.

Everyone has a story to tell. Looking back on your life can be a pleasurable experience. It can inspire you to reconnect to people with whom you've lost touch. Even if some of your memories are painful (and we all have those), it can be therapeutic to confront your own past and then let it go.

Here are some steps you can take to get started on your own memoirs:

✦ Go to the bookstore or explore the Internet for books on writing memoirs.

✦ Check out schools in your community. There are now hundreds of classes offered in writing memoirs.

✦ Do some sense memory exercises to help you remember details of specific incidents. Concentrate on remembering what things looked like, tasted like, how they smelled, and how they felt (physically and emotionally).

✧ Read old newspapers and magazines to remember what was going on in the world at various times of your life. They can help you trigger old memories (for instance, many of us remember what we were doing when John F. Kennedy was killed).

✧ Write about your family, your friends, your accomplishments, your travels—any unique or interesting experiences.

✧ Don't worry about it being perfect or trying to make it great literature. Tell your story from the heart and *have fun*!

Each day of our lives we make deposits in the memory banks of our children.

—Charles Swindoll,
author

I Dare You...

Surround yourself with a wall of information. I do not have the greatest memory. I know that I need reminders—tangible things that can help me stay on course and keep my priorities straight. I need to focus on my agenda and remember critical things that move my business or life forward.

I have these reminders hanging on the walls of my office. I have one board on which I list all the accounts I have in development. On another board, I keep cards with the names and phone numbers of key contacts in various industries. It makes it very easy for me to find their phone numbers when I need them; it also serves as a reminder that these are people with whom I need to keep in constant contact.

The third reminder is a whiteboard where I write specific goals in several different areas. I have lists of goals, and I also draw what looks like a spiderweb. At the end of each "spoke" of the web is a key component of my business. This serves to remind me of how everything I'm doing is connected with everything else I'm doing.

I dare you to create your own walls of information. Keep your lists and contacts out where you can see them—not in the desk, not in a folder, not in the computer—but on the wall where you will see them every day. Then, even when you are out of your office (or wherever your wall might be), you retain the information. It becomes ingrained in you when you see it every day.

Never let your memories be greater than your dreams.

—Doug Ivester,
author

Remember what's most important in life.

Remember that being true to yourself is the only way to live. Never forget who you are. Don't change yourself to please others. Keep finding ways to discover your potential, and then expand it.

Remember your values. Don't make compromises where your values are concerned. Believe in yourself and your ability to know what's right and what's not.

Remember that this too shall pass. Everyone goes through adversity. It's part of life. Unfortunately, these times often bring pain, anger, or depression. Know that these are human emotions and it's normal to have these feelings. But also know that there is a light at the end of every tunnel, and that every challenge also brings opportunity. As time goes on, know that there are always good times ahead.

Remember to set goals and keep moving forward in life. Staying still leads only to discontent and frustration. Moving forward gives us hope, inspiration, and motivation to keep improving all the time.

Remember that it's not the destination, but the journey that is important. Where you're going is never as important as the choices you make on the way there. Never forget that what goes around comes around: The way you treat others is the way you will be treated in the end. You can have all the toys, gadgets, and money in the world, but happiness comes only from who you have loved and what you have learned along the way.

If you don't go far enough back in memory or far enough ahead in hope, your future will be impoverished.

—Art Linkletter,
TV personality

When we take a stroll down memory lane, we usually focus on events that stand out because they were particularly meaningful to us. But it's important to realize that every moment is meaningful. Life is precious, but limited. The one thing we all wish for is more time, especially as we approach the end of our lives. How do we spend the time that we do have? That's probably the most important question we can ask. It's a shame that it usually takes difficult circumstances for us to realize how precious the short time we have on this Earth is. That's why, in the next chapter, you'll find reminders on how to get the most out of every moment you have.

Chapter 17

Time Management:
Making the Most Out of Every Moment

Guard well your spare moments. They are like uncut diamonds. Discard them and their value will never be known. Improve them and they will become the brightest gems in a useful life.

—Ralph Waldo Emerson,
philosopher and poet

What Is Time Management?

To many people, time management means segmenting their lives (especially their work lives) into little boxes, each box representing a certain number of minutes or hours. To me, time management means putting things into perspective. Think about the 4.5 billion years Earth has been in existence. Think about the 70-plus years the average person spends on Earth. Put into that perspective, we are here on Earth for the blink of an eye. We have much to accomplish in such a brief time.

Time management is learning to appreciate the value of every moment you have on Earth. Not every moment will be earth-shattering. There will be moments of excitement and depression, and quiet moments of introspection. But no moment should go to waste. You can't plan every moment of your life. But you can look at how you spend your moments and think about whether or not you are spending your time wisely—and if not, find ways to make necessary changes.

Managing time effectively means more than keeping a schedule and marking a calendar. It means being careful with your time, not careless. It means making value judgments about what you do at work and at home.

It means making the choice to spend your time with people you care about. It means having a greater awareness of the world around and your place in it.

> *Time is the scarcest resource, and unless it is managed,*
> *nothing else can be managed.*
>
> —Peter F. Drucker,
> writer and management consultant

The Power of Time Management

One of the simplest ways to manage time is to try the "two-for-one" principle. This means accomplishing more than one thing at a time. For instance, in my study of martial arts, balance is very important. I don't have a lot of time to practice balance during the day. So every morning when I brush my teeth, I do it standing on one leg. Or when I'm waiting for the train, I discretely stand on one foot (so people don't think I'm crazy). Sometimes I even stand on one foot in the shower. By combining my balancing exercise with these everyday acts, I accomplish two tasks at once.

When you are managing your time efficiently, you gain the ability to do several things at once. Of course, you can't do that all the time. If one task is of great importance, you may need to concentrate fully on its accomplishment. But I don't need full concentration to brush my teeth or to wait for a train.

Doing many things at once can, however, be overwhelming. That's when you have to go back to thinking about goals. You need to keep your goals in front of you as constant reminders of where you want to go. If you get overwhelmed by too many tasks, go back to your reminders. Are your actions taking you toward your main goals? Looking at the big picture gives you a better understanding of where to place your time. Then you can go back to the small steps you need to accomplish your goal, knowing that they are leading you in a specific direction.

When we forget to go back and study the big picture every once in a while, we start living on autopilot. We just exist; we don't really live. When that happens, things tend to fall apart because we're not attuned to what's happening around us. We don't see changes. We don't adapt. We become complacent, we waste time, and we take things for granted.

> *Do not squander time for that is the stuff life is made of.*
> —Benjamin Franklin,
> statesman, writer, and scientist

How Much Time Do You Really Have?

There was a man I knew who I admired very much. Every once in a while I would stop at his shop to ask him questions, to get advice, or just to talk. He gave me knowledge and inspiration. Still, he was really no more than an acquaintance of mine.

Then one day, in a spare moment, I stopped by to say hello. A sign on the store said that the business was closed—my acquaintance had passed away.

I was shocked. I had just seen him—when? A few weeks ago, perhaps. There was so much more I would have asked him, so much more I could have learned from him and about him. It's one of those moments in life that makes you think about time. We are each allotted just so much, and we have no idea what that time may be. It makes you realize that in the time we have, we must appreciate every person we come across. Each and every life has value and things to share. There is no better reminder than death, especially sudden death, that we must treasure our time here, we must wake up every day and grab the most of it.

> *A man who dares to waste one hour of time has not discovered the value of life.*
>
> —Charles Darwin,
> naturalist

The Efficient Use of Time

While putting this chapter together, I thought about who to interview about using time wisely. Perhaps an air-traffic controller for whom every second counts? An agent I know who handles the biggest stars and whose time is extremely valuable? He would have had secrets to share. Then I heard that in this technologically advanced world, information doubles every 90 days and that more information has been generated in the last 100 years than in all previous centuries combined. So I decided to interview someone who knows how to read, process, and understand information faster than anyone else. He is Howard Stephen Berg, "The World's Fastest Reader" (according to *Guinness Book of World Records 1990*), and here is some of what he had to say:

"The reason we read so slowly is because we don't *see* the words, we *hear* them. Think about how you "read" the road while driving a car. You're reading at 60–75 miles per hour; you have to digest what's in front of you, behind you, and to either side. At the same time, you have to keep track of road signs and weather conditions, monitor the dashboard, turn on the radio, talk on the cell phone, or carry on conversations with other people in the car. But when we're reading, we don't see the page like we see the road; we hear the page as a conversation—one word at a time. We need to see a little more and hear a little more to increase our reading speed.

"There are three simple things you can do to increase your speed and comprehension:

> **Skim the material.** Get a sense of what kind of information this particular text is using to provide you with data (charts, pictures, summaries, etc.). Sometimes all the material you need is contained in an appendix at the end. By skimming, you find out what's there before you spend a lot of time on unnecessary material.

> **Read for comprehension at top speed.** While you're reading, mark off any passages that you need to go back to, either to analyze or to memorize.

> **Use study skills to break down information** that you don't understand, and memory skills to lock in concepts and vocabulary you want to retain.

"Using these three steps, you're reading becomes much more effective.

"One of the most important things you can do is read with a purpose. Know what it is you're trying to accomplish. For example, if you're a student, you're trying to get a good grade in the course, which is dependent on test questions. If your goal is to score well on a test, then the information you're searching for could be dramatically different from what you would look for if you were trying to learn the material for use on your job. Knowing the purpose helps you to focus on what is significant, because the brain is designed to selectively filter what's important in the environment.

"Here's a brief demonstration: Look around the room and make a mental picture of everything that is colored green. Memorize this picture. Now close your eyes and try to recall everything around you that is colored blue. Difficult, isn't it? Immediately your brain says, 'That's not fair—you said green!' Whatever you tell your brain to focus on overshadows everything else. You want to have this same kind of focus when you're reading. This is a great time-saver; it helps you focus in immediately on what you need to know."

*There comes a time when for every addition of knowledge
you forget something that you knew before. It is of the
highest importance, therefore, not to have useless facts
elbowing out the useful ones.*

—Sir Arthur Conan Doyle,
British writer

Make Time for Family

There is nothing as important as family, yet it is the one thing in life that most people take for granted. We get so caught up in work—whether we're ambitiously trying to get to the top or simply trying to get out from under—that we forget to make time for family.

Unfortunately, it's not easy to keep family as the highest priority. There are times when, in order to help the family survive, we have to take time away from them and concentrate on work. Sometimes we have no choice but to sacrifice the time we would like to be spending with them. But there are other times when work issues must be sacrificed. Perhaps that promotion should wait until next year. Maybe some of the work you feel can only be done by you can be delegated to others. There is no perfect answer that will work for everyone. It's a matter of balance, and of making the most of the time you do have to spend with your family.

Everyone wants to provide for his or her family. But you can give your family (and especially your children) more by teaching them how to live a life than by giving them money for a life.

If you must sacrifice time with your family for work, at least let them know what's happening. Explain the work you do. Talk about your work with your spouse and your kids. When you bring work home, tell them about what you're doing and why it's important to your job. There may be ways to get your family involved with your work, even if it's just to help you stamp envelopes or do research on the Internet.

Here are two practical tips: Be sure that "family" is one of the headings on your goal board and that it's somewhere they can see it. It helps remind you that you need to set aside time to be with them, and it helps them by letting them see that they're just as important as the work-related goals you're striving to accomplish.

Second, set up projects to do with your children. Instead of taking them to the movies or sitting and watching TV, do something creative.

Take them to the woods and go on hikes. Help them write a book or build a birdhouse. Or simply sit and talk; find out who they really are. Do something that requires interaction without other distractions. One quality half-hour on a project can be more valuable than two hours in front of a movie screen.

> *The happiest moments of my life have been the few which I have passed at home in the bosom of my family.*
> —Thomas Jefferson,
> U.S. president

Making Family Understand Time

When does a possession have the least value to you? When you get it with no time or effort invested. Those are two critical aspects for understanding value.

For instance, most children are constantly asking for (or demanding) things they think they need. If you give in to these demands, the thing they receive has very little value—no matter how much it cost.

My son recently saw a notebook that featured one of his favorite cartoon characters, and he wanted me to buy it for him. Instead of simply shelling out the dough, I gave him a task to do. I asked him to help me put some stickers with my name and address on them onto some products I was sending out. I told him if he worked for so long, he'd get $.50, and if he worked that long, he'd get $1, and so on. When children have to work for what they want, they have a completely different view of the item they desire.

When my son finally added up his earnings, he had $2.50. We went to the store, he picked out his notebook, paid for it, and even got some change. He obviously learned a lesson because he takes very good care of this particular notebook and uses it all the time. He appreciates it more than the things that were given to him.

Children aren't the only ones who can use this lesson—we all can. Something that comes too easily will never have as much value as something that is "bought" with your time and effort.

Time and Pressure

There is an old saying that goes, "one man's meat is another man's poison." When you're talking about pressure, the saying is, "One man's pressure is another man's motivator." A situation that puts pressure on one person might be a creative challenge to another. It all depends on how you look at it.

In this high-energy, got-to-get-it-done-yesterday world, it's almost impossible not to feel the pressure crunch every once in a while. And that's not necessarily a bad thing. As a writer, I know a lot about pressure. I'm constantly under one deadline or another, often several deadlines at once. That kind of pressure can affect you in two ways: It can make you skip over or skimp on details and do a sloppy job—or it can force you to focus your attention to the task at hand and work even harder to get it done and done well.

There are, of course, people who constantly procrastinate—who wait until the last minute to start projects and then complain about all the pressure under which they're working. They claim they work best under pressure. This is not always true, nor is always the best way to work. Too much pressure can cause both physical and mental exhaustion. If you're someone who feels that waiting until the last minute helps you work, try to analyze what it is about those conditions that make you feel that way. Perhaps it's the sense of urgency that spurs you forward. Perhaps the pressure gives you a burst of adrenaline you feel you need to get the job done. Perhaps it's the feeling of accomplishment (real or not) that you get from finishing the job despite the stress.

Whatever the reason, try to find a sense of balance in keeping pressure at bay. Create a time line when you start a project. Give yourself mini-deadlines to meet. Lay out the time for planning, the time for research and preparation, and the time for outlining the necessary steps. Then be sure to give yourself enough time not only to complete the project, but to double-check it at the end so you're sure everything has been done. This kind of time management can help maintain your sanity and relieve a lot of stress.

Too little pressure can result in boredom and frustration. Too much pressure can result in burnout. In the middle ground, when pressure is present but not overwhelming, you are challenged, stimulated, alert, creative, and decisive.

Plan your work for today and every day, then work your
plan.

—Norman Vincent Peale,
author and clerygyman

6 Best Ways to Manage Your Time

1. **Make a list.** To balance your time between work, family, and personal interests, make a list of the top 10 things you want to do in the next 12 months.

2. **Make a daily activity log.** Once every hour, write down how you're spending that time. Then ask yourself, "Is this the most productive use of my time?" If it is, continue what you are doing. If it isn't, make the necessary changes. Notice how much more aware you become of how you use your time as you continue to fill out your daily log.

> *You will never find time for anything. If you want time, you must make it.*
>
> —Charles Buxton,
> statesman, writer, and social reformer

3. **Do not do things by rote.** Swami Sivananda once said, "Put your heart, mind, intellect and soul even into your smallest acts. This is the secret of success." Keep your awareness sharp and make every moment count. Be careful about how you spend your time. The most successful endeavors are those in which the greatest care has been spent on details.

> *Whatever you do, do it with all your might. Work at it, early and late, in season and out of season, not leaving a stone unturned, and never deferring for a single hour that which can be done just as well now.*
>
> —P.T. Barnum,
> showman and entrepreneur

4. **Rearrange your environment.** Are you convinced you're managing time well because you're doing things the way they've always been done? It may be you're just taking the easy way out. You don't have to make major changes to be more efficient; make minor adjustments. Simply moving a file cabinet or changing your filing system may make a huge difference. And if it doesn't work out, you can always put things back the way they were.

5. **Customize your time management method.** There are many useful time management tools and programs on the market today. One of them may work perfectly for you. But none of them work perfectly for everyone. Find one—or create one yourself—that is best suited for you as an individual. Every high achiever I've met has an individual

system that he or she has devised to help manage time. Some are complicated, some are as simple as a little black book. The system you use is less important than using a system that works for you.

6. **Do a pre- and post-evaluation of each of your days.** In the morning, before you even start your day, visualize what you want to accomplish, what your goals are, who you are meeting. What outcomes would you like to see? How can you make the best use of your time each day based on what it is you want to accomplish? At the end of the day, review what you did accomplish and what you need to do tomorrow.

> *Once you have mastered time, you will understand how true it is that most people overestimate what they can accomplish in a year—and underestimate what they can achieve in a decade!*
>
> —Anthony Robbins,
> author

Dialogue With a Time Management Expert: Words of Wisdom From Stephanie Winston

For Stephanie Winston, author of *Organized Executive*, "Time management and organization are not religious or moral issues. People often feel that their character is weak if they are not organized. Rather, I see organization and time management as fundamental tools to enable you to accomplish the things that you value in life, whether they are professional or personal priorities."

In this interview, Stephanie shares her wisdom about managing time and getting more out of life.

BARRY FARBER: What's the most important thing people need to do to get more quality time out of their lives?

STEPHANIE WINSTON: The first thing is to have some sense of commitment to what it is you want to do. A lot of people are disorganized because they're unclear as to what their real intentions are. I use the word intentions purposely, as opposed to priorities. A priority is really a reflection of your intentions. You need to be clear on this because of the tremendous number of claims on your time. Be clear on what you want, and make a personal commitment to it. Once you've articulated an intention, then you can begin to think systematically about priorities, actions, and delegation—the practical aspects of time management.

So your first task is to define your intention, and then to translate that into the actions you will take. Then, as time goes on, measure your success. Are your actions leading you toward your intentions? If so, keep going in that direction. If not, take different actions.

BF: Everyone talks about simplifying their lives. Do you have any simple suggestions for doing that?

SW: Take a few days and analyze how you're spending your time. Every time you undertake an activity, ask yourself, "Is this time expenditure appropriate for me? Can it be eliminated? What would happen if I stopped doing this?" Maybe it is something that can be delegated to someone else. Take voice mail, for instance. If I sit and listen to my voice messages, I could spend half an hour just writing them down. On the other hand, I can have my assistant listen to the messages, then type them up for me, including names and phone numbers. Then I can go through them in just a few minutes. It's a task that needs to be done, but not necessarily by me.

Another thing you can do is get out from under what I call "the curse of e-mail." E-mail has not re-placed the letter or the phone call, it is an add-on. Of course it has its good points, but we somehow feel we are at the mercy of our e-mail—that we have to pay attention to it at all time. People will call and say, "Did you get the e-mail I sent you 15 minutes ago?" The solution is to think of your e-mail as being delivered like your paper mail, and that you will only check it at a specific time. The idea that you must send an instant response is damaging to your work and your life.

BF: I always work on several projects at once. What's the best way to keep many balls in the air at the same time?

SW: First of all, here's a basic rule of time management: Know your own temperament. Some people would find that confusing and overwhelming. You're obviously energized by having many balls in the air. But no matter how many projects you have, you can only concentrate on one thing at a time.

David Allen, a business expert, once said, "You can do anything, but you can't do everything." What I take that to mean is that you can do it all, but you can't do it all at the same time. You have to acknowledge that you are a human being with human limitations. You have to take everything in sequence. Write down the sequence and say, "I'll do this task first, it should take me this long, then I'll do the next one." Otherwise, it's like gridlock with everybody trying to cross the intersection at the same time. No one goes anywhere. This applies not only to business, but to life in general. It's all about setting up a sequence of priorities. It's common sense, but it's difficult to think about when you're caught in the fray. That's why you need to make it a habit in your life.

Lost, yesterday, somewhere between sunrise and sunset, two golden hours, each set with sixty diamond minutes. No reward is offered for they are gone forever.

—Horace Mann,
educator

The Value of Time

Condense value at every turn. The present is always and builds upon the past.

—Barry Farber

Condense value at every turn means at every moment, in every situation, get the most out of it. Focus on it. Get the most benefit out of it. Soak up information.

The present is always. There's only now, right now, this second, then the time is gone. Sometimes the hardest thing to do is to force yourself to pay attention to the minute details, to your present actions. We say, "This isn't important," or, "I'll do this later." We start to put things off because we think we'll always have time later. But that is not necessarily true. We never know how much time we may have.

The present always builds upon the past. The way you do things, the way you understand things, the way you communicate to others, the actions you take—they're all built on what you know, and what you've seen, read, learned, and experienced throughout your life. Every moment you live, your value and the value you bring to others increases. But you have to understand and appreciate that value in order to reap its benefits. Author M. Scott Peck said it best, "Until you value yourself, you won't value your time. Until you value your time, you will not do anything with it."

> *The present moment is a powerful goddess.*
> —Johann Wolfgang von Goethe,
> German author

> *One of the illusions of life is that the present hour is not the*
> *critical, decisive hour. Write it on your heart that every day*
> *is the best day in the year. No man has learned anything*
> *rightly, until he knows that every day is Doomsday.*
> —Ralph Waldo Emerson,
> philosopher

Technology was supposed to make life easier for us. For most of us, however, it has just made life more complicated. That's why time management is so important. Being able to do things faster is a means to end, not an end itself. The goal is to be able to take the time to appreciate those around us, to savor the moments in life that are moving and meaningful. We cannot control time, but we can use the time we have to give ourselves the best in life and to get the best out of it.

> *Time by itself means nothing, no matter how fast it moves,*
> *unless we give it something to carry for us; something we*
> *value. Because it is such a precious vehicle, is time.*
> —Ama Ata Aidoo,
> writer

The best way to make every moment count is to be true to yourself—to do the things that are meaningful to you without worrying that it is not "what everybody else is doing." There's nobody else like you on the planet. Take the time to think about what makes you unique. It's not always easy to be different—but if you want to succeed in life and market yourself, you have to stand out from the crowd and connect with people in a unique way. You're not going to do that if you try to be like everybody else, if you try to conform to the group. The key to marketing yourself is to stick to your convictions, to be innovative, to take a chance. You'll be amazed at what you get in return, as you'll find out in Chapter 18.

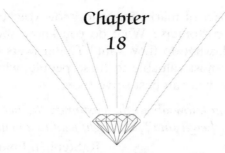

Chapter 18

Marketing Yourself: What Makes *You* Unique

He who has a thing to sell
And goes and whispers in a well
Is not so apt to get the dollars
As he who climbs a tree and hollers

—Anonymous

What Is Marketing?

I read that little poem on the back of a sugar packet in a restaurant. It struck me as the perfect definition of marketing—the only way to get someone to buy your product (or your service, idea, or you, yourself) is to get out and holler. The greatest idea in the world is of no use at all if no one knows about it.

Simply put, marketing is the process of getting a product or service from a seller to a buyer. If you're looking for a new job, you're the seller and the prospective employer is the buyer. If you have a small home business, you're selling a product or service to potential customers. If you're trying to raise funds for a worthy cause, you can't do it unless people hear about your efforts. Marketing is the strategy you apply in order to sell your idea, concept, service, or product to a group of targeted customers.

There are two major foundations for marketing yourself effectively. The first is to know yourself; to really look inside yourself and understand everything you can do, what you're capable of, what your skills are, what your knowledge is, what you want to do, what you're striving for in your life. It's common sense—the more you know about yourself, the better you can market yourself.

The second aspect of marketing is to know your environment: Who are your potential customers? What do you know about these people? What do they need; what do they want? The answers to these questions will tell you what's most valuable to these people, what they would pay money for, and how you can best serve them.

> *The more you know about the customer, the better. You*
> *never know when a small fact might lead to a better product.*
> —R. Stephen Fountaine,
> VP of Market Research, Kimberly-Clark Corp.

The Power of Marketing

A funny thing happens to most of us when we think about marketing ourselves. We shudder at the thought. We're suddenly shy. We're modest. We're embarrassed to talk about ourselves. But think of it this way: If you owned a business, would you simply open a store, sit there, and wait for customers to come to you? If you did, you'd go out of business in a very short time. To succeed, you have to tell people about your product. You have to get the word out. And if you, as the *owner* of the business, are reluctant to sell, who else will do it for you?

Marketing, selling, advertising, and promotion—they're all part of the same overall concept—getting the word out. They're all part of the process of getting an idea across. It's all marketing, and marketing is an art that, once learned, can benefit you in every area of your life. What marketing really does is tell people how you can help them solve particular problems. Because of your special skills, knowledge, invention, or innovation, you can make life easier for someone else. Marketing is getting your message out to people in a way that's stimulating enough to get them to act.

If you want to be successful in the 21st century, you have to become a good marketer. You have to promote your life and your life's work, whether you work for a large company or work for yourself. You'll need an entrepreneurial spirit, managing yourself as if you were running a small business. You have to have a marketing plan, just as any small business would. You have to know your "product" inside out and how to bring that product to the buying public. You have to know where your industry or field of interest is headed so that your product remains a marketable commodity in a rapidly changing world. And you need to have the skills of salesmanship to convince the buyer of the value of the product.

You don't become successful by sitting back and waiting for great things to happen to you. Marketing yourself is the only way to get the word out there. Everyone at the top of his or her profession—from CEOs to movie stars—had to sell themselves to get where they are today. You don't have to be a braggart or a show-off to sell yourself. What you really need is a positive attitude and a belief in yourself and your abilities. Selling yourself to others only proves that you have confidence in yourself and are willing to stand behind your beliefs. When you don't believe in yourself, you're only selling yourself short.

Tips From the Einstein of Infomercials

"I've spent years developing products. Take the Rotisserie, for example. It took two-and-a-half years to perfect. I spent every single one of those days thinking about, improving, and testing that product. The secret to marketing it is not just that it's a great product. It's because I believe in it so much, I have such a passion for it, that people really want to try it."

So says Ron Popeil, one of the greatest inventors and marketers of our time. Everyone knows his products, from the food dehydrator to the Popeil pocket fisherman. When he speaks about his products, he doesn't have to try and "sell" them to you; his enthusiasm and his sincere belief in himself and his products do more than any sales pitch could ever accomplish.

"You have to be passionate about whatever it is you're selling, whether it's a pocket fisherman or yourself or your service. When you believe in something—when that belief is positive—people will listen to you. And if it's priced right, they will try it. Contrary to what most people think, consumers don't want cheap things. They're willing to pay, if you can deliver what you promise. If you can convey your passion, they'll pay the price."

A Child's Guide to Marketing

One summer, I decided to sell my car. I was washing my car, and I asked my then six-year-old daughter, Hallie, to help me make a large "For Sale" sign. We got the car all clean and shiny, and placed the sign in the car window. I gathered up the pails and sponges, and headed back toward the garage.

All of a sudden, I heard Hallie, in her loudest six-year-old voice, shouting, "Car for sale! My daddy's car for sale!" I came out of the garage and said, "Hallie, what are you doing?"

"Daddy," she said, "nobody's going to know the car is for sale if we don't tell them!"

Hallie had a natural understanding of the power of marketing. It's a power that we all have, but we don't always understand. Even though we're not all salespeople, we all sell something. It may be a product, a service, or an idea, but we're selling something. And in every situation—business and social—we're selling ourselves.

There is no reason to be embarrassed or ashamed to let other people know who you are and what you do. Never be afraid to stand at the end of your driveway and shout your message to anyone who will listen.

How Is a Writer Like a Salesperson?

Today, Robert Shook is an extremely successful author, with more than 46 books under his belt. But he, like everyone else, had to start somewhere. His first book was on selling, and in order to get his book sold, he had to do the legwork himself.

"When I first started writing, my books weren't at the top of the publisher's list. They didn't want to spend money on publicizing my book. So I took the situation into my own hands. I was in the insurance business at the time, and traveled all over the country. Whenever I was going to be in a particular city, I'd call the radio and television stations, as well as the local newspapers.

"I'd say, 'I would like to talk to you about an author who is going to be in Pittsburgh on the 2nd and 3rd of next month. His name is Robert Shook. He's a very dynamic guy. He wrote a book called *The Complete Professional Salesman*. He's been on many other talk shows, and he's great. I know you'll want to interview him. He'll be there on Tuesday and Wednesday; which day works best for you?' Then the guy would usually say, "Okay, and who are you? You're my contact, and I need to know how to get in touch with you.' Then I would say, 'I'm Robert Shook. You just heard me give you this pitch, so you know I can sell, and you know I'm going to be a damn good interview!' I got lots of interviews that way, far more than any publicist ever got for me.

"The thing you need to know is that I have none of the natural attributes of a stereotypical salesperson. I have a stutter, I mispronounce words, I talk too fast. I've got every disadvantage. But the one thing I always had was a belief in myself. If you're positive about yourself, your 'customer' will be, too."

*There can be no great courage where there is no confidence
or assurance, and half the battle is in the conviction that we
can do what we undertake.*

—Orison Swett Marden,
founder of *Success Magazine*

5 Points to Remember About Marketing Yourself

1. **Differentiate yourself.** Sometimes the best way to market yourself is
    to take the *Star Trek* approach: to go where no one has gone before.
    When my first book, *State of the Art Selling*, came out, I went out on
    weekends and set up book displays in local diners, video stores, dry
    cleaners, hair salons—places I knew business people patronized (as
    did I). What better place to display a business book? In a bookstore,
    my book could get lost on the shelf. But in the diner, it stood alone.

    Not only did I sell books from these local stores (with the permission
    of the owners, of course), I made many contacts for my seminar
    business—and all because I placed my product in unusual settings. Think
    about it—someone was the first person to look at a gas station and say,
    "All these people stop here anyway; why not build a convenience store
    here as well?" Think about how you might differentiate yourself in your
    own marketplace. Find an unusual niche for your skills and talents that
    will help you stand out and have less competition.

2. **Expose yourself to different environments.** It may be difficult to find
    your unusual niche if you don't learn more about the world around
    you. Most people don't realize that 99 percent of all great breakthroughs
    don't come from the industry you're in. FedEx wouldn't be in existence
    if it hadn't borrowed its check-clearing system from the Federal Re-
    serve Bank. Ban Roll-On wouldn't be in existence if it hadn't borrowed
    the roller ball from PaperMate pens. Right now, outside your indus-
    try, there are new ideas and technologies that might take you in a whole
    new direction. A concept, approach, method, or technology that's as
    common as dirt in one industry can have a powerful impact if you're
    the first to apply it to your field. Go to seminars from different indus-
    tries to find out how you might benefit those people. Join clubs or or-
    ganizations where you'll meet people from a variety of fields and
    circumstances. Change your environment. Step out of your comfort
    zone and look for new networking opportunities. You never know
    what you might find, or whom you might meet.

You are a product of your environment. So choose the environment that will best develop you toward your objective. Analyze your life in terms of its environment. Are the things around you helping you toward success—or are they holding you back?

—W. Clement Stone,
business executive and writer

3. **Do the little things that make a difference.** "The key is to plant seeds," says public relations executive Terrie Williams, whose clients have included Eddie Murphy, Miles Davis, and Janet Jackson. "I read everything I can get my hands on, and keep in mind areas of interest of people I've met. If I find an article someone would like, I send it with a note that says, 'I thought you'd find this interesting.' I stay in touch with people, even if I'm not sure I'll ever see them again. That's how I was able to start my business—this awesome foundation had been built, and I had amassed a really incredible network of contacts."

  I always send hand-written thank-you notes to people who have recommended me for business or have done a favor for me. Never underestimate the power of these little notes. They show you care and keep your name at the top of contacts' minds.

4. **Practice bridging.** If I find out that someone I know needs a job or help with a particular project, I immediately start to think about all the people I know who might be able to help. I get on the phone, set up a conference call with both people, introduce them to each other—then get off the phone and let them connect. I am "bridging" those two people, and it increases my value to both of them. I know that they will do the same for me if the situation ever arises. Bridging is the ability to pull people together to help them market themselves. Even if it doesn't benefit you at that particular moment, your good deed will come back to you in the long run.

5. **Go to the top.** Remember this—82 percent of the CEOs today have a background in selling. They appreciate what it takes to call people at the highest levels. When you're marketing yourself, your product, or a service, you can't be worried about calling someone just because of how "big" he or she is. Often, the "biggest" people have the biggest hearts and are more willing to hear you out. And people with greater authority often have less insecurity than those in lower ranks, which means they may be more willing to give you a chance.

Prime Real Estate: Advice From a Marketing Guru

Jay Abraham is a well-known marketing consultant who is the author of *Getting Everything You Can Out of All You've Got.* Here's what he has to say about marketing yourself:

"The first problem is that most people who are trying to market themselves don't know what that means. They don't have a game strategy. They don't have a particular end in mind. They don't have a picture of what success will look like in their business and personal lives. They don't understand what they're trying to achieve, mentally and financially.

"The first thing you have to do is start with a clear action plan that you can follow. Start with the concept of optimization: getting the highest and best yield from the minimal time, effort, risk, and exposure. Most people don't think about the highest and best, they just think about trying to work hard and hope it all pays off. You need to consider yourself as commercial real estate.

"Suppose you ask a commercial real estate appraiser to look at a parcel of land in a prime commercial area that has a broken-down, two-bedroom clapboard house on it. The appraiser wouldn't judge its worth by the falling-down house that sits on it. He would appraise it at its highest and best use, which might be a 40-story office building or a large retail store. Learn to appraise yourself the same way—not at your current level, but at your highest and best potential."

Business has only two major functions—marketing and innovation.

—Peter Drucker,
management consultant

More than 10,000 businesses fail each year in the United States. The failure rate for new product introductions is more than 75 percent. Why is that? The *first* reason is they don't market well. They don't consider all their employees—from the receptionist to the CEO—as salespeople. What happens when you call a company and the person who answers the phone is rude or unfriendly? That's the impression you have of the entire company.

If you go into a retail establishment and the cashier is slow and distracted and looks like she wishes you would leave her alone—you will. And you won't return. Many companies fail to realize that every single individual in that organization is an extension of their product or service. Just as you are an extension and representative of the service or product you are trying to sell.

The *second* reason companies fail is lack of innovation. Because there are many products on the market that are essentially the same, you have to give the customer a reason to choose one over the other. You have to understand today's customer and anticipate tomorrow's so that you can constantly present new ideas to the marketplace. Even if your product stays the same, you will have to come up with new ideas to get your message across.

> *Strategy and timing are the Himalayas of marketing.*
> *Everything else is the Catskills.*
>
> —Al Reis,
> writer and marketing expert

Strategy and timing are everything. The problem many people have is that they have one, but not the other. They know what they want to do, but feel they need to wait for just the "right time." Or they know when they want to make their move, but they're not sure what that move should be. It takes both to be successful. Here are three ways to make strategy and timing work for you:

1. **Create your own timing.** There is never going to be a perfect time. But you may be able to find a good time to present your product or idea by polling your target audience. Do research to understand just who that audience is—who would use your product or service. Talk to people who are familiar with the market as it is now. Ask them to tell you what problems you might have when introducing your idea, then find solutions to those problems.

   Try merging your product or idea with one in a different market and see if they might complement each other. If you have something to market, take it, test it, do the research. Good timing doesn't happen while you're sitting around waiting for the right market to show up or for people to be screaming for your product. You create your own timing by coming up with solutions that were not available before.

2. **Keep taking action.** Even if you decide the timing isn't right for right now, don't stand still. You don't always need to be taking giant steps, but you always want to feel that you're slowly but surely moving forward. Sometimes it takes years for ideas to come to fruition. If you're always networking, there may come a time when someone you connected with years ago suddenly remembers your idea and is now in a position to do something about it. Constant networking is the key. You never know when someone may come along and say, "I'm ready if you are…"

3. **Build a team to help you strategize.** Sometimes, even when things are going well, there seems to be one or two puzzle pieces that are missing. For instance, you may have the product, but need someone to help you with the distribution. If you find someone to help you with distribution, they may want to be sure this product is supported by publicity.

    Perhaps there are celebrities you could contact who might have a tie-in with the product. Look for people within your industry who's brains you could pick for ideas (and who might even end up becoming your partners). Keep thinking about the different pieces of the puzzle and how you can create the greatest value by putting a strong team together—even if it means sacrificing some of your own dollars or some of your share of the profits. This kind of strategizing creates good timing; it only makes sense to proceed to the next step when all the puzzle pieces come together.

    > *Market leadership is gained by envisioning new products, services, lifestyles, and ways to raise living standards. There is a vast difference between companies that offer me-too products and those that create new product and service values not even imagined by the marketplace.*
    >
    > —Philip Kotler,
    > marketing expert

More Advice From Jay Abraham

Here are three things people can do to market themselves more effectively:

1. **Develop a unique selling proposition.** That's sales talk for find what is unique about yourself and play it up. Today, in our very competitive world, what it really means is figuring out the clearest, most powerful solution you can bring to the marketplace. The marketplace, if you're working for someone else, is your employer. If you're in business for yourself, then the marketplace is your intended customers or clients. You've got to be able to present to them that you're not just the best alternative, you're the only viable solution they can choose.

2. **Eliminate the risk.** In order to own the world, you've got to realize what's keeping people from beating a path to your door. Usually, it's because they're reluctant to take a risk. In anything you

do where you've got to persuade someone else to embrace your point of view, one side is always being asked to assume most of the risk. If it's an employer, for instance, and she makes the decision to hire you, she's risking all the things that could go wrong if it doesn't work out. If a client buys from you, he's risking his money on your product or service. If you can identify the other person's risk and then devise a way to reduce or eliminate it, you own the world. You make it easier for people to say "yes" than "no," because you've taken their risk out of the equation.

3.   **Take the leadership role.** Adapt a strategy of preeminence, which means taking the authoritative role of advisor, counsel, or trusted friend. Shift your focus from falling in love with your job, product, or service, to falling in love with your client. Try to do everything you can to make life easier for them and help them be the best they can be. When you serve your customers with that focus, you increase your own value.

Looking for a New Job? I Dare You to...

✦ **Learn everything you possibly can about the company to which you are applying.** Get a copy of their annual report. Talk to people who work for the company. Talk to some of the company's customers. Look up the company in *Standard & Poors*. Check newspapers and magazines for recent articles about the company and the industry in which you're interested.

✦ **Skip human resources and go right to the top.** Call the president, chairman, or CEO of the company. Studies have shown that more than 82 percent of CEOs were in sales at some point in their careers; therefore, they respect someone who has the courage to make a "sales" call (which is what you're doing when you're trying to get a job) right to the top. Even if you don't get through to the CEO, you can get a recommendation of someone else in the company to call. Then you can say, "Mary Fox of the CEOs office suggested I call..."

✦ **Dare the employer to hire you.** Say that you'll work 30 days for free. Say this: "I know that you are probably looking at other candidates who have more experience than I do or have a more compatible background. But I ask you to hire me for 30 days. Then watch my work ethic, my passion, and my innovative thinking. If I'm not worth more than the salary you're offering for this position, then you can let me go and not pay me a penny. But when I prove to you that I can deliver, give me my 30 days' salary and keep me on board." I guarantee you'll be the only candidate to make such an offer. So first, you've differentiated yourself from the competition. Second, you've shown a strong belief in yourself and your abilities. Third, you've already demonstrated your passion and persistence by everything you've done to get your foot in the door.

Selling yourself to others only proves that you have confidence in yourself and are willing to stand behind your beliefs. When you don't believe in yourself, you're only selling yourself short.

—Dorothy Leeds, author

Becoming the Expert

Marc Friedfertig is the founder of a company called Broadway Trading that offers brokerage services to individuals who want to day-trade for a living. Here is his insight into marketing:

"What I saw happening in 1995 was that changes in regulation and changes in technology were making it possible for an individual at home to have the same instant access to information and the ability to get very quick executions as I did. So I recognized that it was possible to take what I was doing on the floor and apply it electronically.

"What I did differently than everybody else, was that I recognized that just giving people the technology wasn't enough. In fact, in many cases it was detrimental. When we started giving people this technology and this access to markets that were previously only available to professionals, we recognized that the most important thing about giving them this technology was to teach them how to use it. As a result, we started doing training programs. Then people wanted to get a more in-depth understanding of what we were teaching. They couldn't grasp all the information. So we wanted to document the key points that we were teaching. We started drafting handouts and exhibits. Ultimately, these things formed a book.

"Writing a book was something I never dreamed I would do. I really did it out of demand from my customers who were seeking more information.

"It differentiated us. I became the person who wrote the book on the subject. Everybody wanted to learn from the person who wrote the book.

It branded us as the guys who wrote the book. It became the first of many books that came out on the subject, many that borrowed topics that we discussed. It differentiated our business, and that was a key to our success. We differentiated ourselves by recognizing key aspects of the business. And that was educating the customers to use our product properly, by teaching our customers to use our product effectively and efficiently. Having done that we created tremendous demand for our product. Successful customers breed a successful business.

Remember the Children

It's not necessary to write a best-selling book to market yourself. My daughter Hallie was not afraid to shout to the world what we had to offer. Children don't have set ideas about what they can and cannot do. They don't give themselves limitations. Imagine what you could do if you were freed from the idea that you can't—or shouldn't—do something because you're too old, too young, too inexperienced, overqualified, or whatever reason you've given yourself.

Remember that every word you say, every action you take is a marketing tool. This means you always have another chance to present yourself in the best possible light. Believe in yourself and believe in your value to others, then the marketing will take care of itself.

To get what you're worth and to be able to know how to market yourself successfully, you have to understand how to negotiate your value—what makes you valuable to other people. In the next chapter, you'll find out how negotiating well can ensure that everybody wins and that every relationship you have is a positive one.

Chapter 19

Negotiation:
Creating Win-win Scenarios

A candle is not diminished by giving another candle light.
—Earl Nightingale,
writer

What Is Negotiation?

Negotiation can be a really simple concept. It is a deal or bargain we make with one or more parties. We're negotiating all the time. It's something we all do frequently in our daily lives without being aware of it.

We usually think of negotiations as involving a major deal, but we negotiate every day. We negotiate about which movie to see or whether to have Chinese food delivered or go out to eat, what restaurant to go to, or where to go on vacation. When I asked my children what negotiating meant, they said, "Talking it over."

We even negotiate with ourselves; we've all had those inner dialogues that go, "If I do this, then I'll do that. If I buy this, I'll do without that…" We give a little, we get a little.

On a broader scale, we're negotiating in all social encounters. When we're getting to know each other, we're negotiating our positions. When we meet someone new we're negotiating our terms of relationship. Will we be friends? Will we be good friends? Will we be more than friends? These are the kinds of unconscious negotiations that go on throughout our lives.

Negotiation depends on communication.

—Art Windell,
writer

The Power of Negotiation

Although we often think of negotiation as something that happens between two "warring" parties (union vs. management, buyer vs. seller), the best negotiations take place when both parties are willing to compromise, or to reach agreement by modifying their initial demands. You do this by posing "What if...?" situations. "What if I give you this and you give me that? Would that satisfy both our needs? What if I take less of this and more of that? Would that be agreeable?" The more options you come up with, the more room you have to compromise.

There are four major principles that make for successful negotiations:

1. **Understand your own value.** Know what you bring to the table. Keep in mind that your knowledge and experience are strengths you can use as bargaining tools. You must have a complete understanding and appreciation of your value if you expect to communicate it to the other parties involved. The more you know about the benefits you can offer to the other side, and the better you are able to express them, the more excited they will be about making a deal with you.

2. **Understand the other party's value.** Know what they bring to the table; understand their point of view. Put yourself in their shoes. Do research and ask questions. Look at the big picture the way they see it, that way you can tailor your solutions and options to the needs of the other side. Learn as much of the specifics of what the other party is looking for before you begin negotiation. A negotiation is really a sale (you're selling your ideas and positions), and the secret to being a successful salesperson is to meet the buyer's needs.

3. **Understand your goals.** If you don't know what you want out of a negotiation, you'll be tempted to take anything that's offered without examining the consequences. Clarify your goals and your limits. Start with what is least acceptable, and then determine the maximum you can ask for within reason. Set your acceptable parameters. Or, as they say, "Know when to hold them, know when to fold them." Start with the maximum reasonable request and negotiate down from there. If you ask for too much, you can always settle for less. But if you ask for too little, it's almost impossible to bargain upward. Ask yourself the following questions:

- What do I want to get out of this negotiation?

- What are my real needs (money, prestige, benefits)?

- What is the most I could get?

- What is my bottom line?

- Where specifically can I compromise?

4. **Trust is the most important factor.** Most negotiations take place in a climate of shared expectation. We expect that when we give in a little, the other side will give a little, too. We expect that when we bargain in good faith, so will the other side. If you do not feel that these things are true, you should not be negotiating in the first place.

Visible good will is the strongest negotiation strategy. Don't let somebody else determine your behavior.

—Dr. SU Sunrei,
Chinese writer

The G.I. Joe School of Negotiation

Have you ever heard of Don Levine? Probably not. But you've definitely heard of his most famous creation—G.I. Joe. I met Don a few years ago, when he was a guest on my radio program. We've been friends ever since. So when I thought about negotiation, I thought about Don Levine. He has spent his life negotiating—selling his ideas to retailers, manufacturers, and licensers of his products. But his greatest negotiation took place when he first came up with the notion of a doll for boys:

"In 1963, Barbie was the hottest selling toy around," says Levine. "Everyone in the industry was looking for the 'next big idea.' It suddenly came to me that girls had their Barbies to emulate and look up to, but boys had no equivalent. So I came up with the concept of G.I. Joe. But my boss wasn't too keen on the idea. He kept saying, 'Boys don't play with dolls.' My answer was, 'This isn't a doll, it's an action figure.' I just made up the term.

"We went back and forth for months. Finally my boss, who was also my mentor, said, 'I'll tell you what. I'll invite some of the biggest buyers in the toy industry to listen to your idea. If they think you're wrong, promise me you'll be a big boy and stop driving me crazy with this idea!'

"The men came in, and they all loved the G.I. Joe concept. I said to my boss, 'Okay. Now you be a big boy and let's go ahead with this.'

"Thirty-five years later, more than a billion G.I. Joes have been sold. And young men all over the world still come up to me and say, 'I didn't have much when I was growing up, but I had my G.I. Joe. Thank you for giving me so many hours of fun.' It also gave many of them the surrogate father, big brother, or hero they were looking for. Being a part of the G.I. Joe phenomenon is an amazing feeling. And the genesis of it was two men who had to negotiate to make sure each felt secure in what the other was doing.

"Most of us think of negotiating as sitting at a table with your 'opponent' and being a tough business person. But it isn't about that. It's not as tough a word as we think it is. It's not a win-lose situation. It's about compromise. We negotiate every day in order to get by in the world. The greatest negotiation of all is, in fact, life."

It is better to be defeated on principles than to win on lies.
—Arthur Colwell,
writer

3 Crucial Negotiating Skills

Negotiation expert Peter Wink, author of the best-selling book *Negotiate Your Way to Riches*, talks about 3 crucial negotiating skills used by success salespeople:

1. **Negotiate on non-cash deal components.** For instance, you may offer a far superior credit policy or better payment terms than your competitors. You may also carry a far better guarantee. Your prospect may not know this. Do you assemble merchandise where your prospects are located? Do you offer same-day delivery? Does your company have superior expertise that your prospect can benefit from? If so...let your prospect know!

2. **Never take the first offer or counteroffer.** When a prospect gives you their first offer or counteroffer for your product or service...ALWAYS reject it. Chances are they'll make a higher offer the second time around.

3. **Walk away from a bad deal.** If a deal isn't right—walk away from it. Never get emotionally involved in completing any deal. Some deals just aren't worth the time and effort. Another prospect will always come along.

My father said, 'You must never try to make all the money that is in a deal. Let the other fellow make some money, too, because if you have a reputation for always making all the money, you won't have many deals.'

—J. Paul Getty,
founder of Getty Oil

Negotiating for a Raise

For many people, there is nothing more frightening or intimidating than asking for a raise. Most of the time, it's because they're not 100 percent certain they deserve a raise. They know they've been working hard, but has it been hard enough? They don't have a standard against which to judge themselves.

If you're training for the Olympics, you know exactly what the standard is. You know how fast the gold medal winner ran last year, or how high the pole-vaulter vaulted. You wouldn't just train and hope that you get somewhere near the winning time. You set your sights and your training program toward beating the established mark.

How do you know what the winning mark is on your job? There's only one way to find out, and that is to ask. Don't wait for a job review, sit down for a job preview.

Ask your boss these questions:

✧ What are the things you're looking for me to perform in the next year?

✧ What are your goals, and the goals of the department?

✧ What exactly is in my job description?

✧ What could I do that would go beyond the job description?

When you get the answers to these questions, you can start documenting your achievements. That way, when it's time to negotiate for a raise, you can come to the table armed with facts and figures that show just how you have met (and hopefully exceeded) expectations.

The 5 Biggest Negotiating Mistakes

Terry Bragg, founder of Peacemakers Training in Salt Lake City and author of *31 Days to High Self-Esteem*, says that there are five critical mistakes you can make during the process of negotiation:

1. **Defend or attack.** Try to understand any moves the other party makes. If they do something you don't understand, don't get defensive. Say, "That's one way we could do it. What other options do we have?" If you attack their ideas or motives, you lose your credibility. If someone attacks you, instead of defending yourself, say, "I'm sure you have good reasons for saying that. Can you help me understand them?"

2. **Insult.** Don't try to gain leverage by putting other people down. Getting angry or frustrated because things don't go your way doesn't help at all; it only gives the other person an advantage. Stay focused on your outcome—closing the deal.

3. **Blame.** If a problem arises, even if it's the other person's fault, don't place blame. The other person will only become defensive. Instead, concentrate on finding a workable solution.

4. **Present lengthy justifications or arguments for your position.** Present your most compelling arguments first. If they agree with you, move on. If they disagree, try to understand their objections before offering additional arguments.

5. **Use poker tactics.** Great negotiators do not use tricks or manipulation. Avoid bluffing or misleading the other person. Be honest and sincere.

Negotiating in the classic diplomatic sense assumes all parties are more anxious to agree than to disagree.

—Dean Acheson,
U.S. statesman

The Smallest Negotiators

Kids are naturally great negotiators. They'll trade peanut butter for American cheese or a toy truck for a frog, and everyone comes out a winner. They know what they want and they go after it.

But what happens when you want to negotiate with your children? Then it's not so easy. They've got it all figured out. Every parent (and child) in the world knows the high-low strategy: "Daddy, can I have 10 cookies?" "You can have one." "Come on Dad, eight cookies." "You can have two." Usually, they settle for four.

When you really want to negotiate with kids, however, you have to make them understand the meaning of commitment. That's what my father did with me. When I was about eight years old, I was fascinated with reptiles. We were studying them in school. All I wanted was a boa constrictor. My father said I could have a boa if I would sign a contract saying that I would take trumpet lessons for the next five years. It was a big commitment, and it made me really stop and think about how much I wanted that snake.

I got my boa. And for the next five years, even though my father occasionally had to chase me around the house to get me to practice, I took trumpet lessons. I can still play today, and I never forgot the meaning of commitment.

Of course, you can't use this tactic too often. You can't have your children sign contracts for everything. But when it really counts, it may just be the help you need to make them understand that "winning" a negotiation can be a long-term commitment.

8 Traits of Great Negotiators

1. **Know their own needs.** They have a clear vision of what they want to accomplish. They know the minimum they will accept and the maximum they can ask for.

2. **Know what the other side needs.** They do as much research as possible before the negotiations begin. They speak to people who have been in similar situations, people who understand where the other is coming from. They are concerned with meeting the other party's needs, as well as getting what they want themselves.

3. **Focus on the long-term.** They're not interested in a quick fix. They're usually interested in more than just money, whether it's building a relationship, getting better benefits, or bargaining for extended service. They may give up some immediate benefits for future considerations.

4. **Build strong relationships.** The word "negotiate" usually brings up images of aggression and threatening behavior. In reality, it is about trusting each other and making compromises on friendly terms. Morty Davis says he always tries to find out about the personal lives of the people with whom he's negotiating—he asks about their families, their interests and hobbies. He tries to get to know the whole person, not just the business angle.

5. **Build strength in numbers.** Great negotiators don't put all their eggs in one basket. They have many deals going on so that if one doesn't come through, another will take its place. When you are totally dependent on the current negotiation, you're coming from a position of weakness—and there's nothing worse than being weak and coming to the table to try to convince the other party that you're strong. If you have a lot of activity going on, it allows you to keep your principles intact and to stick to your goals and parameters.

> *Don't compromise yourself. You're all you've got.*
>
>   —Janis Joplin,
>   musician

6. **Sell the benefits.** You'll never get what you want if the other party can't see what they will get out of the deal. Most people are afraid that they won't get what they need out of a deal; it's your job to help them see that there are a variety of ways you can both get what you need.

7. **Have patience—with limits.** Good things come to those who wait, but only the good things left after those who hustle. Patience is valuable in negotiations, but you may also need to be quick—to alter your strategy, to pick up on a new factor, or to go in a different direction altogether. Trust your instinct and allow yourself to absorb new facts as they are presented. Remember that one of the best negotiating skills is adaptability.

8. **Use a combination of emotion and logic.** Negotiation is, above all, an exercise in logic and clear thinking. Think about shopping for a house. You fall in love with a house, its features, and the neighborhood. You love everything about it—and the buyer can see right through you. He knows you'll pay big bucks for it because you're buying with your emotions. Whenever your emotion supersedes your reasoning power, you have lost.

> *Strategy is better than strength.*
>
>   —Hausa (Nigerian) proverb

I Dare You...

When you feel as though your negotiating skills can use some pumping up, take action using these 5 strategies:

✦ **Ask for more than you think you can get.** Whether you're asking for a raise or a dollar amount in a deal, ask for the maximum you can get within reason. A successful negotiation is a win-win situation—but the person who asks for more usually gets it. In her book *Marketing Yourself*, Dorothy Leeds states, "Studies show that a negotiator who initially asks for more and offers to give less usually winds up obtaining more and giving less." If you're not worth what you're asking, then you're just being arrogant and the request will probably backfire. If you're worth the maximum, however—and you have the documentation to prove it—then go ahead and ask for it.

✦ **Come to the table with a "why should I..." attitude.** If you've done everything you can to build your own value, then you can say, "Why should I do business with you?" If you go on a job interview, for instance, you don't want to just sit there and answer the interviewer's questions. You should also be asking, "Why should I come to work for your company? What can you offer me?" You may not want to use those exact words, but you want to make them sell themselves to you.

✦ **Get yourself an agent.** An agent is someone who negotiates on your behalf. Of course, in the real world, it's not always possible to have someone else negotiate for you. But you can certainly call on other people who can give you advice. Say, "Here's what I'm trying to do, here's the situation, here's what they're offering. What would you do?" Find someone who is on your side, someone you can bounce ideas off of. They can be invaluable in helping you to avoid mistakes.

✦ **Think more of yourself.** We are our own worst critics. Keep a log of your own accomplishments. We never like to brag about ourselves, but we also tend to forget the things that we have achieved. Even if you don't actually mention these achievements to bolster your negotiations, you can use them to bolster your confidence.

✦ **Let's think about it.** You don't always have to make a deal on the spot. There's nothing wrong with saying, "Let me think about this," or, "Why don't we both think about ways we might be able to work this out and come back together next week?" Sometimes people are uncomfortable talking about money on the spot. It allows you time to send them materials that may increase or reinforce your value. It also shows that you're not desperate to get the business.

The Eyes Have It

Your eyes can reveal a lot about you. When you're asking for what you want, look directly at the other person. If you're constantly shifting your gaze or looking down, the implication is that you don't believe in what you're saying. You have nothing to be embarrassed about. It's okay to ask for what you deserve. Direct eye contact can also help you read the other person. Eye contact is often our best connection to the truth.

> *There is at least one thing more brutal than the truth, and that is the consequence of saying less than the truth.*
>
> —Ti-Grace Atkinson,
> writer

Establish Your Ground

When you're negotiating, don't forget that the other party needs something you have—otherwise they wouldn't be bargaining with you.

J.P. Morgan once wanted to buy a large Minnesota ore track from John D. Rockefeller. Rockefeller merely sent John D., Jr. around to talk. Morgan asked, "Well, what's your price?" John D., Jr. said, "Mr. Morgan, I think there must be some mistake. I did not come to here to sell. I understood you wished to buy."

Don't Sell Yourself Short

Always remember your own value. Don't sell yourself short. You're not asking for anything you don't deserve. Negotiating is a way for both parties to come out ahead. Keep this in mind, and you'll always be a winner. Don't settle for less than you want or less than you deserve.

> *If one is out of touch with oneself, then one cannot touch others.*
>
> —Anne Morrow Lindbergh,
> writer

Your value doesn't exist in a vacuum. It lies in how you relate to the rest of the world and to the people around you. Albert Einstein, one of the greatest thinkers of all time, was thought by some to be an alien from another planet because he was so much more advanced than anyone else on Earth. He studied not only physics, but metaphysics as well. Who better, then, to answer the ultimate question: Why are we here? When he was asked that question, Einstein answered, "To serve mankind." That's why the final chapter is on service. When we live to serve others, we also serve ourselves. That is the true power we all possess.

Chapter 20

Service:
Finding Value Within to Benefit the World

An unshared life is not living. He who shares does not lessen, but greatens, his life.

—Stephen S. Wise,
clergyman and activist

What Is Service?

The definition of service is simple: It is an act of helpful activity. There are many different ways of giving service, but the bottom line is that it is a contribution of your talents, knowledge, and experience to benefit others around you.

We often think of service as giving up something (time or money, for example) to give to someone else. But often service is giving more of yourself to everything you do. Whatever you do in life, your goal is to serve people to the best of your ability. If you are a gas station attendant, your goal is to give 110 percent to your customers—to give them more than they expect. If you're a CEO of a large corporation, your goal is the same.

Life is not meant to be lived selfishly. The true key to successful living is to turn the focus from "How can I help myself?" to "What can I do for others?" Whenever you find yourself off track, recognize that your center of focus is turned inward, toward yourself. As soon as you turn yourself around, everything will come back to you tenfold as you focus on helping others. The more you impact other's lives for the better, the greater your success becomes. The greater your service is, the greater your rewards in life.

Some rewards are tangible—you may make more money, have a nice home and car. Some rewards are intangible—they come in the form of inner satisfaction, happiness, and self-worth. When you give service, you don't necessarily get an immediate reward. The reward may never come, or it may come at a totally unexpected time. The more people you help in this life, the greater the chances that some of them will come back to help you.

Some people you serve may never help you at all. Some may not even say thank you. Some people say that you should give service without looking for rewards—that giving service is in itself reward enough. This may be true. But what's wrong with giving service knowing it will help you as well as somebody else? If my motive is to help you, and by helping you I help myself, where's the harm in that? It's the classic win-win situation.

> *The greatest good you can do for another is not just to*
> *share your riches, but to reveal to him his own.*
>
> —Benjamin Disraeli,
> British prime minister

The Power of Service

Over the years, I have worked with highly successful people from sports, science, business, education, and entertainment. A common sentiment I heard from all of them is that at the end of their lives, they would look back and ask, "How much did I learn, and how much did I serve others?"

Your most important role in life is to help other people succeed. There may be substantial monetary rewards in the way you make your living, but the greatest reward is to have helped others reach their goals. When we're gone, our material possessions don't really matter. Our greatest legacy is the people we've helped build, who are left to build others in the same way.

You can build some people up by giving them money, by giving them a helping hand, or by sharing your knowledge or expertise with them. There is another way of giving service, however, that is not often discussed—and that is respect.

Not too long ago, I started studying martial arts. Having been somewhat of a rebel in my youth, I initially balked at some of the things I was being taught. For instance, when you want to come into the room, you must ask, "Permission to enter, sir?" If you are thirsty, you must ask, "Permission to get a drink of water, sir?" And if you walk by a black belt, you must raise your hand to your chest in a kind of salute. I soon realized that this was a system of respect within the martial arts world, and I could see how this respect not only builds camaraderie amongst the students, it also teaches you to respect the strengths and weaknesses of your opponents, and of yourself as well.

It is this kind of respect—respect for another's strengths and weaknesses—that is needed in business and in the home. Businesses do better when they respect their customers as individual human beings, not just as a means to making a profit. Bosses get more productivity out of employees they respect and praise for jobs well done. And in the home, couples communicate better when they learn to truly respect their partners.

You show respect for your partner in the little things you do. That could be something as simple as cleaning up the dishes after a meal, giving your partner some "alone time" after he or she has been with the kids all day, or really listening to what is most important to the other person. Sometimes the greatest service we can do for someone else is just to make time for them, and to show them you care. To paraphrase an old saying, "Service is in the details." It's the little things you do that show you care about and respect those around you.

Kindness in words creates confidence. Kindness in thinking creates profoundness. Kindness in giving creates love.

—Lao-Tzu,
Chinese philosopher

What Makes Exceptional Service?

Ken Blanchard is the author of *Raving Fans: A Revolutionary Approach to Customer Service*. Here's what he has to say on the subject of service:

"This is my advice for everyone in business today: If you're going to put your energy into being the best at something, make sure that it's serving your customers. You can't just satisfy customers today, you've got to blow them away. You've got to create raving fans—customers who are so excited about what you do for them that they want to brag about you. When that happens, customers virtually become part of your sales force.

"I became a raving fan of a Marriott hotel in Orlando just recently. Why? Because of a wake-up call. If you've stayed in a hotel lately, you know that the most common wake-up call you get is when the phone rings, you pick it up and there's nothing there. The second most common wake up call is when the phone rings and you get a recording that says, 'This is your wake-up call.' Not very customer-friendly.

"When I was at the Marriott, however, the phone rang and a real human being said, 'Good morning, Dr. Blanchard. It's 7 a.m. It's going to be 75 degrees and beautiful in Orlando today. But I see that you're checking out this afternoon. Where are you going?'

"'New York City,' I answered.

"'Well, I have a *USA Today* weather map here and it says it's going to be 40 degrees and rainy in New York today. Are you sure you can't stay in Orlando another day?'

"I did have to fly to New York that day, but you can bet the next time I go to Orlando I'm going to stay at the Marriott, just so I can speak to Theresa in the morning!

"Here's another example of exceptional service, and it comes from a store that is famous for making raving fans. A friend of mine went into Nordstrom's to buy some perfume for his wife. The woman behind the counter said, 'We don't sell that perfume here, but I know where you can get it.' Then she asked my friend how long he would be in the mall. He said another half-hour. She said, 'Fine. Come back in half-an-hour.'

"When he came back, he found that the saleswoman had gone to another store in the mall, bought the perfume, brought it back to Nordstrom's, and had it waiting for him—gift-wrapped. She only charged him what the perfume had cost. So Nordstrom's didn't make a dime on that sale—but they made a customer for life.

"Remember that there is only one thing your competition can't steal from you. They can steal your price, they can steal the quality of your product. The only thing they can't steal is the relationship your people have with your customers. That must always be your number one priority."

> *It is the willingness of people to give of themselves over and above the demands of the job that distinguishes the great from the merely adequate organization.*
>
> —Peter Drucker,
> writer and management consultant

Why is it that these examples of service seem so unusual? Unfortunately, it's because many businesses have forgotten the importance of customer service. They've forgotten that they wouldn't have a business at all without their customers. Common sense and common courtesy have taken a beating in the 20th century, but they're making a comeback in the 21st. Customers now have a choice of shopping anywhere in the world, without even leaving their homes. So if you want your business to be their choice, you have to give them good reason. And there is no better reason than good service.

The man who will use his skill and constructive imagination
to see how much he can give for a dollar, instead of how little
he can give for a dollar, is bound to succeed.

　　　　　　　　　　　　　　　　　　—Henry Ford,
　　　　　　　　　　　　　　　　　　industrialist

A Legend About the Spirit of Giving

A wanderer in the desert happens upon a spring of clear water. He fills a jug with the water and hurries off to give this precious gift to the king. But the king is far away, and it takes the wanderer many days to reach him. When the wanderer arrives, the king tastes the water, smiles, and gives him many thanks. The others in the court rush up, wanting to take their taste of the cool, clean water. But when they do, they find it is hot and stale, and spit it out. One of them asks the king, "How could you smile and give thanks, when this water is spoiled?"

"Ah," said the king, "it was not the water I tasted but the spirit in which it was given."

No person was ever honored for what he received; honor
has been the reward for what he gave.

　　　　　　　　　　　　　　　　　　—Calvin Coolidge,
　　　　　　　　　　　　　　　　　　U.S. president

A True Story About the Spirit of Giving

Mother Theresa was in Calcutta when a six-year-old boy came up to her with his hands outstretched. His own mother had told him that Mother Theresa and the Sisters didn't have any sugar. So he had collected his family's sugar for the whole week, which he held in the palm of his hand and gave to Mother Theresa, saying, "Mother, I heard you had no sugar." When Mother Theresa told the Sisters about this little boy's gift, she said, "People give us wonderful gifts, truckloads of medicines and money for missionaries and charities. And that is a wonderful thing. But when I looked at that little boy and his handful of sugar, I realized that it's not how much we give in life or how much we do in life that counts, it's how much love we do it with."

...One drop of water helps to swell the ocean; a spark of fire helps to give light to the world. None are too small, too feeble, too poor to be of service. Think of this and act.

—Hannah Moore,
English novelist

The Wealthiest Clown in the World

Dr. Gerald Jampolsky, a physician, and Diane Cirincione, Ph.D., travel the world as internationally known lecturers and authorities in the fields of psychiatry, health, business, and education. In 1975, Dr. Jampolsky founded the Center for Attitudinal Healing where children and adults with life-threatening illnesses may find peace of mind. There are now 130 Centers in 24 countries.

A few years ago, Jampolsky and Cirincione were traveling to Boston to a conference on laughter and healing. They were picked up at the airport by four clowns. Dr. Jampolsky asked one of the men, who was about 65 years old, how he came to be a clown. "Well," he said, "about three years ago I lost my business and all my money in a stock market crash. I was broke and terribly depressed. Then one day I saw a notice about a class for becoming a clown. I took the class and loved it. I began to volunteer at homes for the elderly and at pediatric wards. I may not have money anymore, but today I'm the wealthiest man I've ever been."

"This man was rich in service," says Jampolsky. "The most important thing we can do in this world is to serve others. That means focusing on loving others without judgment. It means keeping this question constantly in mind: 'What can I do today to be helpful to another person?'

"When I think of service, I think of the quote we use as the motto for our foundation," says Dr. Cirincione, "which is, 'I reach my hand out into the darkness to help another hand back into the light, only to discover that it's my own.' That's the essence of service—we think we're doing something to help another person, but as we do, we help ourselves as well.

"When Mother Theresa told us the story about the little boy and the handful of sugar, it transformed our lives. We realized that giving is not about numbers; it's not about quantity. It's about the quality of what we do and the purity of our hearts. I thought more about this one day as I was cleaning out the toilet bowl.

"The day before, I had been lecturing to 5,000 people at Madison Square Garden. Yet suddenly, as I was scrubbing out the bowl, I had an incredible sense of presence and awareness. I realized that with service, whether I was cleaning the bowl or speaking in front of 5,000 people, it was my state of mind that mattered most. It was only my ego that made one form of service better than the other."

"The most rewarding type of service, though, is when you touch people in a personal way," says Dr. Jampolsky. "It's not enough to just give money. If you don't know how to help, look in the newspaper or on the Internet for places you can call to volunteer. If you have limited time, make a commitment that once a month you will give one day of your time. Not just sort of a commitment, but a real commitment—you'll find it can change your life.

"Ask yourself some major questions as you go through life: What is my purpose in life? Do I go through life being a fault-finder or a love-finder? Do I want to hold on to my grievances? Or am I willing to forgive? It's difficult to want to help anyone when you're holding on to old grievances. Let them go and you'll find that helping others will help you heal.

"Finally, teach your children about service when they are young. We believe it should be part of the K-12 curriculum so that children understand that the world works far better when we are giving and receiving."

What do we live for if not to make life less difficult for each other?

—George Eliot,
English novelist

Top 6 Things to Do to Improve Your Service

1. **Do everything, even the smallest task, with all your heart and soul.** Do not measure what you're doing by how large a service you think it is. Measure what you're doing by the sense of value you create within yourself. You may never know whom you are serving; just as you may never know that someone nearby may be watching, see the effort you are making, and reward you for it.

2. **Look for holes that you can fill.** Ask people in your profession or industry what they're missing. What do they need?

What are some of their challenges? What would help them run their life or business better? When you find out what's missing, use your knowledge, tools, and experience to fill that gap.

3. **Give of your time, not just your money.** Even if it's just an hour here or there, it is much needed and will be much appreciated. If nothing else, you are guaranteed to meet some wonderful people who are also giving their time. The world needs more people who give with their hands and minds, not just pay or pray.

4. **No matter what you're doing, enjoy the process of serving.** Don't do something of service to others if it is a chore. Those whom you are serving will know if you do so freely or because you feel you have to. Have fun, get involved, enjoy your times of service, and help others enjoy it too.

5. **Share your knowledge with as many people as you can.** Don't be afraid that others will steal your ideas. The more you give, the more you get. As William Danforth, founder of the Ralston Purina Company and author of *I Dare You!* once said, "Our most valuable possessions are those which can be shared without lessening; those which, when shared, multiply; our least valuable possessions are those which, when divided, are diminished."

6. **Make a list of every area in which you have knowledge or skill.** What do you know that can benefit others? List everything, whether it has to do with your profession, hobbies, interests, or personal experience. From that list, see if you can put together some product or service that can make others' lives easier. Then make a list of those you think could be helped by your product or service. Don't always expect an immediate reward for service you provide. Often the inner reward you get is greater than any other compensation.

To give real service, you must add something which cannot be bought or measured with money, and that is sincerity and integrity.

—Douglas Adams,
English novelist

The Impact We Have...Whether We Know It or Not

*We must not, in trying to think about how we can make a
big difference, ignore the small daily differences we can
make which, over time, add up to big differences that we
often cannot foresee.*

—Marian Wright Edelman,
social activist

"Just recently I was walking down the street and a young man I didn't recognize approached me," says Jonar Nader, author of *How to Lose Friends and Infuriate People*. "But he said, 'I want to thank you, Mr. Nader. Because of you I am now directing movies.'"

"I asked, 'How is that?'

"He replied, 'Ten years ago we talked at a party, and you told me I'd be good at movie direction. I started to think about that, and that's the profession I pursued.'

"I didn't even remember this young man, and he told me I had changed his life. It made me realize how often what we do affects other people. Sometimes we don't even know we're doing it. Even so, every gesture, every movement, every word we speak does, in fact, impact people. The more we become aware of this incredible power that we have, the more we feel responsible for our actions and begin to take them more seriously.

"When you make a comment about another person, whether it's about their hairstyle or their behavior, realize that they are listening, watching, and absorbing. The point is, that whether you know it or not—and whether you like it or not—you are always serving people. It could be for good, it could be for worse. You don't have to go somewhere special or do something out of the ordinary to give service. Every moment you're with other people, there's some act of service that can be done to elevate someone else."

Gamble, Cheat, Lie, and Steal

Imagine that it's the end of your life. You're in a large room in your custom-built mansion with priceless art on the walls. You're lying on a satin sheet in a brass bed. All around you are precious jewels, designer clothes, drawers full of money. What's wrong with this picture? You are all alone.

Sometimes we get so caught up in the pursuit of "things," we forget what is really important in life. Life is not about being poor, but happy; neither is it about being a millionaire. It is about using everything you've been given, and everything you can get, and doing something worthwhile with it. The more you can enrich other people's lives, the greater your success becomes.

There are many ways of giving back. You can give to charity or do volunteer work. You can mentor someone starting out in your profession. You can treat everyone kindly and honestly. But you can't begin to give back unless you give yourself the same treatment. In order to do that, you must gamble, cheat, lie, and steal.

✧ **Gamble.** Gamble your best shot in life. Take a risk. Go after what you want and give it your all.

✧ **Cheat.** Cheat those who would have you be less than you are. The best way to cheat people who would pull you down is to gain success. Success is the best revenge.

✧ **Lie.** Lie in the arms of those you love, those who surround you and support you—family, friends, teammates, and colleagues. Treasure the people who treasure you.

✧ **Steal.** Steal every second of happiness you can, and then spread it around. There is nothing more precious.

> *Just as a wave cannot exist for itself, but is ever a part of the heaving surface of the ocean, so must I never live my life for myself, but always in the experience which is going on around me. It is an uncomfortable doctrine which the true ethics whisper into my ear. You are happy, they say; therefore you are called upon to give.*
>
> —Albert Schweitzer,
> humanitarian

I Dare You...

Ask questions of the people around you. Ask them about their problems and challenges; then come up with solutions according to the research you've done. Apply this to your business and personal lives, and see how much more valuable your service to others becomes.

Serve with all your heart and soul in all your actions for seven days straight. No matter how small the act, no matter how minute you think the impact might be on others, serve with all your heart for seven days. Then examine the difference not only in what others see around you, but in how you feel.

> *Only a life lived in the service to others is worth living.*
> —Albert Einstein,
> scientist

Premeditated Acts of Altruism

We do not live on this Earth alone. Everything we do affects the world around us. We cannot expect to take what we need all the time without giving something back. We all have the ability to serve others. In fact, serving others is what makes us human. In their book *Animal Behavior: Readings from Scientific American,* Thomas Eisner and Edward O. Wilson write:

> *A vertebrate society is little more than a loose confederation of families and individuals. Even when they exist as subordinate members of societies, vertebrates remain relatively selfish and aggressive. The single outstanding exception to this trend is man himself, who has retained the basic vertebrate traits, but has managed to balance them with coalitions, contracts, vastly improved communication, and long-range planning that includes premeditated acts of altruism.*

Being of service to others doesn't mean that we have to give up everything we have or want to do for the benefit of others. It means that whatever we choose to do, we should include others in our vision. There are an infinite variety of ways you can give back to others. You can give money, you can give time, you can give praise and encouragement—anything that comes from your heart to someone else's.

> *If you want to lift yourself up, lift someone else.*
> —Booker T. Washington,
> U.S. educator and social reformer

Bibliography

Abraham, Jay. *Getting Everything You Can Out of All You've Got: 21 Ways You Can Out-Think, Out-Perform, and Out-Earn the Competition.* Irvine, Calif.: Griffin Trade Paperback, 2001.

Adubato, Steve. *Speak from the Heart: Be Yourself and Get Results.* New York: Free Press, 2002.

Arnot, Dr. Bob. *The Biology of Success.* New York: Little Brown & Co., 2001.

Attenborough, David. *The Trials of Life: A Natural History of Animal Behavior.* New York: Little Brown & Co., 1991.

Blanchard, Ken and Sheldon Bowles. *Raving Fans: A Revolutionary Approach to Customer Service.* New York: William Morrow, 1993.

Borysenko, Joan. *Inner Peace for Busy People: 52 Strategies for Transforming Your Life.* Carlsbad, Calif: Hay House, 2001.

Bragg, Terry. *31 Days to High Self-Esteem: How to Change Your Life So You Have Joy, Bliss and Abundance.* Richmond, Va.: Peacemakers Training, 1997.

Brown, Tom Jr. *The Way of the Scout.* New York: Berkley Publishing Group, 1997.

Carper, Jean. *Your Miracle Brain: Maximize Your Brain Power, Lift Your Mood, Improve Your IQ and Creativity, Prevent and Reverse Mental Aging.* New York: Quill, 2002.

Costanzo, Charlene. *The Twelve Gifts of Birth.* New York: HarperResource, 2001.

Culligan, Joseph. *You Can Find Anybody.* San Diego, Calif.: Jodere Group, 2000.

Danforth, William H. *I Dare You!* Belle Fourche, SD: Kessinger Publishing Company, 2003.

Deng, Ming-Dao. *356 Tao: Daily Meditations.* San Francisco, Calif.: Harper San Francisco, 1992.

Eisner, Thomas and Edward O. Wilson, editors. *Animal Behavior: Readings from Scientific American.* New York: W.H. Freeman and Company, 1975.

Farber, Barry. *The 12 Clichés of Selling and Why They Work.* New York: Workman Publishing Company, 2001.

———. *Diamond in the Rough.* New York: Berkley Publishing Group, 1995.

Garcia, Oz and Sharyn Kolberg. *The Balance: Your Personal Prescription for Super Metabolism, Renewed Vitality, Maximum Heath, and Instant Rejuvenation.* New York: ReganBooks, 2000.

Gray, John. *Men are from Mars, Women are from Venus.* New York, NY: HarperCollins, 1993.

Harrell, Keith. *Attitude is Everything: 10 Life Changing Steps to Turning Attitude into Action.* New York: HarperBusiness, 2002.

Langer, Ellen J. *The Power of Mindful Learning.* New York, NY: Perseus Publishing, 1998.

Laroche, Loretta. *Life is Not a Stress Rehearsal: Bringing Yesterday's Same Wisdom into Today's Insane World.* New York: Broadway Books, 2001.

Leeds, Dorothy. *The 7 Powers of Questions: Secrets to Successful Communication in Life and At Work.* New York: Perigee, 2000.

Leeds, Dorothy. *Marketing Yourself: The Ultimate Job Seeker's Guide.* New York: HarperCollins, 1991.

Legge, Peter. *It Begins with a Dream.* Burnaby, British Columbia, Canada: Eaglet Publishing, 1996.

Lorayne, Harry. *Harry Lorayne's Page-a-Minute Memory Book.* New York: Ballentine Books, 1996.

Luoma, Jon R. *The Hidden Forest: The Biography of an Ecosystem.* New York: Henry Holt, 1999.

Nader, Jonar. *How to Lose Friends and Infuriate People: Leadership in the Networked World.* Miami, Fla.: Plutonium Publishing, 2002.

Phillips, Bill. *Body for Life: 12 Weeks to Mental & Physical Strength.* New York: HarperCollins, 1999.

Pinker, Seven. *How the Mind Works.* New York: W.W. Norton and Company, 1999.

Rosenbluth, Hal and Diane McFerrin Peters. *The Customer Comes Second: Put Your People First and Watch 'em Kick Butt.* New York: HarperBusiness, 2002.

Shook, Robert. *The Complete Professional Salesman.* New York: Barnes & Noble, 1976.

Watson, Lucinda. *How They Achieved: Stories of Personal Achievement and Business Success.* New York: John Wiley & Sons, 2001.

Winik, Jay. *April 1865: The Month that Saved America.* New York: HarperCollins, 2001.

Wink, Peter. *Negotiate Your Way to Riches: How to Convince Others to Give You What You Want.* Franklin Lakes, NJ: Career Press, 2003.

Winston, Stephanie. *The Organized Executive: The Classic Program for Productivity: New Ways to Manage Time, People, and the Digital Office.* New York: Warner Books, 2001.

Index

About the Author

Barry Farber is the author of nine books (several of which have been translated into 18 foreign languages) on sales, management, and personal achievement, including *Superstar Sales Secrets* and *Superstar Sales Manager's Secrets*. He is also the president of three successful companies: Farber Training Systems, a sales and management training company; The Diamond Group, a literary agency; and Profound Products Inc., a company that creates and markets innovative products.

A well-known public speaker and writer, as well as a television guest and host, Barry is also a monthly columnist for *Entrepreneur Magazine*, host of *Selling Power Live*, and one of the nation's highest-rated speakers on sales, leadership, and motivation. He is a black belt in tae kwon do and is currently training in aikido and jiu-jitsu. Barry received first-place rankings in state and regional weapons competitions and achieved second place in a National Karate Tournament in the Black Belt division. He often uses his martial arts experience to tie into his messages on sales, marketing, and success. For more information about Barry and his products, visit *www.barryfarber.com*.

About the author